BLOCKCHAIN REGULATION AND GOVERNANCE IN EUROPE

In *Blockchain Regulation and Governance in Europe*, Michèle Finck examines the relationship between blockchain technology and EU law and introduces the theme of blockchain governance. The book provides a general introduction to blockchains as both a regulatable and a regulatory technology and outlines the interaction between distributed ledger technology and specific areas of EU law, such as the General Data Protection Regulation. It should be read by anyone interested in EU law, the relationship between law, innovation and technology, and technology governance.

MICHÈLE FINCK is a Senior Research Fellow at the Max Planck Institute for Innovation and Competition in Munich as well as a lecturer in EU law at Keble College, University of Oxford. She holds law degrees from King's College London, the Sorbonne and the European University Institute as well as a doctorate in law from the University of Oxford. Prior to joining the Max Planck Institute Michèle worked as a fellow at the London School of Economics and Political Science. She is the author of *Subnational Authorities in EU Law* (2017) and an editor of the *Cambridge Handbook on the Law of the Sharing Economy* (2018).

Blockchain Regulation and Governance in Europe

MICHÈLE FINCK

Max Planck Institute for Innovation and Competition (Munich)

CAMBRIDGE
UNIVERSITY PRESS

University Printing House, Cambridge CB2 8BS, United Kingdom

One Liberty Plaza, 20th Floor, New York, NY 10006, USA

477 Williamstown Road, Port Melbourne, VIC 3207, Australia

314–321, 3rd Floor, Plot 3, Splendor Forum, Jasola District Centre, New Delhi – 110025, India

79 Anson Road, #06–04/06, Singapore 079906

Cambridge University Press is part of the University of Cambridge.

It furthers the University's mission by disseminating knowledge in the pursuit of education, learning and research at the highest international levels of excellence.

www.cambridge.org
Information on this title: www.cambridge.org/9781108474757
DOI: 10.1017/9781108609708

© Michèle Finck 2019

First published 2019

Printed and bound in Great Britain by Clays Ltd, Elcograf S.p.A.

A catalogue record for this publication is available from the British Library.

ISBN 978-1-108-47475-7 Hardback
ISBN 978-1-108-46545-8 Paperback

Contents

v

Contents

Acknowledgements

It is often said that writing a book is a solitary enterprise. This is in many ways true as you need to spend considerable time reading, thinking and writing alone. Yet, in at least as many ways even writing a monograph is a collaborative enterprise where you build on what you have learned from others.

I am grateful to the institutions that have allowed me to discuss some of the ideas in this book with them. These include the Oxford Internet Institute, the London School of Economics, Seoul National University, the European Blockchain Observatory and Forum and the European Commission, the University of Freiburg, the University of Oxford, the University of Ferrara and the European Law Institute, Wharton Business School, Cardozo Law School, the Sorbonne, University College London, various institutions of various EU Member States as well as others. I should also single out a few individuals that have read parts of this book or provided valuable inspiration in conversations: the entire MPI data group, Oliver Beige, Tatiana Cutts, Primavera De Filippi and the COALA crew, Jörn Erbguth, Robert Riemann, Edmund Schuster, Daniel Resas, Christian Sillaber, Kevin Werbach and the entire Reg@Tech Group at Wharton, Aaron Wright, Karen Yeung and Vlad Zamfir. The vibrant Twitterverse also deserves an honorable mention as well as Liz Fisher, Giorgio Monti and Steve Weatherill who taught me about scholarly research in the first place.

I must also thank the Max Planck Institute for Innovation and Competition and in particular Reto Hilty for having provided me with an extraordinary working environment. This book was written between the fall of 2017 and the spring of 2018, something that I could not have done without the outstanding research environment I was able to enjoy. I moreover owe particular thanks to the London School of Economics and my former colleagues at the LSE Law Department. It was my fellowship at the LSE (from 2015-2017) that enabled me to discover new academic terrains, including blockchain. Finally, I would also like to thank Felix Hoerl and Domagoj Pavic for superb research assistance.

Most importantly I owe thanks – for everything – to my family, in particular to my parents Martine and Jean-Claude and my husband Moritz.

1

Blockchain Technology

[Blockchains] will be the biggest disruptor, not only causing every single back office for every single corporation to be re-thought but also leading to the emergence of new business models and new companies. Smart contracts, in particular, will turn into an invention on par with the invention of written laws and with the emergence of corporations.[1]

This monograph sets out to examine blockchains and other forms of distributed ledger technology (DLT) from a legal and governance perspective.[2] A blockchain is, essentially, a database that is replicated across a network of computers updated through a consensus algorithm. Whereas innovations in database design may once have appeared bland and uninspiring, they no longer are in an age in which the economy and close to all aspects of life have become datafied. Blockchains promise to constitute a profound paradigm shift regarding data collection, sharing and processing and to trigger related revisions of socio-economic and political arrangements.

Much hype currently surrounds the potential of DLT, as it is hailed as a solution to 'virtually every human problem in existence'.[3] Distributed ledgers are widely considered to be 'radically disruptive'[4] and 'to fundamentally shift the way in which

---

[1]   Wilson, 'Interview With Emin Gun Sirer, Professor And Cryptocurrency Researcher At Cornell, And His Thoughts On Smart Contracts' (*CryptoMeNow*, 18 March 2018) <http:// insider.cryptomenow.com/interview-with-emin-gun-sirer-professor-and-cryptocurrency-researcher-at-cornell-and-his-thoughts-on-smart-contracts/> accessed 28 March 2018.

[2]   From a technical perspective, 'blockchains' cannot necessarily be assimilated with other forms of DLT that do not group data in blocks. For the sake of simplicity, I use this terminology interchangeably and also occasionally rely on 'distributed ledgers' as a synonym.

[3]   Angela Walch, 'The Fiduciaries of Public Blockchains' (2016) <http://blockchain.cs.ucl.ac.uk/ wp-content/uploads/2016/11/paper_20.pdf> accessed 20 March 2018.

[4]   Mark Walport, 'Executive Summary' in Government Office for Science, 'Distributed Ledger Technology: Beyond Block Chain. A Report by the UK Government Chief Scientific Adviser' 14   <www.gov.uk/government/uploads/system/uploads/attachment_data/file/492972/gs-16-1-distributed-ledger-technology.pdf> accessed 3 April 2018.

society operates'.[5] It has been argued that the technology's eventual impact 'on British society may be as significant as foundational events such as the creation of the Magna Carta'.[6] Blockchains are thus seen as an entirely novel socio-economic paradigm.[7]

While many are profoundly optimistic about the technology, others are deeply sceptical. It is striking that most observers either venerate or condemn the technology, with little middle ground in between these camps.[8] Indeed, many caution that blockchains are the most inefficient of all databases and susceptible to trigger environmental disaster through the high-energy consumption required to power some of them.[9]

Hype is an unavoidable component of each technological revolution.[10] Further, according to Clayton Christensen, we must distinguish between 'sustaining innovations', which simply improve the performance of established products, and 'disruptive technologies', which typically perform poorly at first but bring an entirely different value proposition, resulting in subsequent large-scale adoption.[11] Blockchains might fall into the latter category. There can be no certainty regarding the technology's eventual impact, however. Right now blockchains are inefficient by design and need to be upgraded to be functional at scale. The technology suffers from technical limitations that must be resolved to match expectations. The starting point of my analysis, and of any policy-maker compelled to engage with the blockchain phenomenon, must therefore be that this is an area in full development and that the outcome of current innovation processes cannot be predicted.

In a climate of fast-paced development and extreme opinions, objective and timeless analysis proves challenging. Referring to the first blockchain, Bitcoin, Andreas Antonopolous notes the following: 'I wrote a book that answers the question

5   Aaron Wright and Primavera De Filippi, 'Decentralized Blockchain Technology and The Rise of Lex Cryptographia' (2015) 2 <https://papers.ssrn.com/sol3/papers.cfm?abstract_id=2580664> accessed 28 February 2018 (hereafter Wright and De Filippi, 'Lex Cryptographia').

6   Catherine Mulligan, 'Applications in Government' in Government Office for Science, 'Distributed Ledger Technology: Beyond Block Chain. A Report by the UK Government Chief Scientific Adviser' (n 1) 65 <www.gov.uk/government/uploads/system/uploads/attachment_data/file/492972/gs-16-1-distributed-ledger-technology.pdf> accessed 3 April 2018.

7   Jason Potts, Ellie Rennie and Jake Goldenfein, 'Blockchains and the Crypto-City' (2017) 1 <https://papers.ssrn.com/sol3/papers.cfm?abstract_id=2982885> accessed 3 April 2018.

8   According to the Gartner hype cycle for emerging technologies, it will take between five and ten years for blockchains to reach mainstream adoption. See Amy Forni and Rob van der Meulen, 'Gartner Identifies Three Megatrends That Will Drive Digital Business Into the Next Decade' (*Gartner*, 15 August 2017) <www.gartner.com/newsroom/id/3784363> accessed 13 April 2018.

9   For a critical account, see David Gerard, *Attack of the 50 Foot Blockchain: Bitcoin, Blockchain, Ethereum & Smart Contracts* (CreateSpace Independent Publishing Platform 2017).

10   Carolta Perez, *Technological Revolutions and Financial Capital: The Dynamics of Bubbles and Golden Ages* (Edward Elgar 2003).

11   Clayton Christensen, *The Innovator's Solution: Creating and Sustaining Successful Growth* (Harvard Business School Press 2003).

"What is Bitcoin?" It's 300 pages long, was obsolete the moment it was printed and has to be corrected and updated every three months just to keep up with changes."[12] This, no doubt, is a fate my book also faces. I nonetheless remain convinced of the importance of contributing to the debate about blockchain's regulatory and governance implications at this early stage of the technology's development. Let me explain why. Immature technologies are malleable technologies. It is now – not at the stage of widespread deployment – that the parameters of how technological change affects the human condition, and its socio-economic, normative and institutional underpinnings, are defined.

Blockchains create great opportunities and serious problems. In order to grapple with related challenges we must look beyond the narratives of innovation and technology to come to terms with their significance. Even if the promises currently associated with a distributed ledger do not deliver, current innovation efforts will still result in innovation, even if not in the form currently projected. Even if blockchains do not materialize in the form currently predicted, many of the pain points that manifest in this context are of a general significance in an age of profound technological transmutation. The key themes examined in this book relate to legal automation, the regulatory potential of technology, the difficulties in regulating decentralized global networks, principles of data law[13] and technology governance (that is to say, the rules and principles surrounding software maintenance). These themes will dominate regulatory debates in the years to come, and this also outside of the blockchain context. Extraordinary amounts of capital and talent are flowing into distributed ledger development, triggering technical sophistication, new business ideas and socio-political momentum. Innovation processes are open-ended by nature, and, although precise outcomes cannot be predicted, it appears undeniable that current efforts will cause lasting change. Indeed, whereas the technology itself suffers from severe shortcomings, it inspires people to think of a decentralized future. This vision may be the core value proposition of the technology at this moment in time.

In light of the above it is maybe not surprising that the term 'blockchain' has come to simply be used as a synonym for 'technology' or 'innovation'. This pinpoints a collective perception that we're currently at a crossroads of how technological innovation affects human civilization. For lack of understanding of the precise components and consequences of this evolution, 'blockchain' has evolved to become a code word for these broader evolutions, which are not limited to DLT but, equally, pertain to developments in artificial intelligence (AI) (especially machine and deep learning), smart robotics, new forms of computing, automation and machine-to-machine communications, to name just a few. It is worth noting that it is in combination with these dynamics that blockchains' most appreciable potential lies.

---

12 <www.youtube.com/watch?v=A6kJfvuNqtg&feature=youtu.be&t=83>, at 1:24.
13 I use this expression to refer to the body of legal rules governing personal and non-personal data under EU law.

The wide interest in blockchains testifies to the need for new mental models as we transition from knowledge to information societies, in which data becomes the source of everything. Blockchains open up a new way of thinking about technology and its impact on our lives. Through the power of collective imagination, the technology serves to dream up a new world, especially in light of current problems associated with the tech industry.[14] In one way or another, the 'blockchain' is thus here to stay. The objective of my analysis consists in offering an account of related regulatory and governance challenges and laying the groundwork for future research.

The focus on regulation and governance to examine emerging technologies is warranted for a number of reasons. First, distributed ledgers, like any technology, are in and of themselves neutral but will not be used neutrally. Blockchains are capable of serving benevolent or malicious ends. Just as any other technology, they are a 'technical artefact with a particular architecture, which inevitably has both social and political motivations, as it facilitates certain actions and behaviours more than others'.[15] Blockchains can be used for good, such as in bringing banking services to the unbanked or in adding transparency to areas where it is currently sparse. Blockchains can also be used maliciously, however, and pose a threat to public order. They have already been used to facilitate tax evasion[16] and other crimes[17] and could in the future be relied on to, for example, operate automated unstoppable drone armies or assassination markets.[18] Regulation is thus one important factor that determines how a technology unfolds.

My second focus lies on questions of governance. In the blockchain context, governance is understood as the process of maintaining a technical protocol. This highlights that distributed ledgers are governed by the interplay of endogenous and exogenous regulation. I aim to distil both influences and delineate their mutual influence. My focus rests predominantly on public and permissionless projects, though not exclusively, as I engage with their private and permissioned counterparts where opportune.

I. STRUCTURE OF THE BOOK

This is the first book that examines blockchains from the perspective of European Union law. Therefore, it seeks to provide much of the groundwork needed for future

[14] Nathaniel Popper, 'Tech Thinks It Has a Fix for the Problems It Created: Blockchain' *The New York Times* (1 April 2018) <www.nytimes.com/2018/04/01/technology/blockchain-uses.html?smid=tw-nytimes&smtyp=cur> accessed 13 April 2018.

[15] Primavera de Filippi and Samer Hasan, 'Blockchain Technology as a Regulatory Technology: From Code is Law to Law is Code' (*firstmonday*, 5 December 2016) <http://firstmonday.org/ojs/index.php/fm/article/view/7113/5657> accessed 21 March 2018.

[16] Omri Marian, 'Are Cryptocurrencies Super Tax Havens?' (2013) 112 University of Michigan Law Review First Impressions 38.

[17] <https://en.wikipedia.org/wiki/Silk_Road_(marketplace)> accessed 25 May 2018.

[18] Whether the State needs to directly intervene to prevent this or whether these objectives can be achieved through self-regulation is a question we turn to in the final two chapters.

research and discussions.[19] I combine insights from EU law with regulatory theory and the 'law and innovation' and 'law and technology' schools of thought to provide impetus as to how we ought to approach an emergent and potentially disruptive technology. This tale unfolds in eight parts.

Chapter 1 introduces blockchain technology. It provides an overview of its central technical components and offers a functional perspective in highlighting its main characteristics and related implications. I will illustrate that, in its current configuration, the technology is limited and probably cannot be deployed at scale. I will also highlight the rapid technical developments that occur in this area and potential future consequences. The chapter further outlines the various layers of a blockchain ecosystem and speculates about what the predominant future use cases and implications of the technology might be.

Chapters 2 and 3 examine the technology from a regulatory perspective in focusing on the two general and overarching themes of how a complex global technology can be regulated and, conversely, how such a technology regulates those who engage with it. Chapter 2 addresses claims that, due to their decentralized and transnational peer-to-peer structure and the use of encryption, blockchains cannot be regulated. I draw parallels to early debates of Internet regulation and rebut that narrative, highlighting various centralized regulatory access points to the decentralized network that enable regulatory intervention. Chapter 3 evaluates the potential of distributed ledgers to serve as regulatory agents. In highlighting that blockchains are an aspect of the increasing automation of law, I introduce associated promises and drawbacks. This analysis further stresses that DLT forms a potent behaviour-constraining tool in the hands of those who operate it.

After this general examination of distributed ledgers and their regulatory implications, I turn to examine the data they store from the perspective of two specific areas of EU law. Chapter 4 examines the data stored on blockchains from the perspective of the European Union's General Data Protection Regulation (GDPR) whereas Chapter 5 explores the technology in relation to the provisions of supranational law governing non-personal data and current debates concerning the need for legal reform in this domain. Taking data law as my looking glass, I highlight, on the one hand, that DLT can stand in considerable tension with established legal frameworks and their underlying technical and economic assumptions (in the case of personal data). On the other hand, however, distributed ledgers could provide a technical solution in areas where law is currently falling short of achieving desired normative objectives (in this case, promoting the sharing of non-personal data between undertakings).

---

[19] For a general account of the relation between blockchains and law, with particular references to the US, see Primavera De Filippi and Aaron Wright, *Blockchain and the Law* (Harvard University Press 2018) (hereafter De Filippi and Wright, 'Blockchain and the Law').

From that conclusion I will move on to explore the wider policy implications of blockchain technology. In Chapter 6 I ponder the complex interaction between law, technology and innovation to formulate concrete recommendations for policy-makers faced with emerging technologies. I advance a concept of polycentric co-regulation, which constitutes an attempt to reconcile the established benefits of public regulation with the newer challenges and opportunities of the participatory and regulatory potential of technology. Chapter 7 is dedicated to the specific governance challenges presented by blockchain technology. I survey ongoing debates echoing the uncertainties as to how these technological artefacts, designed to replace trust in human beings, should be governed amidst realizations that technology doesn't eliminate the need for human consensus. The legal implications of governance decisions are also debated. My analysis closes by offering a conclusion that highlights the book's main arguments and suggests themes for further research. Considering the fast pace of development in this area, it is worth noting that this book takes into consideration developments up until the early spring of 2018.

II. BLOCKCHAINS AND OTHER FORMS OF DISTRIBUTED LEDGER TECHNOLOGY

This chapter is designed to set the scene for subsequent analysis in providing an introduction to the technology and its potential impact. My approach consists in trying to make technological concepts accessible while maintaining the necessary details and terminology needed to meaningfully engage in this space. Overall, I try to set out the technology from a functional perspective; focusing on what it does and where its most pivotal impacts might lie.

A. *Definition*

In essence, a blockchain is a shared and synchronized digital database that is maintained by an algorithm and stored on multiple *nodes* (the computers that store a local version of the distributed ledger). Blockchains can be imagined as a peer-to-peer network, with the nodes serving as the different peers.[20] Some chains operate a distinction between 'full' and 'lightweight' nodes, whereby only full nodes store an integral copy of the ledger from the *genesis block* (the first block) whereas light-weight nodes store only those parts of the ledger of relevance to them.

As its etymology reveals, a blockchain is a chain of *blocks*.[21] A block groups together multiple transactions and is then added to the existing chain of blocks.

---

[20] A 'peer' of course doesn't have to be a private individual but can also be a corporatione or, in the future, a machine.

[21] It is worth noting that as the technology evolves this structure might eventually cede way to other forms of data-storage.

Data is grouped into blocks that, upon reaching a certain size, are chained to the existing ledger through a hashing process. A *hash* is, essentially, a unique fingerprint that represents information as a string of characters and numbers.[22] The ledger's blocks have different key components, including the hash of all transactions contained in the block (its 'fingerprint'), a *time stamp* and a hash of the previous block (which creates the sequential chain of blocks).[23] Because blocks are continuously added but never removed a blockchain can be qualified as an *append-only data structure*. Cryptographic hash-chaining makes the log *tamper-evident*, which increases transparency and accountability.[24] Indeed, because of the hash linking one block to another, changes in one block change the hash of that block, as well as of all subsequent blocks.

Blockchain networks achieve resilience through *replication*. The ledger's data is resilient as it is simultaneously stored on many nodes, so that, even if one or several nodes fail, the data goes unaffected. In light of such replication, there is no central point of failure or attack at the hardware level.[25] Through its design, a distributed ledger moreover reduces verification costs (the verification of a transaction's attributes) and networking costs (the ability to bootstrap and operate a marketplace without the need for an intermediary).[26]

The replicated data stored in blocks is synchronized through a *consensus protocol*, which enables the distributed network to agree on the current state of the ledger in the absence of a centralized point of control. The consensus protocol governs how new blocks are added to the chain. Through this process, data is chronologically ordered in a manner that makes it difficult to alter data without altering subsequent blocks. Consensus refers to the mechanisms that coordinate data held by the various nodes, providing assurance to network participants that their versions of the ledger are consistent and accurate.

Blockchains are both a new technology for data storage and a novel variant of programmable platform that enables new applications such as smart contracts.[27] It is crucial to note that a blockchain ecosystem is *multi-layered*. First, blockchains themselves rely on the Internet and Transmission Control Protocol/Internet Protocol (TCP/IP) to operate, and can in this respect be seen as 'new application protocols that sit on top of the transport layer'.[28] Second, distributed ledgers

---

[22] A hash is a one-way cryptographic function, designed to be impossible to revert.

[23] Andreas Antonopoulos, *Mastering Bitcoin* (O'Reilly 2017) xxiii.

[24] Ed Felten, 'Blockchain: What is it Good For?' (*Freedom to Tinker*, 26 February 2018) <https:// freedom-to-tinker.com/2018/02/26/bloc> accessed 3 April 2018.

[25] In Chapter 7 we will see that there can be a central point of attack or failure at the software governance level.

[26] Christian Catalini and Joshua Gans, 'Some Simple Economics of the Blockchain' (2016) Rotman School of Management Working Paper No. 2874598, 1 <https://papers.ssrn.com/sol3/papers.cfm?abstract_id=2874598> accessed 3 April 2018.

[27] A smart contract essentially is self-executing software code. I examine smart contracts in further depth just below.

[28] De Filippi and Wright, 'Blockchain and the Law' (n 19) 48.

themselves provide not just an infrastructure for data management and a new infrastructure that can anchor diverse applications (the *'infrastructure layer'*). Third, a blockchain itself serves as an infrastructure on which decentralized applications (the *'application layer'*) run.

Distributed ledgers provide a replicated database that is updated in a decentralized manner. While this database can be used independently, such as to record transactions in cryptoassets or register information, it can also serve as the ground level on which further edifices are constructed, which in the blockchain case are usually labelled 'decentralized applications' because they reflect the decentralized structure of the underlying network.[29] These applications can take a wide variety of forms and serve a wide variety of use cases.[30] While some applications sit directly on top of a blockchain, others use an intermediary layer in the form of a decentralized application framework that implements their own protocols for the creation and maintenance of decentralized applications.[31] A blockchain ecosystem accordingly has different vertical layers. In addition, it can have different components from a horizontal perspective, as blockchains can be interoperable, or when a single DLT relies on child chains or side chains that can serve different purposes.[32]

Blockchain ecosystems are still under construction, and, as these networks become more refined, it will be more straightforward and common to distinguish between their diverse aspects, such as the protocol and second-layer applications, but also different forms of storage and computing.[33] I now turn to consider the broader context from which blockchains in their current form emerged and take a deeper look at their technical details. Thereafter, I offer an overview of the technology's broader applications and implications.

B. *History and Evolution*

The first blockchain was created to provide the technical infrastructure of *Bitcoin* in 2009. At the time the technology itself was considered to be but a by-product of the cryptocurrency, and the term 'blockchain' doesn't even figure in Satoshi Nakamoto's famous White Paper.[34] Rather than being a completely novel technology, DLT is better understood as an inventive combination of existing

---

[29] This terminology reflects, on the one hand, that these are applications running on an infrastructure and that they can be managed in a decentralized fashion just as the infrastructure itself.

[30] See further below.

[31] See, by way of example: <https://daostack.io/>.

[32] Side chains allow data to be stored in another chain and then be moved back to the main chain.

[33] Note the analogies with 'the Internet'.

[34] Satoshi Nakamoto, 'Bitcoin: A Peer-to-Peer Electronic Cash System' (2009) <https://bitcoin .org/bitcoin.pdf.> accessed 20 March 2018 (hereafter Nakamoto, 'Bitcoin White Paper'). Nakamoto is the pseudonymous mastermind behind Bitcoin.

mechanisms. Indeed, nearly all its technical components originated in academic research from the 1980s and 1990s.[35]

In the aftermath of Bitcoin's creation, observers noticed the technology's capacity to serve as a decentralized record of data and digital assets that can be operated between parties that do not know or trust each other without the need for a trusted third party. This has led developers to build on the Bitcoin blockchain, to create new blockchains (such as *Ethereum*),[36] as well as other forms of distributed ledger technology that do not store data in blocks (such as hashgraphs). These networks promise to facilitate a wide range of uses in the private and public sectors.

In the private sector, DLT is currently being experimented with to enable various forms of digital money[37] and mobile banking,[38] track goods in international trade,[39] manage software licences,[40] power machine-to-machine electricity markets[41] and replace centralized sharing economy platforms,[42] among many others. More generally, blockchains promise to enable 'business governance structures that are more transparent, more flat, and more participatory'.[43] Equally, the public sector is trialling the technology. The European Union is currently exploring the option of a supranational blockchain infrastructure[44] while a UK report suggests using the technology to protect critical infrastructure against cyberattacks, for operational and budgetary transparency and traceability and to reduce tax fraud.[45] Such variegated applications are possible because blockchains are simultaneously a programmable platform that enables new applications as well as a method for data storage (essentially, an accounting system).

---

[35] Arvind Narayanan and Jeremy Clark, 'Bitcoin's Academic Pedigree' (2017) 60 Communications of the ACM 36.

[36] Ethereum is a so-called second generation blockchain, which not only allows to track transactions (as Bitcoin) but also provides computer programming language that allows for the construction of decentralized applications on top of the network infrastructure.

[37] Such as Bitcoin.

[38] <https://www.bitpesa.co/>.

[39] <https://www.everledger.io/>.

[40] Walter Blocher, Alexander Hoppen and Peter Hoppen, 'Softwarelizenzen auf der Blockchain' (2017) 33 Computer und Recht 337.

[41] Janusz Sikorski, Joy Haughton and Markus Kraft, 'Blockchain Technology in the Chemical Industry: Machine-to-machine Electricity Market' (2017) 195 Applied Energy 234.

[42] Steve Huckle et al., 'Internet of Things, Blockchain and Shared Economy Applications' (2016) 98 Procedia Computer Science 461.

[43] Carla Reyes, Nizan Packin and Benjamin Edwards, 'Distributed Governance' (2017) 59 William & Mary Law Review Online 1, 19.

[44] European Commission, 'Study on Opportunity and Feasibility of a EU Blockchain Infrastructure' (Call for tenders) <https://ec.europa.eu/digital-single-market/en/news/study-opportunity-and-feasibility-eu-blockchain-infrastructure> accessed 13 April 2018.

[45] Mark Walport, 'Executive Summary' in Government Office for Science, 'Distributed Ledger Technology: Beyond Block Chain. A Report by the UK Government Chief Scientific Adviser' 14 <www.gov.uk/government/uploads/system/uploads/attachment_data/file/492972/gs-16-1-distributed-ledger-technology.pdf> accessed 3 April 2018.

C. *Blockchains as an Accounting System*

Blockchain infrastructure is basically a common asset registry, an innovation in database design that either directly stores data or links to data. These shared accounting systems can be used by different entities to standardize and link data and 'enable credible accounting of digital events'.[46] Through their structure, they present the potential to coordinate information between many stakeholders. With these characteristics, blockchains help track and store evidence about transactions and participants.

While these distributed and verifiable records only ever store data, this data can be taken to represent anything we believe and agree it represents. Bitcoin is, essentially, data that is valuable because people have come to believe it is. Similarly, over time other forms of *digital assets* have emerged that are still nothing but raw data taken to represent a good, service or entitlement. Blockchain-based assets can purely have on-chain value (as in Bitcoin) or be the avatar of a real-world asset, whether a good (such as a token representing a bike), a service (such as a voucher for a haircut) or an entitlement (such as a legal right).

Often labelled as *the Internet of Value*, distributed ledgers thus promise to disrupt the online circulation of value.[47] Whereas the Internet provides a protocol for the exchange of information, blockchains provide a protocol for the exchange of value. Indeed, right now economic assets are but a different kind of information expressed in bits and bytes on the Internet. Blockchains empower value transfers without the need for a traditional intermediary. Distributed ledgers allow for value to be administered in a decentralized fashion, providing a transparent and secure record of transactions. For example, the Bitcoin blockchain provides a 'public append-only and tamper-proof log of all transactions ever issued'.[48] Given that data stored on a DLT can be personal or non-personal data from the perspective of EU law, I will examine its status under the relevant legal regimes in Chapters 4 and 5.

In providing a distributed and verifiable record of data, blockchains may come to transform record-keeping systems. While this may sound underwhelming, it can have far-reaching implications as the importance of accounting in socio-economic settings must not be ignored. To illustrate, Max Weber considered that the invention of double-entry bookkeeping founded capitalism.[49] Blockchains are an innovative system for determining 'who did what when' that can be deployed to enable

---

[46] Roman Matzutt et al., 'A Quantitative Analysis of the Impact of Arbitrary Blockchain Content on Bitcoin' (26 February 2018) 1 <https://fc18.ifca.ai/preproceedings/6.pdf> accessed 3 April 2018 (hereafter Matzutt, 'A Quantitative Analysis').

[47] Amy Cortese, 'Blockchain Technology Ushers in "The Internet of Value"' (*cisco*, 10 February 2016) <https://newsroom.cisco.com/feature-content?articleId=1741667> accessed 3 April 2018.

[48] Matzutt, 'A Quantitative Analysis' (n 46) 1.

[49] Max Weber, *General Economic History* (Frank Knight 1927) 276 ('the most general presupposition for the existence of this present-day capitalism is that of rational capital accounting').

coordination between parties that was not previously possible. This is not the only characteristic of DLT that may have momentous repercussions, however. Beyond supplying an accounting infrastructure, blockchains are also a programmable database, or, more poetically, 'a magic computer'.

D. *Blockchains as Application Infrastructure*

Vitalik Buterin, the inventor of Ethereum, has defined blockchains as

> a magic computer that anyone can upload programs to and leave the programs to self-execute, where the current and all previous states of every program are always publicly visible, and which carries a very strong cryptoeconomically secured guarantee that programs running on the chain will continue to execute in exactly the way that the blockchain protocol specifies.[50]

A distributed ledger's infrastructure layer can host a wide range of second-layer applications, including smart contracts (which are examined separately below). Below I observe that applications can be deployed on a DLT infrastructure that reflect the underlying infrastructure's characteristics of resilience, decentralization and tamper evidence. In Chapter 7 we will see that these different layers are interconnected so that governance decisions regarding one layer may have repercussions for others. The possibilities raised by this application layer are perceived to inaugurate the third era of the Internet.

Web 3.0 has been defined as a new phase of the Internet's continued development in which many of the current problems associated with concentration, such as data silos and growing platform power, are remedied through blockchains' decentralization paradigm.[51] According to this vision, multiple profit centres will henceforth share value across an open network.[52] Blockchain-based applications are projected to enable us to move away from concentrated data behemoths towards a global Internet characterized by the absence of centralized points of control, in which data subjects control their own personal data, data breaches are minimized and applications are increasingly interoperable.[53] Blockchains enable such decentralization through their ability to replace traditional trust intermediaries with trust based in numbers.

---

[50] Vitalik Buterin, 'Visions part I: The Value of Blockchain Technology' (*Ethereum Blog*, 13 April 2015) <https://blog.ethereum.org/2015/04/13/visions-part-1-the-value-of-blockchain-technology/> accessed 20 March 2018 (hereafter Buterin, 'Visions').

[51] On platform power, see Orla Lynskey, 'Regulating 'Platform Power'' (2017) LSE Legal Studies Working Paper No. 1/2017 <https://papers.ssrn.com/sol3/papers.cfm?abstract_id=2921021> accessed 25 May 2018.

[52] Matteo Zago, 'Why the Web 3.0 Matters and you should know about it' (*Medium*, 30 January 2018) <https://medium.com/@matteozago/why-the-web-3-0-matters-and-you-should-know-about-it-a5851d63c949> accessed 13 April 2018.

[53] See further Chapter 5.

E. *Algorithmic Trust*

The absence of trust is a central assumption of blockchain systems. Their replicated structure and decentralized management echoes a hypothesis that the involved parties cannot be trusted, so the ledger must not be held or administered in a centralized fashion. Satoshi Nakamoto, the pseudonymous mastermind behind Bitcoin, produced private money to provide 'an electronic payment system based on cryptographic proof instead of trust, allowing any two willing parties to transact directly with each other without the need for a trusted third party'.[54] The removal of the human or institutional third party forms a core value proposition of blockchain networks. Reid Hoffmann has put forward that DLTs provide *trustless trust*, as '[p]arties no longer need to know or trust each other to participate in exchanges of value with absolute assurance and no intermediaries'.[55] Rather than relying on trust in humans or institutions, blockchain-based transactions are powered by trust in technology. Importantly, this doesn't remove trust; it just changes the instance in which it is placed. Human decision-making cannot be replaced entirely, as humans are still needed to, for example, maintain blockchain protocol and reach agreement on the terms of a smart contract.

The trustless trust narrative is anchored in what game theory maps as *the problem of cooperation*.[56] When two strangers trade, they face a prisoner's dilemma of cooperating (honouring their promise) or not (defecting). Vili Lehdonvirta has explained that this problem is conventionally solved by parties' incentives to maintain their reputation or through reliance on a trusted third party, such as the state and its legal system.[57] Blockchains promise to replace these mechanisms with a technical *protocol*.[58] Seen from this perspective, DLTs are 'IT artefacts that replace organizational trust'.[59]

---

[54] Nakamoto, 'Bitcoin White Paper' (n 34) 1.

[55] Reid Hoffman, 'The Future of the Bitcoin Ecosystem and "Trustless Trust" – Why I Invested in Blockstream' (*LinkedIn*, 17 November 2014) <www.linkedin.com/pulse/20141117154558-1213-the-future-of-the-bitcoin-ecosystem-and-trustless-trust-why-i-invested-in-blockstream/> accessed 13 April 2018.

[56] See further Douglass North, *Institutions, Institutional Change and Economic Performance (Political Economy of Institutions and Decisions)* (Cambridge University Press 1990).

[57] Vili Lehdonvirta, 'The Blockchain Paradox: Why Distributed Ledger Technologies May Do Little to Transform the Economy' (*Oxford Internet Institute*, 21 November 2016) <www.oii.ox.ac.uk/blog/the-blockchain-paradox-why-distributed-ledger-technologies-may-do-little-to-transform-the-economy/> accessed 3 April 2018.

[58] In computer science, a protocol refers to a set of rules and procedures for transmitting data between electronic devices: <www.britannica.com/technology/protocol-computer-science> accessed 15 March 2018. In the blockchain context, the protocol enables communication between nodes and the addition of new blocks.

[59] Roman Beck et al., 'Opportunities and Risks of Blockchain Technologies' (2016) 7 Dagstuhl Reports 99, 119 (hereafter Beck, 'Opportunities and Risks of Blockchain Technologies').

This explains why, to some, blockchains are an ideology rather than a technology, expressing the preference for a world without institutions where trust is put into cryptography rather than humans.[60] This is indeed in line with Bitcoin's origins in the *cypherpunk movement*, which works at the nexus of cryptography and politics.[61] Cypherpunks perceive peer-to-peer technology and encryption as tools of personal freedom and mechanisms that could undermine government power and render government operations more transparent.[62]

Indeed, the history of blockchain cannot be disconnected from a desire for wide-reaching politico-institutional reform.[63] Karen Yeung notes that blockchains' trust function is one now performed by the rule of law, which anchors the capacity and legitimacy of legal systems 'to provide an effective response to the problem of cooperation'.[64] Examining the relation between blockchains and regulation is thus worthwhile not only for determining how law should react to this new technology but also because replacing trust generated by the legal system with machine-based trust may have lasting implications for the rule of law. Further, blockchain threatens to disrupt other core legal concepts, such as jurisdiction and legal personality.[65]

It is worth repeating that blockchains do not make trust disappear; they simply replace trust in humans and institutions with trust in technology. Trust in machines does not, however, resolve from the need to trust humans, as we'll discover in Chapter 7 when examining governance arrangements. Indeed, the rules and principles comprised in blockchain code are not a product of the technology itself but, rather, of the humans who create it. Software is, accordingly, never neutral but the reflection of the objectives and beliefs of those who use it as a means of expression. Trusting a blockchain or blockchain-based application ultimately requires trust in the collectivity of individuals who architect this technology, as well as in the procedures that govern their behaviour and manage their accountability – or the absence of such norms and institutions.

---

[60] Michael Seemann, 'Digitaltechnologie Blockchain: Eine als Technik getarnte Ideologie' *Deutschlandfunk Kultur* (15 March 2018) <www.deutschlandfunkkultur.de/digitaltechnolo gie-blockchain-eine-als-technik-getarnte.1005.de.html?dram:article_id=413022> accessed 3 April 2018.

[61] Phillip Rogaway, 'The Moral Character of Cryptographic Work' (December 2015), 17 <http://web.cs.ucdavis.edu/~rogaway/papers/moral-fn.pdf> accessed 25 May 2018; see also Arvind Narayanan et al., *Bitcoin and Cryptocurrency Technologies* (Princeton University Press 2016) 201–02 (hereafter Narayanan, 'Bitcoin and Cryptocurrency Technologies').

[62] Eric Hughes, 'A Cypherpunk's Manifesto' (*activism.net*, 9 March 1993) <www.activism.net/cypherpunk/manifesto.html> accessed 13 April 2018.

[63] See further Chapter 2.

[64] Karen Yeung, 'Blockchain, Transactional Security and the Promise of Automated Law Enforcement: The Withering of Freedom Under Law?' (2017) TLI Think! Paper 58/2017, 4 <https://papers.ssrn.com/sol3/papers.cfm?abstract_id=2929266> accessed 3 April 2018.

[65] We'll observe in Chapter 6 that Malta is considering attributing legal personality to software in the form of a smart contract.

It's also worth noting that, although it often is, the ideal of trustless trust doesn't necessarily have to be the expression of strong ideology. It can simply address practical necessities, such as in supply chains in which many suppliers and manufacturers interact that don't necessarily know or trust another.[66] Here, DLT has much to add, as its time-stamping function allows for the tracking of activities, intermediaries become less prominent, self-executing code can enforce contractual clauses, the ledger can hold proof of provenance, quality or other characteristics of the good in question and on-boarding of new participants can be facilitated through related digital identities. While the technology initially emerged with a strong ideological message, which continues being carried forward in many realms, it is now also being adapted to many other contexts divorced from such ideology. Indeed, both from a contextual and technical perspective, there is a continuously expanding variety of DLTs.

F. *A Large Variety of Blockchains*

There is immense variance in blockchains and their internal governance structures.[67] Rather than constituting a singular technology with a predefined set of characteristics, blockchains are more adequately seen as 'a class of technologies'.[68] There is pronounced diversity regarding software management, the visibility and identifiability of transactions on the ledger and the right to add new data to a ledger.

Distributed ledgers can be configured in various fashions. They can be public or private, permissioned or unpermissioned and centralized or decentralized in their technological set-up and governance structures. In *public and permissionless* blockchains, anyone can entertain a node by downloading and running the relevant software; no permission is needed. In such an unpermissioned system, there are no identity restrictions for participation.[69] Transparency is an important feature of these systems, moreover, as anyone can download the entire ledger and view transaction data (which is why they are sometimes also referred to as 'public' blockchains). For example, any interested party can create a Bitcoin or Ethereum account (both are permissionless systems) using public key cryptography (introduced further below)

---

[66] For the benefits of blockchains in trade, see Lin Cong and Zhiguo He, 'Blockchain Disruption and Smart Contracts' (2018) NBER Working Paper No. 24399, 14 <www.nber.org/papers/w24399> accessed 3 April 2018.

[67] Blockchain governance refers to the process of maintaining the software. Chapter 7 is dedicated to this theme.

[68] Roman Beck, Christoph Müller-Bloch and John King, 'Governance in the Blockchain Economy: A Framework and Research Agenda' (2018) 3 <www.researchgate.net/publication/323689461_Governance_in_the_Blockchain_Economy_A_Framework_and_Research_Agenda> accessed 3 April 2018 (hereafter Beck et al., 'Governance in the Blockchain Economy').

[69] This is true at least in theory as over time informal restrictions for participation in mining (of an economic nature) and software governance have emerged.

without the need for prior permission from a gatekeeper. Permissionless blockchains rely on open-source software that anyone can download and then participate in the network without the need for prior approval by a gatekeeper. Conversely, on such ledgers, transactions are publicly auditable, which ensures transparency but minimizes privacy.

Blockchains can also be *private and permissioned*, however, which means that they can run on a private network, such as intranet or a virtual private network (VPN), and an administrator needs to grant permission to individuals wanting to maintain a node. The key distinction between permissioned and unpermissioned blockchains is simply that, while one needs access permission to join the former, this is not necessary in respect of the latter. Whereas unpermissioned blockchains are often a general-purpose infrastructure, permissioned ledgers are frequently designed for a specific purpose. These systems are not open for anyone to join and see. Rather, a single party or a consortium acts as a gatekeeper. Permissioned blockchains can be internal to a specific company or joint venture (which is why they are also often referred to as 'private' or 'enterprise' blockchains). Permissioned systems are a spin-off from the original permissionless systems that do not share the same ideology. Rather, parties experiment with them to achieve efficiency gains or to more easily operate transactions in a context devoid of trust (remember the complex supply chain example above). While public/permissionless and private/permissioned are currently the predominant combinations, blockchains can also take hybrid forms.

In permissioned systems, parties' identities are known, and only parties with specific attributes are admitted to the system. Because these systems involve fewer participants they can process transactions much more quickly than their unpermissioned counterparts. Where such solutions are relied on for specific purposes and in existing networks, there needs to be mediation regarding participation in the network. While the objectives of relying on a permissioned chain can also often be achieved by reliance on a conventional database, the case for using a DLT is stronger when a large number of parties are involved, when the actions of others need to be overseen and verified and when parties want to enjoy a degree of autonomy – e.g. to be able to specify smart contracts.[70] On the other hand, however, it is easier for participants in these networks to collude, as often only a few parties need to agree to validate information and record it thereto.

It is difficult to predict the design of the blockchains of the future. Some speculate that it lies in public permissionless blockchains, which could become a new generalized layer on top of the Internet (just as the Internet phased out intranets). Others, however, bet on current experiments with public chains merely paving the

[70] Jatinder Singh and Johan Michels, 'Blockchain as a Service: Providers and Trust' (2017) Queen Mary School of Law Legal Studies Research Paper No. 269/2017, 8 <https://papers.ssrn.com/sol3/papers.cfm?abstract_id=3091223> accessed 3 April 2018.

way for the private 'enterprise blockchains' of the future. Other possibilities include a coexistence of both systems, such as where unpermissioned systems serve as the network infrastructure for private chains. In the years to come more hybrids will probably emerge. It is also worth noting that some providers have started offering blockchain-as-a-service (BaaS) solutions; similarly to the cloud computing scenario, a firm here offers access to blockchain infrastructure to other firms.[71]

Although there are clear divergences between permissionless and permissioned blockchains, considerable divergences can also be pinpointed concerning the technical set-up, governance principles and underlying purposes of various projects within each of these categories. The same variety, if not more, exists in relation to emerging blockchain-based applications. Just as there is large variety in blockchains and their respective governance structures, the data stored on these ledgers can be equally diverse. It can represent anything from currency to property, intellectual property, equity, collectibles, contracts and other kinds of digital assets.

G. *Cryptoassets*

Private money in the form of Bitcoin was blockchains' first use case, and some continue to consider it as its killer app. Beyond cryptocurrencies, additional cryptoassets have emerged over time in the form of *tokens* or *coins*.[72] A token or coin is, essentially, a digital good that is artificially rendered scarce and tracked through a blockchain or blockchain-based application. These cryptoassets are artificially scarce, as the prohibition of *double spending* prevents an owner from spending a coin more than once.[73] This is one of the central benefits of relying on a blockchain as a form of accounting.

Tokens can have different purposes and represent anything from goods or services to rights, including voting rights. At this stage a common terminology for and conceptualization of different cryptoassets is still lacking. Some tokens exist to power blockchain infrastructure. For example, Ether is the native token of the Ethereum blockchain. It serves to pay transaction fees and to incentivize particular behaviour, such as securing the network.[74] Many blockchain-based applications also have their own token, which can be used to incentivize specific actions or, maybe more often, to raise capital for the development of the application.

Indeed, over the past few years there have been countless *initial coin offerings* (ICOs). In an ICO, coins or tokens are sold to the public. This often happens in

---

[71] ibid.

[72] I use 'cryptoasset' as a general terminology encompassing what is sometimes referred to as 'cryptocurrencies', as well as 'tokens' and 'coins'.

[73] Jean Bacon et al., 'Blockchain Demystified' (2017) Queen Mary University of London, School of Law Legal Studies Research Paper No. 268/2017, 5 <https://papers.ssrn.com/sol3/papers.cfm?abstract_id=3091218> accessed 28 May 2018 (hereafter Bacon et al., 'Blockchain Demystified').

[74] Ethereum White Paper at <https://github.com/ethereum/wiki/wiki/White-Paper> (accessed 3 May 2018).

various stages, first at a discounted rate to selected investors and then at a higher price to the public. ICOs are heralded as a more democratic alternative to venture capital, as they have turned into 'a way for innovative firms...to raise substantial amounts of funding'.[75] A question that has kept regulators busy over the past months is whether the cryptoassets sold in the context of an ICO always qualify as a security, and accordingly trigger the application of securities regulations.[76] Whereas some if not most cryptoassets undoubtedly are securities, a related debate highlights that this qualification will impose considerable regulatory burdens on innovators in this area, and that some tokens are noticeably distinct from a security and should be governed by an alternative legal framework.

In this context, suggestions have been made that the alternative legal classification of *utility tokens* should be a legally recognized category, to reflect that these tokens should not be qualified as securities.[77] Utility tokens have been defined as being 'primarily functional and consumptive in nature', so that they 'grant holders the right to access or a license to use an online service'.[78] In addition, however, they can also imbue holders with a right to vote or other decision rights in relation to the protocol or another online service.[79]

Utility tokens are best thought of as avatars of real-world goods, services or rights. For example, my bike could be represented by a token on the BikeChain, and, if I were to sell it to you, we would trade ownership of the token on-chain.[80] There are important distinctions, as, when an on-chain asset purely has on-chain value, the ledger can provide 'a complete record of the relevant assets'.[81] With respect to the BikeChain token, this would not be the case, as a theft of the bike would not be automatically reflected on-chain. This hints at the need for interoperability between the on-chain and off-chain worlds, which I'll address in Chapter 3.

The still unsettled discussions concerning utility tokens highlight that, through the development of blockchain technology, a broader phenomenon of 'tokenization' has been inaugurated. Tokenizing data has potentially far-reaching consequences. When an asset is tokenized, its on-chain version can be kept valuable

---

[75] European Commission, 'Remarks by Vice-President Dombrovskis at the Roundtable on Cryptocurrencies' (Speech) <http://europa.eu/rapid/press-release_SPEECH-18-1242_en.htm> accessed 28 March 2018.

[76] For a discussion, see Phillip Hacker and Chris Thomale, 'Crypto-Securities Regulation: ICOs, Token Sales and Cryptocurrencies under EU Financial Law' (2017) <https://papers.ssrn.com/sol3/papers.cfm?abstract_id=3075820> accessed 25 May 2018; Jonathan Rohr and Aaron Wright, 'Blockchain-Based Token Sales, Initial Coin Offerings, and the Democratization of Public Capital Markets' (2017) University of Tennessee Legal Studies Research Paper No. 338 <https://papers.ssrn.com/sol3/papers.cfm?abstract_id=3048104> accessed 28 May 2018.

[77] Some jurisdictions are now recognizing this category, such as the US State of Wyoming.

[78] De Filippi and Wright, 'Blockchain and the Law' (n 19) 100.

[79] ibid.

[80] If this is the future of tokens we may need to ponder under which fundamental economic freedom they fall under EU law.

[81] Bacon et al., 'Blockchain Demystified' (n 73) 5.

(because it is artificially scarce) and it can be easily shareable and transferable (because all changes can be reflected in the ledger in a relatively straightforward and decentralized manner). Through tokens 'real property, intellectual property and debt could become more liquid and could transfer around the world without the need to pass through layers of intermediaries'.[82]

We are just beginning to understand the function and different categories of tokens, and much more research into their micro- and macroeconomic implications is required. According to economist Susan Athey, cryptoassets, including cryptocurrencies, 'potentially expand international commerce, support financial inclusion, and transform how we shop, save and do business in ways we probably cannot even yet fully understand'.[83] In the future we might witness the 'tokenization of everything', powered by decentralized DLT networks.

H. *Decentralization and Disintermediation*

Where data is replicated across various nodes, a decentralized structure emerges provided that the governance of that network is also decentralized.[84] The distributed storage of data indeed offers numerous benefits, such as (i) it prevents a single centralized party tampering with the data; (ii) there is no master copy, hence no single point of failure, reducing the chances of a possible attack succeeding; and (iii) there is less risk of a denial-of-service attack.[85]

Disintermediation is the technology's related promise. As a consequence of their very structure, blockchains are widely considered to decentralize and disintermediate economic relations. When value is transferred through blockchain networks, the traditional intermediaries responsible for verifying and validating transactions – human-based institutions – may become obsolete.[86] As a consequence, it has been argued, 'the institutional structure of society could shift to one that is computationally based and thus has a diminished need for human-operated brick-and-mortar institutions'.[87]

Consensus guarantees that every transaction on the ledger is valid, which (at least in theory) obliterates the need for third-party intermediaries. It is worth noting, however, that this promise has not yet been realized, as for the time being more intermediaries have been added through the development of blockchain technology

---

[82] Wright and De Filippi, 'Lex Cryptographia' (n 5) 28.

[83] Susan Athey, '5 ways digital currency will change the world' (*World Economic Forum*, 22 January 2015) <www.weforum.org/agenda/2015/01/5-ways-digital-currencies-will-change-the-world/> accessed 13 April 2018.

[84] I return to this theme in Chapter 7.

[85] Bacon et al., 'Blockchain Demystified' (n 73) 12–13.

[86] Melanie Swan and Primavera de Filippi, 'Toward a Philosophy of Blockchain: A Symposium: Introduction' (2017) 48/5 Metaphilosophy, 604 <https://onlinelibrary.wiley.com/doi/full/10.1111/meta.12270> accessed 28 May 2018.

[87] ibid.

than removed. For example, centralized exchanges have emerged to allow people to buy and sell cryptoassets in a convenient manner. Similarly, wallet providers make it easier for people to manage their accounts.[88] Smart contracts necessitate oracles, a new class of intermediary, whereas miners and mining pools can also be considered as new intermediaries operating DLT networks.[89] These new intermediaries now coexist with older intermediaries. Over time some of the latter could be replaced with the former, such that parties rely on the technology, rather than a human institution, to verify and validate their transactions.

When it comes to narratives of decentralization and disintermediation, however, it is imperative to separate fact from fiction. Blockchains are not by definition decentralized. Rather, they can be centralized at both the software and the hardware levels. First, one may have a blockchain that runs only on very few nodes, which can all be located in the same room. Second, even when DLT is highly decentralized at hardware level, it can still be centralized at the software governance level. When protocol maintenance is managed by a single party or small group, decentralization is hardly a given. Often, permissioned blockchains are centralized at vendor or consortium level. Yet even the most well-known permissionless blockchains, such as Bitcoin and Ethereum, can be considered to be centralized, as the software development process is dominated by a few individuals.[90] I return to this theme in Chapter 7.

When decentralization occurs, it presents various advantages, but it also adds challenges, as a decentralized system will always be less efficient then a centralized one. Indeed, due to decentralization, blockchains are inefficient by design. Further, decentralized public permissionless blockchains are inherently transnational: a global network of computers not controlled by a single entity. As a consequence of this set-up, complex jurisdictional questions emerge, which I examine in Chapter 2. The removal of the central point of access indeed burdens the determination of jurisdiction and the imposition of legal obligations and responsibility.[91] Consensus protocols are the mechanism that makes it possible for blockchains to operate in a decentralized fashion without the need for a central controlling party.

I. *Consensus Protocols*

Consensus protocols provide consistency among the many copies of the ledger. Consensus is established when the protocol can ensure that each node adds the same new blocks to its local version of the blockchain. The fact that all actors follow

---

[88] Wallets can be stored offline, on a personal computer or be accessed through online applications.

[89] I introduce miners and their role in blockchain networks just below.

[90] Adem Efe Gencer et al., 'Decentralization in Bitcoin and Ethereum Networks' (*Cornell University Library*, 11 January 2018) <https://arxiv.org/abs/1801.03998> accessed 28 May 2018.

[91] See further Chapter 2.

the protocol's predetermined rules in deciding how to update the ledger can be considered the source of trust in the system. Indeed, it is the essence of consensus mechanisms that parties can have confidence that a certain outcome is reached *before* it is effectively reached.[92] It is in this way that trust in technology is said to replace trust in humans.

Blockchains are thus essentially protocols for reaching consensus. They enable users to agree through a consensus mechanism that confirms the ledger's accuracy by reconciling each version against all other copies. For nodes to accept new blocks, they need to be generated by *miners* (the nodes that group transactions into new blocks and suggest them to the network) in accordance with the consensus protocol.[93] Depending on the consensus protocol that is used, miners have diverse names, such as 'validator'. When a user signs a transaction, the transaction record is broadcast to nodes that are invited to process the transaction.[94] Miners assemble transactions into new blocks and subsequently broadcast them to the network. In return for their processing, they are rewarded with newly minted coins in the form of a *block reward*, and they potentially also receive transaction fees paid by users to secure the fast processing of their transactions.[95]

Whereas only some nodes participate in mining (only miners do), all nodes participate in the validation of new blocks. Upon finding a valid hash for a block, the miner broadcasts its hash to the network, and other nodes subsequently run a computation to verify whether the hash is valid – i.e. whether it meets the specifications of the protocol. When the node concludes that the new block is valid, it adds it to its local copy of the ledger and broadcasts it to other nodes in the network.[96]

There is large diversity in consensus protocols currently being discussed and experimented with. At this stage, *proof-of-work* is the most commonly used consensus mechanism for public and permissionless blockchains, relied on in Bitcoin and Ethereum. Through this consensus mechanism, nodes contribute computing power to secure and maintain the system and engage in an economic competition (requiring them to solve a computational puzzle) before they can propose a valid block to the nodes.[97] The difficulty of the mathematical puzzle is adjusted by the protocol to ensure consistency in transaction processing.[98]

---

[92] I owe this insight to Vlad Zamfir.
[93] Blockchains rely on asynchorous protocols in accordance with which nodes don't wait to synchronize with their peers to validate specific blocks, rather they validate blocks on the basis of the next block available to them. See Bacon et al., 'Blockchain Demystified' (n 73) 13.
[94] In many systems users can add a transaction fee to incentivize nodes to process their transaction swiftly.
[95] Narayanan, 'Bitcoin and Cryptocurrency Technologies' (n 61).
[96] Bacon et al., 'Blockchain Demystified' (n 73) 12.
[97] ibid. 15.
[98] This explains why on the Bitcoin blockchain a new block is added approximately every ten minutes.

Proof-of-work requires an investment in the form of money paid for electricity. Indeed, considering that in permissionless systems anyone can become a miner or node, the system needs safeguards against malicious actors that seek to control the network. Under a so-called *Sybil attack*, an attacker could flood the system with new nodes and newly mined blocks.[99] The investment in electricity is designed to make this prohibitively expensive.[100] It also causes serious environmental concerns. It was estimated that in June 2017 Bitcoin alone was using more energy than 150 individual countries in the world.[101] This is one of the main reasons why alternative consensus protocols are currently being developed with a view to being deployed in the future.

In permissionless systems, in principle any user can become a miner. Over time the required equipment has become prohibitively expensive, however, so that related costs function as a hurdle for participation in mining operations. Miners now need specialized and expensive hardware to mine a new block.[102] As a consequence, *mining pools* – a consolidation of miners – have emerged particularly in relation to Bitcoin. In a mining pool, block rewards and transaction fees are shared between participants, so that miners increase the probability of touching a monetary reward through participation.[103] As a consequence, mining can be extremely consolidating, confirming that there can be elements of stark centralization in allegedly decentralized networks.

The agglomeration of mining operations raises concerns from an economic and political perspective and may further undermine the security of the network.[104] Indeed, where mining is concentrated, the risk of a so-called *51% attack*, whereby the network is taken over by miners controlling the majority of the overall hash rate, increases. Some argue that this is merely hypothetical, as miners have an incentive to protect the system to continue benefiting financially through mining rewards and transactions.[105] This position neglects the incentives of actors not motivated by such costs, however.

In light of the problems associated with proof-of-work, alternative consensus protocols are currently being developed. The most discussed alternative is *proof-of-stake*, whereby participants show a 'stake' in the system (in the form of coins) in

---

[99] Bacon et al., 'Blockchain Demystified' (n 73) 14.
[100] For the mechanics of such energy consumption, see Narayanan, 'Bitcoin and Cryptocurrency Technologies' (n 61) 146–49.
[101] Eric Holthaus, 'Bitcoin Mining Guzzles Energy – And Its Carbon Footprint Just Keeps Growing' (*wired*, 12 June 2017) <www.wired.com/story/bitcoin-mining-guzzles-energyand-its-carbon-footprint-just-keeps-growing/> accessed 1 June 2018.
[102] Miners use application-specific integrated circuits ('ASICs').
[103] Users conventionally insert transaction fees into their blocks to incentivize miners to process their block. The higher the fee, the quicker the block will be processed.
[104] Daniel Conte de Leon et al., 'Blockchain: Properties and Misconceptions' (2017) 11/3 Asia Pacific Journal of Innovation and Entrepreneurship, 294 <www.emeraldinsight.com/doi/full/10.1108/APJIE-12-2017-034> accessed 28 May 2018 (hereafter Conte de Leon, 'Blockchain: Properties and Misconceptions').
[105] Nakamoto, 'Bitcoin White Paper' (n 34) 4.

order to participate in consensus. Stake can be combined with other factors, such as a randomized ballot, to determine who gets to suggest a new block to the network in order to lessen the oligopolistic tendency of this consensus protocol. In addition to proof-of-stake, many additional consensus protocols are being explored and might be relied on in the future.[106] I now turn to examine decentralized applications.

J. *Decentralized Applications and D(A)Os*

Decentralized applications (DApps) are programs that are stored on a decentralized ledger and executed by multiple nodes. For example, decentralized file-sharing protocols permit the storage of files in peer-to-peer networks in which access to a file is controlled by a smart contract.[107] Such solutions seek to provide safe and resilient file storage options without a centralized point of control.[108] The idea is that many peers store small portions of files in exchange for compensation in the form of tokens that are reassembled by the protocol upon demand.

Decentralized organizations (DOs) and *decentralized autonomous organizations* (DAOs) constitute a subcategory of decentralized applications. A DO is a form of organization that 'relies on blockchain technology and smart contracts as their primary source of governance'.[109] They are a nexus of smart contracts that is combined to 'form an interconnected system of technically enforced relationships that collectively define the rules of an organization'.[110] Decentralized organizations accordingly provide individuals with an option to cooperate or transact on a peer-to-peer basis without the need for a conventional intermediary.

The potential of such organizations has been explored in the sharing economy context.[111] The idea is that the platforms intermediating the relation between participants could be replaced by a DO (and possibly a DAO in the future).[112] Airbnb and Uber would be swapped for a nexus of smart contracts and transactions paid for in tokens. The result would be a modern-day cooperative powered by code that could be run by those using the platform on the supply side, aiming to split profits between themselves rather than seeing a large share go to the centralized intermediary.

---

[106] For an early overview, see Narayanan, 'Bitcoin and Cryptocurrency Technologies' (n 61) 216–36.

[107] On smart contracts, see further below.

[108] See, by way of example: <https://filecoin.io/>; <https://github.com/ethersphere/swarm-guide/blob/master/contents/runninganode.rst>.

[109] De Filippi and Wright, 'Blockchain and the Law' (n 19) 136.

[110] ibid.

[111] On the sharing economy generally, see Nestor Davidson et al., *Cambridge Handbook of the Law of the Sharing Economy* (Cambridge University Press 2018).

[112] Alex Pazaitis et al., 'Blockchain and Value Systems in the Sharing Economy: The Illustrative Case of Backfeed' (*ScienceDirect*, December 2017) <www.sciencedirect.com/science/article/pii/S0040162517307084> accessed 25 May 2018.

In a decentralized autonomous organization there is only very little human control. A DAO expresses a reciprocal relationship between individuals, firms or machines to create a 'complex ecosystem of autonomous agents interacting with one another according to a set of pre-determined, hard-wired, and self-enforcing rules'.[113] Instead of an institution managed by 'humans interacting in person. . .via the legal system', a DAO involves 'humans interacting with each other according to a protocol specified in code, and enforced on the blockchain'.[114] Decentralized autonomous organizations at this stage remain largely an idea – but a potent one, according to which human interaction would be replaced by technical protocols.[115]

The DAO concept also illustrates why some consider that blockchains could accelerate a structural shift of power 'from legal rules and regulations administered by government authorities to code-based rules and protocols governed by decentralized blockchain-based networks'.[116] D(A)Os allow individuals to construct their own systems of rules that are automatically enforced by the blockchains' protocol, and hence create customized governance solutions that could decrease coordination costs in (large) groups.[117] Some welcome it as a 'new form of democracy' that is stable and less prone to erratic human behaviour.[118] The governance challenges of these systems should not be underestimated, however. Indeed, code doesn't make human problems and the need for human agreement go away. These elements will still be required in relation to software development and maintenance. The sharing economy example above may ultimately fail not because of technical shortcomings but, rather, the inability of humans to efficiently reach decentralized consensus.

It is further unlikely that such systems will develop outside the confines of established legal orders. Whereas D(A)Os can be designed to operate on the basis of rules and principles distinct from those mandated by law, compliance with law is required to secure interoperability with the real world. At least in the short to medium term, we are more likely to observe D(A)Os being integrated into existing companies and used as part of corporate governance mechanisms rather than as a tool to redefine democracy in line with Pierre-Joseph Proudhon's vision of running society through individual contracts.[119] Smart contracts are the most well-known example of applications running on a blockchain.

---

[113] Wright and De Filippi, 'Lex Cryptographia' (n 5) 17.

[114] Vitalik Buterin, 'DAOs, DACs, DAs and More: An Incomplete Terminology Guide' (*Ethereum Blog*, 6 May 2014) <https://blog.ethereum.org/2014/05/06/daos-dacs-das-and-more-an-incomplete-terminology-guide/> accessed 13 April 2018.

[115] I return to this theme in Chapter 7.

[116] De Filippi and Wright, 'Blockchain and the Law' (n 19) 7.

[117] This theme is examined further in Chapter 3.

[118] Ralph Merkle, 'DAOs, Democracy and Governance' (2016) 1 <http://merkle.com/papers/DAOdemocracyDraft.pdf> accessed 3 April 2018.

[119] Pierre-Joseph Proudhon and John Robinson, *General Idea of the Revolution in the Nineteenth Century* (Courier Corporation 2004) 4.

K. *Smart Contracts*

Smart contracts are one of the varied decentralized applications that can run on a blockchain infrastructure.[120] Buterin considers blockchains to be about 'the freedom to create a new mechanism with a new ruleset extremely quickly and pushing it out'.[121] Smart contracts are a means of achieving that goal.[122] The terminology dates back to 1994, when Nick Szabo defined a smart contract as 'a set of promises, specified in digital form, including protocols within which the parties perform on these promises'.[123] Szabo envisaged the creation of computer software resembling contractual clauses. These artefacts would be able to link parties to another in a manner that would make it difficult for one of them to unilaterally terminate the agreement.[124] Others were similarly fascinated by the idea of creating contracts that could be read and used by humans and machines alike.[125]

Digital contracts are not, of course, novel. Agreements have long been translated into machine-readable code, and performance has been based on computers. For example, contracts concluded between consumers and online service providers and large corporations often rely on electronic data interchanges.[126] Algorithmic contracts are already used in high-frequency trading, such that machine learning allows algorithms to react quickly to changes in the market.[127] What distinguishes smart contracts from earlier digital contracts is *automated execution*. Indeed, per se smart contracts have little to do with contracts that are smart but are rather automatically executing computer programs. While automated execution can also exist in other networks, it is considered to be particularly powerful in public and permissionless blockchains, as, here, no single party or group of actors can interfere with the software's execution.

Smart contracts are essentially software that executes automatically and the execution of which cannot be halted unless this possibility is specifically built into the code. These artefacts are neither smart nor contracts, however. Smart contracts are *not smart in the AI sense*, as they are unable to understand natural language

---

[120] Buterin, 'Visions' (n 50).
[121] Smart contracts can be coded on the Bitcoin blockchain but Bitcoin's native language is limited in this regard and often the Ethereum blockchain will be preferred as a general-purposes computing platform that is Turing complete.
[122] Nick Szabo, 'Smart Contracts: Building Blocks for Digital Markets' (1996) <www.fon.hum.uva.nl/rob/Courses/InformationInSpeech/CDROM/Literature/LOTwinterschool2006/szabo.best.vwh.net/smart_contracts_2.html> accessed 13 April 2018.
[123] ibid.
[124] See Ian Grigg, 'The Ricardian Contract' <http://iang.org/papers/ricardian_contract.html> accessed 14 April 2018.
[125] See also Harry Surden, 'Computable Contracts' (2012) 46 UC Davis Law Review 629.
[126] Lauren Scholz, 'Algorithmic Contracts' (2017) 20 Stanford Technology Law Review 128.
[127] Ari Juels, Ahmed Kosba and Elaine Shi, 'The Ring of Gyges: Using Smart Contracts for Crime' 2 <www.arijuels.com/wp-content/uploads/2013/09/Gyges.pdf> accessed 3 April 2018 (hereafter Juels et al., 'The Ring of Gyges').

(such as contractual terms) or to independently verify whether an execution-relevant event occurred. For this, *oracles* are needed. An oracle can be one or multiple persons, groups or programs that feed the software relevant information, such as whether a natural disaster has occurred (to release an insurance premium) or whether online goods have been delivered (to release payment). Oracles are the necessary bridge between blockchains and the real world in the absence of adequate machine intelligence.

Smart contracts also *cannot be qualified as contracts in the legal sense*. They're a computer-programmable 'if'/'then' relation unable to account for wider contextual factors. A smart contract is, essentially, a sequence of instructions that a miner runs in exchange for compensation. As such, these technical artefacts are better defined as 'an autonomously executing piece of code whose inputs and outputs can include money'.[128] Further, a smart contract can be used to organize transactions between two addresses belonging to the same person whereas a contract is concluded between at least two parties. While smart contracts can, accordingly, be useful in contractual settings (such as to automatically execute a contractual clause), they are not legal contracts per se but computer code that can be used to produce legal effects.

The fact that smart contracts are neither smart nor contracts does not imply, however, that they're an insignificant innovation. Rather, the opposite is the case. Smart contracts' automated execution enables transactions in situations devoid of human and institutional trust, lowers transaction costs and reduces counterparty risk and interpretative uncertainty.[129] Further, because smart contracts are machine-readable they present great potential in the Internet of Things (IoT) context. As second-layer applications, smart contracts benefit from the tamper-proof nature of the underlying blockchain infrastructure and thus cannot be stopped by a single party.[130] Given that many nodes run smart contract code, it 'is not controlled by – and cannot be halted by – any single party'.[131] This is considered to inaugurate a new era of computing in which 'software applications are no longer controlled by a central authority but rather operate autonomously on a decentralized, peer-to-peer network'.[132]

---

[128] For an overview of smart contracts' advantages, see Mark Giancaspro, 'Is a "smart contract" really a smart idea? Insights from a legal perspective' (2017) 33 Computer Law & Security Review 825 and Richard Holden and Anup Malani, 'Can Blockchain Solve the Holdup Problem in Contracts?' (2017) 21–24 <https://papers.ssrn.com/sol3/papers.cfm?abstract_id=3093879> accessed 3 April 2018.

[129] It is worth noting that this doesn't make them or their effects 'immutable' as their effects can always be rolled back by a second transaction that has that objective.

[130] De Filippi and Wright, 'Blockchain and the Law' (n 19) 29.

[131] ibid.

[132] Christian Sillaber and Bernhard Waltl, 'Life Cycle of Smart Contracts in Blockchain Ecosystems' (2017) 41 Datenschutz und Datensicherheit 497.

A smart contract has four life cycles: creation, freezing, execution and finalization.[133] During the creative phase it is defined and turned into code. The software is then frozen while being added to the chain through the relevant consensus process, before it is executed – that is to say, read and implemented by the various nodes.[134] Finally, the smart contract is finalized as 'the resulting transactions and the new state information are stored in the distributed ledger and confirmed according to the consensus protocol'.[135] This removes the intervention of an intermediary (other than the oracle) and results in considerable efficiency gains. Through related cost reductions, new business models and markets can emerge, such as peer-to-peer energy markets using neighbourhood smart grids or solutions powered by micropayments. Much hope is placed in smart contracts in relation to machine-to-machine communications in an IoT context and consumer contracts in which the software could automatically process legally mandated refunds.[136]

In a smart contract, performance is hard-wired into the code. For example, the software can be used for the automatic transfer of collateral in the event of default or to disburse employee compensation if performance goals are achieved.[137] Moreover, many possible uses for smart contracts are currently explored in InsurTech concerning event-driven insurance.[138] Ed Felten thinks that cryptocurrencies are most useful when combined with smart contracts, as this will 'allow parties to define the behavior of a virtual actor in code, and have the cryptocurrency's consensus system enforce that the virtual actor behaves according to its code'.[139] Some go so far as to qualify automated execution as the paramount value proposition of this new technology, as 'the blockchain economy extends beyond the digital economy in that agreed-upon transactions are autonomously enforced, following rules defined in smart contracts'.[140]

Thomas Hobbes has already emphasized that 'covenants, without the sword, are but words and of no strength to secure a man at all'.[141] While automated execution accordingly presents many advantages, it also has drawbacks that should not be ignored. Written in programming language, smart contracts remove the ambiguity

[133] ibid.
[134] ibid.
[135] See further Josh Fairfield, 'Smart Contracts, Bitcoin Bots, and Consumer Protection' (2014) 71 Washington & Lee Law Review Online 36.
[136] David Yermack, 'Corporate Governance and Blockchains' (2017) 21 Review of Finance 7, 26.
[137] Stan Higgins, 'AXA is using Ethereum's Blockchain for a New Flight Insurance Product' (*coindesk*, 13 September 2017) <www.coindesk.com/axa-using-ethereums-blockchain-new-flight-insurance-product/> accessed 13 April 2018.
[138] Ed Felten, 'Blockchain: What is it good for?' (*Freedom to Tinker*, 26 February 2018) <https://freedom-to-tinker.com/2018/02/26/bloc> accessed 3 April 2018.
[139] Beck et al., 'Governance in the Blockchain Economy' (n 68) 5.
[140] Thomas Hobbes, *Leviathan* (The Floating Press 2009) Part II Chapter XVII 240.
[141] Jeremy Sklaroff, 'Smart Contracts and the Cost of Inflexibility' (2017) 166 University of Pennsylvania Law Review 263.

inherent to natural language. In some circumstances, parties to an agreement will prefer the flexibility afforded by legal contracts over the rigidity of automated software. Smart contracts are indeed unable to match the linguistic ambiguity and enforcement discretion ingrained in legal contracts.[142] Terms such as 'good faith', 'best efforts' or 'force majeure' cannot be expressed in code. Smart contracts further fall short of contract law's remedial function of adjudicating disputes after the fact.[143] Whereas the role of the law is to fill gaps in agreements with default rules, smart contract code contains no gaps allowing law to intervene.[144]

Furthermore, whereas software is automatically executed on-chain, unwanted transactions cannot be rolled back. This can be problematic, such as when a party lacks legal capacity. The identity of a party to a contract can be difficult to establish, moreover, as digital signatures rather than real-world identities are used. This is problematic, as it cannot accommodate changes such as those mandated as a result of judicial decisions.[145] It could cause particular problems in a number of domains, such as where this software is used for unlawful purposes. Indeed, smart contracts could be used to enable such anti-competitive behaviour as price-fixing[146] and to 'effectively guarantee payment for committed crimes' and, conversely, to fuel new criminal ecosystems.[147]

In light of the above, it is hardly surprising that solutions are being developed to harness the efficiency of smart contracting software while reducing the unavoidability of execution. Rather than being fully automated, the smart contract's execution could in some circumstances be implemented through *multiple-signature verification* (MultiSig) – that is to say, parties would need to agree to its execution.[148] Moreover, in order to remedy disputes arising in respect of smart contracts, new dispute resolution mechanisms are being designed. A number of smart contract protocols are currently being developed that parties can include into the smart contract itself. Mechanisms also still need to be developed concerning the handling of unintended or malicious flaws in smart contract code, a governance question I address in Chapter 7.[149]

---

[142] Kevin Werbach and Nicolas Cornell, 'Contracts Ex Machina' (2017) 67 Duke Law Journal 313 (hereafter Werbach and Cornell, 'Contracts Ex Machina') (emphasis in original).

[143] Usha Rodrigues, 'Law and the Blockchain' (2018) University of Georgia School of Law Legal Studies Research Paper No. 2017–07, 6 <https://papers.ssrn.com/sol3/papers.cfm?abstract_id=3127782> accessed 3 April 2018.

[144] See further Chapter 3.

[145] Werbach and Cornell, 'Contracts Ex Machina' (n 142) 373; Ariel Ezrachi and Maurice Stucke, *Virtual Competition: The Promise and Perils of the Algorithm-Driven Economy* (Harvard University Press 2016).

[146] Juels et al., 'The Ring of Gyges' (n 127) 1.

[147] Werbach and Cornell, 'Contracts Ex Machina' (n 142) 345.

[148] Conte de Leon, 'Blockchain: Properties and Misconceptions' (n 104) 296.

[149] Kevin Werbach, *The Blockchain and the New Architecture of Trust* (MIT Press 2018) 202.

It is important to remember that, although smart contracts can be used for unlawful means and the execution of the software cannot be stopped, legal systems in principle retain control over the effects of the transaction. 'The code made me do it' is not a valid excuse. This is not only why smart contracts' outcomes are subject to the jurisdiction of real-world courts but also why, going forward, we might see increased reliance on code libraries that offer a choice of elements used in legal contracts to the parties to a smart contract. Next, I examine the role of cryptography in blockchain technology.

L. *Cryptography and Cryptoeconomics*

Kevin Werbach considers that *cryptography* is blockchains' distinctive architectural element, as they 'enforce decisions based on the difficulty of reversing cryptographic mathematical transformations'.[150] Two cryptographic tools are particularly important in the context of DLT: public key infrastructure (PKI) and hash functions. Phillip Rogaway has highlighted that cryptography is an inherently political tool, as it 'rearranges power: it configures who can do what, from what'.[151] This is an important theme to bear in mind when evaluating specific DLTs and their governance structures.

In permissionless blockchains, each participant engages through an account comprised of a public address (the identifier) and a private key (the password).[152] *Public key infrastructure* is used as a means of authenticating identities in order to identify the parties associated with each transaction in a pseudonymous manner.[153] This cryptographic tool comprises a function to generate a key pair that consists of a public and a private key, a signing algorithm and a validation function used to check whether a digital signature is correct.[154] This key pair has a number of properties, including that data that is encrypted with the public key can be decrypted only by using the private key, and vice versa.[155] This enables PKI to serve as an identity authentication method, as, if data can be decrypted with the public key, it proves that it was encrypted by the holder of the private key.

It is in this way that PKI is used as a means of creating *digital signatures*. To 'sign' the data item, the sender encrypts data with their private key. If data can be

---

[150] Phillip Rogaway, 'The Moral Character of Cryptographic Work' (December 2015), 1 <http://web.cs.ucdavis.edu/~rogaway/papers/moral-fn.pdf> accessed 25 May 2018.

[151] Quantum computing might in the future come to present a challenge to encryption (in its current form).

[152] Bacon et al., 'Blockchain Demystified' (n 73) 4.

[153] ibid. 9.

[154] ibid.

[155] ibid.

decrypted through the public key, this is taken as proof that the sender held the relevant private key.[156] Through challenge–response interactions it can be verified whether someone holds a particular private key. The use of PKI underlines that transactions on a blockchain are pseudonymous in nature. When digital signatures are used, the identity of a party is not immediately known but can be unveiled when it is matched with additional information.[157] Indeed, while information stored on the ledger is usually encrypted, metadata about the accounts involved in transactions are usually not. It is, accordingly, relatively straightforward to link such pseudonymous identities belonging to the same individual though the statements they make.[158] The current lack of privacy on most blockchains is a subject I return to in Chapter 4.

In blockchain systems, *hash functions* are relied on to maintain data integrity – that is to say, to create a persistent and tamper-evident record of transactions.[159] Hashing can prove the integrity of input data, as when the contents of that data are put through a hash function; the latter creates a string of digits of a fixed length that is unique to the input data item.[160] If the input data is changed even in the slightest, a totally different hash value will result, revealing that the input data has undergone change. The hashing method thus makes the ledger tamper-evident. Any changes to blockchain data are visible, as they alter the hash of the block and of all subsequent blocks. It is worth stressing that hashing is a one-way function. If the range of possible inputs is sufficiently large and unpredictable that all possible combinations cannot be tried, hashing becomes non-invertible.[161]

Cryptography and game-theoretic incentives are used to secure blockchain systems. This combination has led to the emergence of the concept of *cryptoeconomics*. It denotes that blockchains are not only secured by cryptography but further anchored in economics, as they rely on incentives to guide behaviour. Indeed, on DLT, every transaction is ultimately an economic transaction.

According to Buterin, the concept of cryptoeconomics refers to any decentralized cryptographic protocol 'that uses economic incentives to ensure that it keeps going and doesn't go back in time or incur any glitch'.[162] The precise incentivization mechanisms used depend on the specific ledger but generally include transaction

[156] On this, see further Chapter 4.
[157] Narayanan, 'Bitcoin and Cryptocurrency Technologies' (n 61) 42.
[158] Bacon et al., 'Blockchain Demystified' (n 73) 4.
[159] ibid. 6–7.
[160] Gunes Acar, 'Four Cents to Deanonymize: Companies Reverse Hashed Email Addresses' (*Freedom to Tinker*, 9 April 2018) <https://freedom-to-tinker.com/2018/04/09/four-cents-to-dea nonymize-companies-reverse-hashed-email-addresses/> accessed 28 May 2018.
[161] Buterin, Visions (n 50).
[162] On block rewards, see further Narayanan, 'Bitcoin and Cryptocurrency Technologies' (n 61) 62.

fees and block rewards.[163] The concept of cryptoeconomics further underlines the impossibility of understanding blockchains from a singular perspective; rather, interdisciplinary approaches are needed. It is the use of cryptography that turns DLT into a tamper-proof system.

M. *Blockchains as Tamper-Proof Systems*

Blockchains are conventionally branded as 'immutable'. In reality, they are not.[164] Indeed, various participants can collude to change the current state of the ledger. While such efforts would be extremely burdensome and expensive, they are not impossible.[165] Indeed, as per the Bitcoin White Paper itself, there is an 'ongoing chain of hash-based proof-of-work, forming a record that cannot be changed *without redoing the proof-of-work*'.[166] Through human intervention, changes to the network become possible, as I further document in Chapter 7. It is for that reason that it is preferable to refer to distributed ledgers as *tamper-evident*.

Although amending the ledger is not impossible, it is extremely hard and unlikely. Indeed, there are 'no technical means, short of undermining the integrity of the entire system, to unwind a transfer'.[167] Because blocks are linked through hashes, changing information on a blockchain is difficult and expensive. We've already seen that the header of each block contains a hash of the preceding block and even small changes will change the unique hash of the altered block – and of all subsequent blocks. Making changes to blockchain data is thus extremely hard, and when it is done it is probably visible to all those having access to the ledger. This also indicates that the blockchain becomes more secure over time, as the longer the chain is and the older the block subject to modification, the harder this becomes.

Through their tamper-proof nature, blockchains freeze facts (information entered cannot, as a general rule, be changed) and the future (smart contracts' execution cannot be halted even when parties change their mind). We'll observe in Chapter 3 that strictly immutable blockchains are unlikely to coexist with the law, as they must be able to absorb changes required by law, such as token ownership modifications mandated by a court order. Chapter 4 documents, moreover, that tamper resistance is acutely problematic from the perspective of

---

[163] See also Conte de Leon, 'Blockchain: Properties and Misconceptions' (n 104) 290.
[164] Angela Walch, 'The Path of the Blockchain Lexicon (and the Law)' (2017) 36 Review of Banking and Financial Law 713.
[165] Nakamoto, 'Bitcoin White Paper' (n 34) 1 (emphasis added).
[166] Werbach and Cornell, 'Contracts Ex Machina' (n 142) 335.
[167] Regulation (EU) 2016/679 on the protection of natural persons with regard to the processing of personal data and on the free movement of such data [2016] OJ L 119/1.

the European Union's General Data Protection Regulation.[168] It is accordingly unsurprising that there are currently projects that seek to make blockchains redactable.[169] Some are also predicting that in the future there may well be ways for 'automating aspects of reversibility, such as corrective operation that can occur automatically through the use of smart contracts'.[170] These discussions underline that the technology continues to suffer from technical immaturity.

N. *Technical Immaturity*

At this moment in time blockchains suffer from 'severe technical and procedural limitations'. This is no mystery, as prominent voices in the blockchain space have always admitted to this fact while working on solutions to make the system more mature. According to Vlad Zamfir, a researcher at the Ethereum Foundation, 'Ethereum is not safe or scalable. It is immature experimental tech.'[171] Vitalik Buterin, the co-founder of Ethereum, agrees that 'bitcoin and ethereum are both deeply flawed in their current forms'.[172]

In their contemporary set-up, DLTs suffer from numerous overall shortcomings. They lack the scalability for any large-scale deployment. Blockchains are inefficient by design, as every full node must process every transaction and maintain a copy of its entire state. While this process eliminates the single point of failure and presents security benefits, it lowers throughput and slows down transactions.[173] This problem is likely only to increase as ledgers grow in size. This illustrates the constant tension between centralization and decentralization, as solving the scalability problem may require a return to more centralization. Scalability indeed is an important concern

---

[168] Giuseppe Ateniese, Bernardo Magri, Daniele Venturi and Ewerton Andrade, 'Redactable Blockchain – or – Rewriting History in Bitcoin and Friends' (2017) <https://eprint.iacr.org/2016/757.pdf> accessed 3 April 2018.

[169] Bacon et al., 'Blockchain Demystified' (n 73) 24.

[170] Christian Sillaber and Bernhard Waltl, 'Life Cycle of Smart Contracts in Blockchain Ecosystems' (2017) 41 Datenschutz und Datensicherheit – DuD 497.

[171] Vlad Zamfir [VladZamfir] (4 March 2017) 'Ethereum isn't safe or scalable. It is immature experimental tech. Don't rely on it for mission critical apps unless absolutely necessary!' [Tweet] <https://twitter.com/vladzamfir/status/838006311598030848?lang=de> accessed 3 April 2018. See also Vlad Zamfir, 'About my tweet from yesterday..' (*Medium*, 5 March 2017) <https://medium.com/@Vlad_Zamfir/about-my-tweet-from-yesterday-dcc61915b572> accessed 20 March 2018.

[172] Vitalik Buterin [VitalikButerin] (14 September 2017) 'I think bitcoin and ethereum are both deeply flawed in their current forms. And I say this is in some way in most presentations I make.' [Tweet] <https://twitter.com/VitalikButerin/status/908268522890985472> accessed 3 April 2018.

[173] See further Preethi Kasireddy, 'Fundamental Challenges with Public Blockchains' (*Medium*, 10 December 2017) <https://medium.com/@preethikasireddy/fundamental-challenges-with-public-blockchains-253c800e9428> accessed 20 March 2018 (hereafter Kasireddy, 'Fundamental Challenges').

in an append-only and thus ever-growing database in which each new transaction causes the network to grow. Solutions currently experimented with to resolve these issues include off-chain payment channels,[174] sharding,[175] off-chain computations[176] and directed acyclic graphs (DAGs).[177]

Furthermore, on a blockchain, data is stored integrally and perpetually on each node. As a consequence, every node is adding ever more data as the blockchain grows.[178] Decentralized storage models could help remedy this issue, for instance through Swarm,[179] IPFS[180] and Storj.[181] Further issues revolve around the lack of formal verification processes for smart contracts.[182]

Adoption can also be seen as a social challenge; concrete blockchain applications remain rare at this point in time. Hyman Minsky has rightly noted that 'everyone can create money; the problem is to get it accepted'.[183] This denotes the uncertainty of cryptocurrency adoption, but also of blockchains more generally. In their present configuration, blockchains are an attractive technology only when the benefits of decentralization outweigh concerns for scalability, efficiency and speed. Whether these limitations are here to stay remains to be seen. Prominent blockchain researchers have expressed confidence, however, that 'the current performance limitations of blockchain will be solved in the future'.[184]

Above, I have hinted at only some of the many technical insufficiencies of distributed ledgers that need to be addressed in the future. The point was not to discuss these elements or to provide a comprehensive overview thereof but, rather, to emphasize that innovation is in full swing and that the technology's building blocks are constantly evolving. This realization matters, as it underlines not only the speed of innovation but also that the uncertain and changing assumptions that are relied on in policy and regulatory discussions must be borne in mind. Technological immaturity further confirms that, at this moment in time, blockchains are a malleable technology, and that the blockchains of the future will be shaped by the various influences, including those of a regulatory nature, they are exposed to today. DLT is malleable not only at a technical but also at a normative level.

---

[174] Such a micropayment channel network allows to keep transactions off-chain and the block-chain functions purely as a settlement layer. The Lightning Network plans to carry this out on the Bitcoin blockchain. See further <https://lightning.network/> accessed 20 March 2018.

[175] Sharding denotes a process whereby different nodes store and process a small part of the state only.

[176] Through off-chain computations, such as Ethereum TrueBit, computations are carried out off-chain.

[177] A DAG does away with the linear blockchain structure.

[178] Kasireddy, 'Fundamental Challenges' (n 173).

[179] <https://github.com/ethersphere/swarm-guide/blob/master/contents/runninganode.rst>.

[180] <https://ipfs.io/>.

[181] <https://storj.io/>.

[182] Kasireddy, 'Fundamental Challenges' (n 173).

[183] Hyman Minsky, *Stabilizing and Unstable Economy* (McGraw Hill 1986) 255.

[184] Beck, 'Opportunities and Risks of Blockchain Technologies' (n 59) 119.

O. Malleability

In and of themselves, blockchains are a neutral technology. Just like any technology, they can therefore be manipulated to be operated for good or for bad. Whereas the potential benefits of distributed ledgers are naturally put to the fore in most discussions, we must not ignore the fact that they can also be exploited for malicious ends.[185] Stated otherwise, blockchains can be used to bank the unbanked or power autonomous drone armies. They can serve as a backbone for autonomous assassination markets or to bring more transparency to industry and politics. DLT can be used by governments to improve their operations, or as a tool of surveillance and oppression. Of course, there are many shades of grey between these black and white extremes, and beneficial and malicious uses are not mutually exclusive.

Nonetheless, it must be clear that the manner in which blockchains and new technology in general will be used in the future remains undefined, though not for long. It is in these early years that the tone will be set as to what blockchains (and, in a broader sense, technological change) will mean for humanity. Like all technology, blockchains can be used to support or undercut law, or to further or undermine policy objectives.

While an immature technology is a malleable technology, a matured technology is much less so. As a consequence, it should be evident that the time for society, regulators and stakeholders to start learning, thinking and discussing blockchains is now – even if there is no certainty at this stage as to whether and how these technical artefacts will be used in the future.[186] Blockchains trigger both utopian and dystopian visions, and it is up to us to determine which vision will turn into reality. With this in mind, I now turn to the book's substantive analysis.

---

[185] Vlad Zamfir, 'Blockchains Considered (Potentially) Harmful' (*Medium*, 21 August 2017) <https://medium.com/@Vlad_Zamfir/blockchains-considered-potentially-harmful-d039888c3208> accessed 13 April 2018.

[186] It is for this precise reason that Chapter 6 develops a concept of polycentric co-regulation that stresses the importance of broad dialogue since the early stages of technological development.

2

Blockchains as a Regulatable Technology

> The ability of blockchains to facilitate and support autonomous systems will increasingly create challenges for states and regulators seeking to control, shape, or influence the development of blockchain technology.[1]

The preceding chapter illustrated that blockchains represent a still immature technology that could come to considerably redefine socio-economic systems. While use cases continue to crystallize, diverse legal questions have started to surface. There have been ample discussions about, *inter alia*: whether all cryptoassets should be qualified as securities;[2] to what extent software developers are liable for damage caused by their code;[3] how blockchains will transform certain areas of law;[4] and whether urban planning needs to account for cryptocurrency mining.[5] Some even consider that blockchain-based applications might come to unsettle the very social

---

[1] Primavera De Filippi and Aaron Wright, *Blockchain and the Law* (Harvard University Press 2018) 5 (hereafter De Filippi and Wright, 'Blockchain and the Law').

[2] Jonathan Rohr and Aaron Wright, 'Blockchain-Based Token Sales, Initial Coin Offerings, and the Democratization of Public Capital Markets' (2017) Cardozo Legal Studies Research Paper No. 527, University of Tennessee Legal Studies Research Paper No. 338 <https://papers.ssrn.com/sol3/papers.cfm?abstract_id=3048104> accessed 28 February 2018; Philipp Hacker and Chris Thomale, 'Crypto-Securities Regulation: ICOs, Token Sales and Cryptocurrencies under EU Financial Law' (22 November 2017) <https://ssrn.com/abstract=3075820> accessed 28 February 2018.

[3] <https://github.com/ethereum/EIPs/pull/867#issuecomment-365800936> accessed 28 February 2018.

[4] 'Will Blockchain Soon Disrupt IP Protection?' (8 September 2017) <http://blog.dennemeyer.com/blockchain-disrupt-ip-protection> accessed 28 February 2018.

[5] New York State Assembly Bill No. A 09862 (14 February 2018) 'Referred to Economic Development' <http://assembly.state.ny.us/leg/?default_fld=&leg_video=&bn=A09862&term=2017&Summary=Y&Actions=Y&Committee%26nbspVotes=Y&Floor%26nbspVotes=Y&Text=Y&Chamber%26nbspVideo%2FTranscript=Y> accessed 1 March 2018.

contract that grounds contemporary constitutional orders.[6] These are but some of the complex and multifaceted legal questions being discussed in the face of this technology's adoption. Going forward, lawyers and policy-makers will be compelled to determine how existing legal frameworks can be applied to the technology, and to ponder the necessity of legislative intervention.[7]

Before turning to the substantive merits of such debates, I must first consider the *very possibility* of regulatory interference with systems originally designed to be censorship-resistant. Bitcoin stems from the libertarian cypherpunk movement. Its genesis block[8] carried an explicitly political message: the text from a British newspaper of 3 January 2009 concerning controversial bank bailouts.[9] This underlines that the purpose of censorship resistance is not only to generate trust between untrusting parties but also to prevent governmental interference. This can be observed in several features of the Bitcoin blockchain: first, the value of central coordination is dismissed in favour of 'the primacy of economics over politics'; second, blockchains use encryption to enhance citizens' 'freedom and privacy'; third, blockchains are built on the premise of peer-to-peer global networks that 'aim to decentralize hierarchical structures, be independent as far as possible from government powers, and challenge their agenda'.[10]

Some consider blockchains to be inherently immune to state interference, and others go as far as to plead that this is the technology's principal value proposition. A frequent mantra is that of 'code is law' – not used in the Lessigian sense[11] but, rather, as a statement that code is the *only* applicable normative constraint, defeating government regulation.[12] Some consider the 'code is law' mantra to be of equal strength to the laws of physics,[13] while others have stated that tolerating accountability towards courts and law is to be avoided as 'we considered malicious governments as part of our threat model'.[14] Blockchain developers have argued that their

---

6   Marcella Atzori, 'Blockchain Technology and Decentralized Governance: Is the State Still Necessary?' (2015) 15 <https://papers.ssrn.com/sol3/papers.cfm?abstract_id=2709713> accessed 28 February (hereafter Atzori, 'Is the State Still Necessary?').

7   Chapter 4 proposes a general approach that regulators should follow in such contexts.

8   A genesis block is the first block of a blockchain.

9   Jamie Redman, 'Bitcoin's Quirky Genesis Block Turns Eight Years Old Today' (*Bitcoin*, 3 January 2018) <https://news.bitcoin.com/bitcoins-quirky-genesis-block-turns-eight-years-old-today/> accessed 28 February 2018.

10   Atzori, 'Is the State Still Necessary?' (n 6) 15.

11   We'll see further below that Lawrence Lessig considered code to be law, but only one of different sources of law that does not supersede others.

12   Lessig's notion of code is law is introduced just below.

13   Arvicco, 'Code is Law and the Quest for Justice' (*Ethereum Classic*, 9 September 2016) <https://ethereumclassic.github.io/blog/2016-09-09-code-is-law/> accessed 28 February 2018.

14   'Trust is Risk: A Decentralized Trust System' (*openbazaar*, 1 August 2017) <www.openbazaar.org/blog/trust-is-risk-a-decentralized-trust-system/> accessed 28 February 2018.

applications are 'not bound by terms of law and jurisdiction' but only by code.[15] Code, it has been suggested, moreover, 'could be regarded as a base for a new type of digital jurisdiction, rather than subject of regulation'.[16]

This chapter addresses these claims in contemplating the intricacies of blockchain regulation. It will be seen that the narratives pictured above are reminiscent of the cyberlibertarianism of the early days of the commercial Internet, and repeat the familiar error of the 'artificial division of virtual and real-space activity'.[17] Valuable insights can be gained from this comparison, not only because the Internet is the infrastructure that blockchains depend on to operate[18] but also because both are aterritorial global networks. Law, by contrast, continues to be anchored in the notion of territorial jurisdiction.

The past twenty years have revealed that the world of atoms and the world of bits cannot be neatly separated. I revisit the evolution of Internet regulation and related narratives before concluding that the same regulatory technique that has enabled a still swelling regulation of cyberspace – the capture of access points – enables states to influence blockchains and blockchain-based applications. The possibility of regulation should not be mistaken for ease, however. My analysis will conclude with an outline of factors complicating blockchain regulation, some of which are likely to become more prominent as public and permissionless blockchains develop.

I. BLOCKCHAINS AS THE NEW SEALAND?

There are remarkable parallels between the regulation adversity of parts of the blockchain community and initial conceptions of Internet regulation. In the early 1990s it was envisaged that Internet users would create distributed socio-technological systems that self-regulate like biological systems,[19] that users would themselves define the rules that apply to them[20] and that a 'New Magna Carta for the Knowledge Age', repealing existing legal systems, was needed.[21]

---

[15] Paul Vigna, 'Chiefless Company Rakes In More than $100 Million' (*wsj*, 16 May 2016) <www.wsj.com/articles/chiefless-company-rakes-in-more-than-100-million-1463399393> accessed 28 February 2018.

[16] 'Decentralized Arbitrage, Blockchain, Smart-contracts, Jincor and Many Other Crossword Words' (*Medium*, 8 August 2017) <https://blog.jincor.com/decentralized-arbitrage-blockchain-smart-contracts-jincor-and-many-other-crossword-words-2bfa4ce2c32e> accessed 28 February 2018.

[17] Kevin Werbach, 'The Song Remains the Same: What Cyberlaw Might Teach the Next Internet Economy' (2017) 69 Florida Law Review 887 (hereafter Werbach, 'The Song Remains the Same')

[18] Although some consider that blockchains could be operated through radio waves: Collin, 'Nick Szabo has Developed a Method to Send Bitcoin Transactions over the Radio' (*blockinsider*, 15 November 2017) <https://blockinsider.net/2017/11/nick-szabo-has-developed-a-method-to-send-bitcoin-transactions-over-the-radio/> accessed 28 February 2018.

[19] Kevin Kelly, *Out of Control* (Basic Books 1994).

[20] Howard Rheingold, *The Virtual Community* (MIT Press 1994).

[21] Esther Dyson et al., 'Cyberspace and the American Dream: A Magna Carta for the Knowledge Age' (1994) <www.pff.org/issues-pubs/futureinsights/fi1.2magnacarta.html> accessed 28 February 2018.

David Johnson and David Post laid out a cyberlibertarian utopia, arguing that regulation anchored in state sovereignty cannot function in cyberspace, making the Internet effectively unregulatable.[22] Post, moreover, has pictured the Internet as an 'exit-option' from states' territorial jurisdiction.[23] The Declaration of the Independence of Cyberspace has been the most famous and poetic expression of this movement. It proclaims:

> Governments of the Industrial World, you weary giants of flesh and steel, I come from Cyberspace, the new home of Mind. On behalf of the future, I ask you of the past to leave us alone. You are not welcome among us. You have no sovereignty where we gather. We have no elected government, nor are we likely to have one, so I address you with no greater authority than that with which liberty itself always speaks. I declare the global social space we are building to be naturally independent of the tyrannies you seek to impose on us. You have no moral right to rule us nor do you possess any methods of enforcement we have true reason to fear.[24]

The Declaration makes the point not only that state interference was unwelcome but also that it was *impossible*. Cyberlibertarianism culminated in the proposal of an 'Internet State', created to avert interference by other sovereigns. The chosen land was the Principality of Sealand, a fortress island build by British military forces in North Sea international waters during the Second World War.[25] Sealand was first populated by a small community in 1967, which declared it an independent state. In 2000 cypherpunks set up a data-hosting services company in Sealand, intended as a data haven shielding Internet data from government censorship.[26]

The presumption underlying this movement was that, since cyberspace is not anchored in territorial space, states would be unable to exercise territorial competence. The same argument is now being repeated in relation to permissionless blockchains, a network based on nodes replicated around the globe.[27] There appears to be a widespread belief that, because there is no single point of control on a blockchain network, it is immune to regulation and enforcement.[28] Permissionless

---

[22] David Post and David Johnson, 'Law and Borders: The Rise of Law in Cyberspace' (1996) 48 Stanford Law Review 1367.

[23] David Post, 'Anarchy, State, and the Internet: An Essay on Making Law in Cyberspace' (1995) Journal of Online Law art 3 <www.temple.edu/lawschool/dpost/Anarchy.html> accessed 28 February 2018.

[24] John Perry Barlow, 'A Declaration of the Independence of Cyberspace' (*Electronic Frontier Foundation*, 8 February 1996) <www.eff.org/cyberspace-independence> accessed 28 February 2018.

[25] <www.sealandgov.org/> accessed 28 February 2018.

[26] Simson Garfinkel, 'Welcome to Sealand. Now Bugger Off (*wired*, 1 July 2000) <www.wired.com/2000/07/haven-2/> accessed 28 February 2018. It is interesting to note that HavenCo undertook a form of self-regulation in deciding to itself intervene where the data was child pornography, spamming and malicious hacking.

[27] In contrast to debates in earlier decades, the main proponents of crypto-libertarianism aren't intellectuals but industry insiders.

[28] Some have gone as far as to state that blockchains would survive a nuclear war: Nick Szabo [NickSzabo4] (30 January 2018) 'A digital currency that would survive a nuclear war: the full

blockchains indeed rest on many nodes spread across jurisdictions. For the Bitcoin blockchain, there were approximately 11,000 nodes around the planet in early 2018;[29] the Ethereum blockchain was replicated across 22,000 nodes.[30] Miners and core developers are similarly based in multiple jurisdictions, can easily move and do not have absolute control over the system. Considering that key governance participants are distributed across a large number of jurisdictions, states or even coalitions of states may struggle to impose obligations on them, it is argued.

If the evolution of Internet regulation over the past few decades provides any indication, however, cryptolibertarianism will soon be confronted with reality. Jack Goldsmith and Tim Wu have shown that the Internet can be regulated precisely because it is not fully decentralized but, rather, has points of control (the regulatory access points) that can be coerced to comply with law.[31] Internet 'cyber-romanticism' indeed quickly gave way to regulation, as diverse regulatory regimes, anchored in territorial jurisdiction, have been adopted over time.[32] For instance, the European Union has issued the E-Commerce Regulation,[33] the General Data Protection Regulation[34] and net neutrality ('open internet') requirements.[35] The United States adopted the Digital Millennium Copyright Act, based on the 1996 World Intellectual Property Organization Copyright Treaties,[36] and required the telecommunications industry to design its equipment and services to tolerate wiretapping.[37] These are but a few examples of larger regulatory frameworks, which continue to be refined. Their existence refutes claims that virtual

---

Bitcoin transaction history, all the way back to the genesis block, exists in over 11,000 copies located in over 100 countries – and that's just counting the copies running live.' [Tweet] <https://twitter.com/NickSzabo4/status/958584961644285954> accessed 28 February 2018.

[29] See further <https://bitnodes.earn.com/>.

[30] For the Bitcoin blockchain, there are currently approximately 11,000 nodes around the planet, of which about 1800 are in Germany and 800 in France.

[31] Jack Goldsmith and Tim Wu, *Who Controls the Internet?* (Oxford University Press 2006).

[32] Andrew Shapiro, 'The Disappearance of Cyberspace and the Rise of Code' (1998) 8 Seton Hall Constitutional Law Journal 703, 709.

[33] Arno Lodder and Andrew Murray, *EU Regulation of E-Commerce* (Edward Elgar 2017).

[34] Regulation (EU) 2016/679 of the European Parliament and of the Council of 27 April 2016 on the protection of natural persons with regard to the processing of personal data and on the free movement of such data, and repealing Directive 95/46/EC (General Data Protection Regulation) (Text with EEA relevance).

[35] Regulation (EU) 2015/2120 of the European Parliament and of the Council of 25 November 2015 laying down measures concerning open internet access and amending Directive 2002/22/EC on universal service and users' rights relating to electronic communications networks and services and Regulation (EU) No 531/2012 on roaming on public mobile communications networks within the Union.

[36] WIPO Copyright Treaty (WCT); WIPO Performances and Phonograms Treaty (WPPT); 17 U.S.C. §§ 101, 104, 104A, 108, 112, 114, 117, 701 Digital Millennium Copyright Act (DMCA).

[37] Hildegard Senseney, 'Interpreting the Communications Assistance for Law Enforcement Act of 1994: The Justice Department Versus the Telecommunications Industry & Privacy Rights Advocates' (1998) 20 Hastings Communications and Entertainment Law Journal 665.

transnational networks cannot be regulated, or that the only applicable law is that of the jurisdiction where the server is located.[38]

It is worthy of particular emphasis that these regulatory regimes have not targeted 'cyberspace' as such but, rather, various access points more approachable for regulators. Unlike cyberspace, the natural and legal persons involved in its operation cannot escape their physical presence even when their actions take place online. As Lawrence Lessig has noted, 'You are never *just* in cyberspace; you never just *go* there. You are always both in real space and in cyberspace at the same time.'[39] The interaction between the norms of real space – law, social norms and market forces – and those of cyberspace (code) are correspondingly complex. Indeed, before investigating how regulation could come to be imposed on blockchains, I start by evoking the convoluted nature of the reciprocal relation between regulation and code.

II. REGULATING CODE

Blockchains are essentially software code. This mandates an analysis of code's regulatory dimension. There is ample evidence that the synergies between law and code are extraordinarily complex. Code is not only an optimal method of implementing self-regulation but can also be used to reinforce or undermine public regulation. Law, on the other hand, can subvert or strengthen code.

A. *Code as Law*

Two decades ago Joel Reidenberg and Lawrence Lessig contended that 'code is law'. By this, they did not assert that code would replace law but, rather, that it is one of multiple regulatory factors exerting a normative influence on individual behaviour. Together with market dynamics, law and social norms, code has become one of many factors shaping the human condition, as software shapes the behaviour of its users.[40] Today code influences how we communicate, shop and sometimes even date and reproduce. Code informs human conduct by making behaviour possible – or impossible, as system design choices impose rules on participants.

It follows that code 'can be as normative as law – decisions have to be made on the values that code embeds'.[41] To illustrate, Bitcoin is heavily regulated by code. Its protocol sets out highly specific and constraining rules in relation to how the cryptoasset can be stored and transferred.

---

[38] Joel Reidenberg, 'Technology and Internet Jurisdiction' (2005) 153 University of Pennsylvania Law Review 1951, 1056–57 (hereafter Reidenberg, 'Technology and Internet Jurisdiction').

[39] Lawrence Lessig, *Code and other Laws of Cyberspace* (Basic Books 1999) 21.

[40] ibid.; see also Julie Cohen, *On Networked Self: Law, Code and the Play of Everyday Practice* (Yale University Press 2012).

[41] Ian Brown and Christopher Marsden, *Regulating Code* (MIT Press 2013) 303 (hereafter Brown and Marsden, 'Regulating Code').

Just like social norms and legislation, code expresses the objectives, values and beliefs of its creators, which is precisely why we need to ask not only what the rules are but also who is making them.[42] Indeed, code is 'no more neutral than regulation with each subject to monopoly and capture by commercial interests'.[43] While code is a form of regulation, however, it is also shaped by outside norms. For example, although the founders of The DAO claimed that 'code is law',[44] the Ethereum blockchain was subsequently forked to revert the 'theft' in accordance with the Ethereum community's social norms.[45]

B. *Law Constraining Code*

Code is shaped not just by market forces and social norms but also by regulation. It can be a means of expressing and enforcing the self-regulatory efforts of a given company or industry. For instance, Uber relies on code to exclude drivers with low ratings from its platform.[46] Code can also constitute a means of implementing externally imposed regulatory constraints, as illustrated by Airbnb's tweaking of its code to collect tourist taxes in select jurisdictions.[47]

Regulatory constraints inform developer choices. Most software projects seek to be compliant so that regulation shapes the design of code. In this way, code can be a regulation-implementing tool. To illustrate, legal frameworks have outlawed the reverse engineering of encryption in digital rights management (DRM) to enforce copyright law.[48] The European Union's Directive on Copyrights and Related Rights in the Information Society bans the import, sale, rental and possession for commercial purposes of all tools designed to circumvent encryption systems.[49] Another example of how law influences network architecture can be found in the General Data Protection Regulation, which is essentially a code-constraining scheme that subjects the modalities of personal data processing to plentiful qualifications.[50]

---

[42] See further Chapter 7.
[43] Brown and Marsden, 'Regulating Code' (n 41) xix.
[44] Stephan Tual [stephantual] (21 March 2016) 'Customer protection on blockchain is insured via smart contracts, not legal systems. Code is law.' [Tweet] <https://twitter.com/stephantual/status/711874685156376576> accessed 28 February 2018.
[45] See further Chapter 7.
[46] Tom Simonite, 'When Your Boss Is an Uber Algorithm' (*MIT Technology Review*, 1 December 2015) <www.technologyreview.com/s/543946/when-your-boss-is-an-uber-algorithm/> accessed 28 February 2018.
[47] Michèle Finck, 'Digital Co-Regulation: Designing a Supranational Legal Framework for the Platform Economy' (2017) 43 European Law Review 47.
[48] See also Articles 11 and 12 of the World Property Organization Copyright Treaty (1996).
[49] Article 6(2).
[50] See further Chapter 4.

Court decisions can have a similar effect. In the European Union, the most famous illustration of how law affects software is the *Microsoft* decision.[51] The European Commission had accused Microsoft of having abused its dominant position in the market for the supply of client PC operating systems.[52] The European Court of Justice (ECJ) agreed that Microsoft had refused to supply competitors with the option of interoperability and had tied the Windows Media Player with Windows PC, weakening competition for media players.[53] It not only fined Microsoft almost €500 million but also ordered it to offer a version of the Windows operating system that did not include its media player.[54] Future versions of Microsoft's software were thus shaped by the judicial decision.

The fate of Napster demonstrates not only that law forms the design of code but also that it can bring it to its demise. Napster was a peer-to-peer file-sharing tool, designed to facilitate the sharing of digital audio files in MP3 format, that operated between 1999 and 2001.[55] Essentially, it enabled the circumvention of copyright law through technology. Napster was forced to shut down in 2001 as a result of *A&M Records, Inc.* v. *Napster, Inc.*, in which a US court held that Napster was guilty of copyright infringement under the Digital Millennium Copyright Act.[56] Although the law eventually shut down Napster, it was able to function as a method of law avoidance for some time.

C. *Code as Law Avoidance*

When code is designed to avoid regulatory compliance it acts as an aspect of interest group behaviour used to minimize legal costs.[57] The history of peer-to-peer file-sharing software is a case in point. Napster was short-lived, but other systems, such as BitTorrent, have been more persistent.[58]

Code is particularly powerful in avoiding regulation when coupled with social norms.[59] The combination of code and social norms has allowed for the large-scale avoidance of obscenity laws with respect to online pornography. While many

---

[51] Case T-201/04 *Microsoft Corp. v Commission of the European Communities* [2007] ECR II-3619 ECLI:EU:T:2007:289 (hereafter *Microsoft v Commission*).

[52] Article 102 TFEU.

[53] *Microsoft v Commission*, paras 1031–90.

[54] ibid. paras 1222–29.

[55] Peter Jan Honigsberg, 'The Evolution and Revolution of Napster' (2002) 36 University of San Francisco Law Review 473.

[56] *A&M Records, Inc. v Napster, Inc.*, 239 F.3d 1004 (2001). For a comment, see Michael W. Carroll, 'Disruptive Technology and Common Law Lawmaking: A Brief Analysis of A&M Records, Inc. V. Napster, Inc.' (2002) 9 Villanova Sports and Entertainment Law Journal.

[57] Tim Wu, 'When Code Isn't Law' (2003) 89 Virginia Law Review 103, 105.

[58] Bryan Choi, 'The Grokster Dead-End' (2006) 19 Harvard Journal of Law and Technology 393, 402–03.

[59] Annemarie Bridy, 'Why Pirates (Still) Won't Behave: Regulating P2P in the Decade after Napster' (2009) 40 Rutgers Law Journal 565.

jurisdictions have dated obscenity laws that could be applied to online pornography, they are not usually enforced. Faced with the widespread consumption of such materials, which has become possible through code, states have had the choice to 'either invest large sums to attempt to enforce the law in the digital environment, or they could de facto deregulate adult obscenity and focus their attentions on more pressing problems such as child-abuse images'.[60] Most states have chosen the second option, also in light of changed social norms regarding sexuality.

These examples underline that code can empower individuals to exit a regulatory system in the Hirschmanian sense. Albert Hirschman's book *Exit, Voice, and Loyalty* lays out that members of an organization, whether a firm, state or other forms of human grouping, have two possible responses when they are less satisfied with their membership: exit (leave the organization) or voice (actively try to repair shortcomings).[61] Loyalty to the organization reduces the risk of exit. Code can be a means of achieving exit from legal systems. Blockchains have already been relied on as a law avoidance mechanism. When Argentina banned credit card companies from processing transactions for Uber as a consequence of its violation of local law, some consumers used a Bitcoin-based debit card to circumvent the ban, which in turn enabled Uber to continue its operation.[62]

What remains questionable is whether code is a realistic law avoidance mechanism at scale considering that most citizens are not motivated to evade the law but, rather, prefer the defaults of legality and convenience. The example of peer-to-peer file sharing is a case in point. Such methods are an effective means of avoiding regulation. Tim Wu has even compared them to a 'temporary repeal of copyright law'.[63] Yet only a minority of end users rely on this option, while most adhere to the legal default. Governments may indeed tolerate law avoidance only because it does not scale to cause systemic problems. Torrents, which are computer files that contain only metadata about files to be distributed, and which have been used to distribute files in contravention of copyright law, may work only because those acting unlawfully can take advantage of the continued compliance of regular consumers to finance the industry.[64]

While code doubtlessly can be used as a law avoidance technique, probably also at scale, it has thus far never disrupted regulatory systems. The question to ask, then, is whether this will be different with regard to blockchains. Whereas the

---

[60] Andrew Murray, *Information Technology Law* (Oxford University Press 2016) 56.

[61] Albert Hirschman, *Exit, Voice and Loyalty: Responses to Decline in Firms, Organizations and States* (Harvard University Press 1970).

[62] Alison Griswold, 'Uber Has Found a Clever Way to Bypass a Roadblock in Argentina Involving Bitcoin' (*QUARTZ*, 7 July 2016) <https://qz.com/725822/uber-has-found-a-clever-way-to-bypass-a-roadblock-in-argentina-involving-bitcoin/> accessed 28 February 2018.

[63] Tim Wu, 'When Code Isn't Law' (2003) 89 Virginia Law Review 103, 107.

[64] ibid.

technology's constitutive features can be operated to facilitate law evasion, it is not clear that most citizens would want to rely on systems outside the default of legality.[65] Indeed, although many forecast that Bitcoin would facilitate large-scale tax avoidance and money laundering, this is not what recent figures appear to indicate.[66] There are thus no indications that blockchains more easily lead to systemic law avoidance than existing technology. This highlights that we should not think of law and code as simply adversarial systems. To the contrary, there is ample evidence that they can be mutually reinforcing.

D. Code Can Help Law

Code can be used as a substitute for law when technology is better suited to resolve policy issues.[67] Code can support the achievement of regulatory objectives in implementing law more efficiently. To highlight, geolocation technology has enabled courts to impose sanctions on activity related to citizens in their jurisdiction, while digital rights management has been the means of enforcing copyright law in cyberspace.[68] China has, moreover, fashioned its Great Firewall to censor Internet traffic in accordance with its policy of prohibiting politically and morally undesirable content.[69]

Seen through this lens, technology provides potent tools for the enforcement of policies and decisions. RegTech, the use of informational technology to enhance regulatory processes, is now being employed to ease regulatory monitoring, reporting and compliance in replacing manual by digital processes.[70] Technology can enforce regulation more easily.[71] This leads me to argue in the subsequent chapter that technology may facilitate the emergence of more detailed regulation, with compliance being monitored through code. Because software is a potent tool to enforce norms, it matters who creates it, and to what end. The synergetic relation between law and code also manifests where regulation helps code.

---

[65] Whereas code can be used as a means of law-avoidance it can also be used as a more efficient means of law enforcement. We engage with this in further detail in the next chapter.

[66] Neeraj Agrawal, 'A New Study Finds less than 1% Of Bitcoin Transactions To Exchanges Are Illicit' (*Coincenter*, 17 January 2018) <https://t.co/sklD4zDMpN> accessed 28 February 2018.

[67] Joel Reidenberg, 'Lex Informatica: The Formulation of Information Policy Rules Through Technology' (1998) 76 Texas Law Review 3, 552, 583.

[68] Jonathan Zittrain, 'Internet Points of Control' (2002) 44 Boston College Law Review 653.

[69] Margaret Roberts, *Censored: Distraction and Diversion Inside China's Great Firewall* (Princeton University Press 2018).

[70] Douglas Arner, Janos Nathan Barberis and Ross Buckley, 'FinTech, RegTech and the Reconceptualization of Financial Regulation' (2017) 37 Northwestern Journal of International Law & Business 371.

[71] See further Chapter 3.

E. *Code Needs Law*

Technology and regulation are often 'posed as adversaries': technology represents 'markets, enterprise and growth' while regulation symbolizes 'government, bureaucracy and limits to growth'.[72] The less-emphasized story is that there are many blockchain projects that seek to build legally compliant products. The history of Internet regulation confirms that industry might eventually welcome regulation, as it facilitates its operation.[73] Internet companies did not end up settling in Sealand but in jurisdictions with solid legal and institutional structures, and the required human capital. Ultimately, Internet companies sought out regulation to get the consumer confidence that comes with it and to have predictability on the actions of their competitors. There are thus abundant benefits to cooperation between regulators and technology companies, which are further delineated in Chapters 3 and 6.

Code needs law for stability and for its real-world expressions to be legally recognized. This may be even more accurate in relation to blockchains than it was for the Internet. The Internet is inherently about communication and information. Copyright law has been hard to enforce online precisely because files are nothing but data. While this content may have real-world consequences (think about material inciting hatred), it itself remains in cyberspace. Regulating online content has been difficult and controversial, moreover, because it involves speech and expression. Regulating blockchain content may be easier because many use cases focus on the exchange of value rather than pure information. What is more, distributed ledgers' success ultimately hinges on legal recognition.

Given that blockchains do not exist in isolation from the real world, their success will largely depend upon recognition not only through lay politics and popularity but also through law. For example, cryptocurrencies lose appeal when they cannot be transferred into fiat or are not broadly accepted as currency. Similarly, when tokens act as avatars of real-world goods, related actions must be enforceable in the real world. As net neutrality is being abandoned in the United States, observers have expressed concerns that internet service providers (ISPs) may autonomously decide to block traffic coming from blockchains or undermine users' ability to run a node.[74] Law will thus serve as a factor of stability and legal recognition, necessary to translate code into facts.

Regulation can, furthermore, support the development of code. It can provide certainty to developers wishing to pursue a certain option, or create incentives for development. When code is 'slow to evolve, law can assist by removing bottlenecks

---

[72] Jonathan Wiener, 'The Regulation of Technology, and the Technology of Regulation' (2004) 26 Technology in Society 483, 483.

[73] See further Chapter 3.

[74] Jordan Pearson, 'The End of Net Neutrality Means ISPs Could Crack Down on Cryptocurrencies' (*Motherboard*, 27 November 2017) <https://motherboard.vice.com/en_us/article/kz34ay/net-neutrality-repeal-affect-cryptocurrency-bitcoin-ethereum> accessed 28 February 2018.

to innovation'.[75] Regulatory uncertainty nowadays affects many aspects of block-chains' operation. Appropriate and clear legal frameworks can prevent innovation paralysis due to fear of legal consequences and provide a stepping stone towards the design of more sophisticated software.

I have argued that the relationship between regulation and code is multifaceted. Each may stand either in an antagonistic or supportive relation depending on the specific circumstances at issue. This emphasizes that code does not exist in a vacuum but constantly interacts with other normative postulates. The manifest interdependence of the world of bits and the world of atoms underlines the fact that distributed ledgers cannot be extra-legal constructs immune to regulation.

III. THE REGULATORY ACCESS POINTS OF THE BLOCKCHAIN SPACE

Law has perpetually been challenged by the emergence of new technologies, yet legal systems have never been undermined.[76] This does not mean that these systems have been unaffected by technological change. When the printing press was first disseminated, many debated whether law should be printed: some worried about the potentially destabilizing effects of individuals being able to read the law without fully understanding its inner workings.[77] Similar concerns were expressed in relation to the Internet and personal computers.[78] Nowadays we can identify concerns that 3D printing may lead to patent infringements[79] and that the emergence of the platform-enabled 'gig economy' will eradicate labour law protections.[80] Blockchains trigger comparable anxieties. Chapter 4 underlines that it is far from clear how these networks should be treated under existing legal frameworks. If the technology is more widely adopted, similar riddles need to be answered in multiple contexts.

Just as in earlier periods of technological upheaval, a process of mutual adaptation is likely to occur, whereby technology grows to be compliant with existing legal principles while the law adapts to new technology. The existence of regulatory access points confirms that nothing renders blockchains intrinsically immune to regulation. Even Satoshi Nakamoto knew that blockchains would not be entirely resistant to state intervention. Shortly after the release of Bitcoin he was asked in an

---

75 Brown and Marsden, 'Regulating Code' (n 41) 31.
76 Andreas Manolopoulos, 'Raising Cyberborders: The Interaction Between Law and Technology' (2003) 11 International Journal of Law and Technology 40, 55.
77 Richard Ross, 'The Commoning of the Common Law: The Renaissance Debate Over Printing English Law, 1520–1640' (1998) 146 University of Pennsylvania Law Review 323–461.
78 Richard Ross, 'Communications Revolutions and Legal Culture: An Elusive Relationship' (2002) 27 Law and Social Inquiry 637–84.
79 Timothy Holbrook and Lucas Osborn, 'Digital Patent Infringement in an Era of 3D Printing' (2015) 48 UC Davis Law Review 1319–85.
80 Brhmie Balaram, 'What is the Gig Economy?' (RSA, 13 July 2017) <www.thersa.org/discover/publications-and-articles/rsa-blogs/2017/07/what-is-the-gig-economy> accessed 14 February 2018.

e-mail conversation whether cryptography could solve political problems. He conceded that this was not the case, but argued that 'you can win a major battle in the arms race and gain a new territory of freedom for several years'.[81] Although blockchains' first decade was marked by an overall absence of regulatory intervention (and, for the most part, interest), the tide is now turning.

When evaluating the relation between blockchains and regulation, we must distinguish between the various network layers.[82] Blockchain-based applications can be regulated by targeting the application itself, especially when it takes the form of a legally incorporated entity. The same is true for permissioned blockchains, which are often centrally controlled by a corporate structure. There are, however, scenarios in which regulatory access points are harder to define, such as in respect of a smart contract deployed by peers, or if more strongly decentralized blockchain-based applications emerge.[83]

In centralized regimes, regulation can focus on a central regulatory control point. In decentralized peer-to-peer contexts this becomes more burdensome, as peers do not have the same capacity to 'absorb' regulation as their centralized counterparts. Chapter 4 underlines that, if blockchain nodes are data controllers for GDPR purposes, it is unlikely that they will be able to comply with all related requirements. Similarly, when individuals exchange cryptoassets through decentralized exchanges, they might not be in a position to comply with the European Union's complex anti-money-laundering (AML) requirements.[84] Historically, intermediaries have often been tasked with absorbing complex legal specifications, especially as a placeholder for smaller actors – a factor that cannot be relied on in absolute peer-to-peer contexts. In such circumstances, blockchain applications become intangible, either because they are not managed by a legally incorporated entity or because they simply are not centrally managed at all. When reaching for applications to regulate blockchain-based activity becomes futile, we need to think about the possibility of regulating the activity occurring on the network itself.

The modalities of Internet regulation provide telling insights into how blockchains can be regulated. Even though cyberspace is spread across jurisdictions, regulators continue to impose various requirements through diverse access points.[85] Blockchain regulation can be expected to follow a similar path. While these systems are difficult to target in and of themselves, policy-makers have started exploiting access points to impose regulatory constraints.[86] The following analysis introduces

---

[81] See <https://satoshi.nakamotoinstitute.org/emails/cryptography/4/>.
[82] See further Chapter 1.
[83] On DApps and DAOs, see further Chapter 1.
[84] Decentralized exchanges are introduced further below.
[85] Giancarlo Frosio, 'Reforming Intermediary Liability in the Platform Economy: A European Digital Single Market Strategy' (2017) 112 Northwestern University Law Review 19, 39.
[86] For a parallel with virtual worlds, see Viktor Mayer-Schönberger, 'Napster's Second Life? The Regulatory Challenges of Virtual Worlds' 100 Northwestern University School of Law 1775, 1819 (hereafter Mayer-Schönberger, 'Napster's Second Life') ('Virtual world providers are the

several potential regulatory access points and ponders the advantages and disadvantages of the suggested solutions.

A. *Internet Service Providers*

Internet service providers have been a crucial access point for Internet regulation. ISPs are easy to identify and are formally incorporated in a specific jurisdiction. To illustrate, net neutrality requirements have been imposed on ISPs to shape cyberspace.[87] EU net neutrality confirms that ISPs manage the traffic of data in a prescribed manner, as they are prohibited from blocking or slowing down traffic except when necessary, such as to comply with legal constraints.[88] The underlying objective of net neutrality legislation is to safeguard the free access of EU-based users, to distribute information and content and to decide which services and applications to use. This is designed to 'preserve a Darwinian competition among every conceivable use of the Internet so that only the best survive'.[89]

Elsewhere, regulators have similarly relied on ISPs to enforce normative objectives through content blocking. As access points to the underlying network, ISPs have been compelled to restrict access to websites containing child abuse images in many jurisdictions.[90] In China, ISPs must, moreover, enforce the ban on online pornography and censor politically sensitive materials.[91] In 2012 the United Kingdom's High Court ordered five ISPs to block The Pirate Bay (TPB), a peer-to-peer file-sharing system, arguing that its operators had induced and incited users to infringe copyright law.[92]

---

most obvious targets of real-world government regulation. Because they maintain the virtual world's infrastructure, they control the central bottleneck of virtual community interaction.').

[87] Christopher Marsden, *Network Neutrality: From Policy to Law to Regulation* (Manchester University Press February 2017); <http://eur-lex.europa.eu/LexUriServ/LexUriServ.do?uri=OJ: L:2009:337:FULL:EN:PDF> accessed 13 April 2018.

Article 3 of Regulation (EU) 2015/2120 of the European Parliament and of the Council of 25 November 2015 laying down measures concerning open internet access and amending Directive 2002/22/EC on universal service and users' rights relating to electronic communications networks and services and Regulation (EU) No 531/2012 on roaming on public mobile communications networks within the Union (Text with EEA relevance).

[88] Tim Wu, 'Network Neutrality, Broadband Discrimination' (2003) 2 Journal of Telecommunications and High Technology Law 141.

[89] ibid. 142.

[90] Brett Danaher, Michael Smith and Rahul Telang, 'The Effect of Piracy Website Blocking on Consumer Behavior' (2015) 1 <https://papers.ssrn.com/sol3/papers.cfm?abstract_id=2612063> accessed 28 February 2018 (hereafter Danaher et al., 'The Effect of Piracy Website Blocking').

[91] Dong Han, 'From Vagueness to Clarity? Articulating Legal Criteria of Digital Content Regulation in China' (2016) 12 Global Media and Communication 211–17 <http://journals .sagepub.com/doi/abs/10.1177/1742766516675495> accessed 28 February 2018.

[92] *Dramatico Entertainment Ltd & Ors v British Sky Broadcasting Ltd & Ors* [2012] EWHC 268 (Ch) [2012].

ISPs are, accordingly, key access points through which Internet traffic can be controlled. They could, equally, become focal points of blockchain regulation. When governments wish to prevent their citizens from using blockchains or specific blockchain-based applications, they could order ISPs to block encrypted data that passes through their network or prevent ISPs from transmitting data to and from decentralized applications.[93] Moreover, ISPs can, at least in some circumstances, use IP addresses or hostnames to identify which nodes are connected to a blockchain as well as the data that is recorded onto a blockchain.[94] In the past ISPs have indeed already relied on deep packet inspection[95] to 'throttle' (restrict the speed) of BitTorrent uploads and downloads.[96] Through throttling in this way, ISPs can apportion bandwidth by inspecting data packets to discriminate against certain kinds of data.[97]

There are limits to what ISPs can do, however. Unlike shutting down entire sites (as occurred with Megaupload.com),[98] website blocking through ISPs merely blocks users' access to the site.[99] The manipulation of Internet traffic must, moreover, always be proportionate so as to not unduly infringe users' rights. The flexibility of software also enables a blocked site to return under a new domain a few days later.[100] This implies that, when a website is blocked, developers can quickly resurrect it under a new domain name within a very short time period, defeating regulatory intervention.

There are further limitations to the effectiveness of ISP intervention. Given that content remains available on the servers of the blocked sites, users can circumvent the block through Tor or virtual private networks to access it via another route.[101] Through VPNs, the effects of deep packet inspection are limited, as an attacker sees only encrypted data, preventing it from knowing what services are accessed. Yet, unless such techniques are turned into default configurations, these exit options

---

93 Aaron Wright and Primavera De Filippi, 'Decentralized Blockchain Technology and The Rise of Lex Cryptographia' (2015) 51 <https://papers.ssrn.com/sol3/papers.cfm?abstract_id=2580664> accessed 28 February 2018.
94 Maria Apostolaki, Aviv Zohar and Laurent Vanbever, 'Hijacking Bitcoin: Routing Attacks on Cryptocurrencies' (2017) IEEE Symposium on Security and Privacy <https://btc-hijack.ethz.ch/files/btc_hijack.pdf> accessed 28 February 2018.
95 This technique allows ISPs to scan and analyze Internet traffic.
96 Milton Mueller and Hadi Asghari, 'Deep Packet Inspection and Bandwidth Management: Battles Over Bittorrent in Canada and the United States' (2011) TPRC.
97 ibid. 6.
98 Brett Danaher and Michael Smith, 'Gone in 60 Seconds: The Impact of the Megaupload Shutdown on Movie Sales' (2013) <https://papers.ssrn.com/sol3/papers.cfm?abstract_id=2229349> accessed 28 February 2018.
99 These sites host the tracker files required in order to download data through the BitTorrent protocol.
100 Matt Kamen, '85 "new" pirate sites now blocked in the UK' (*wired*, 14 December 2015) <www.wired.co.uk/article/85-new-pirate-sites-blocked-uk> accessed 28 February 2018.
101 Tor is an anonymity network that makes it difficult to trace a user's online activity.

from governmental control are costly, financially and in terms of the required expertise, which relegates them to the status of a marginal phenomenon.[102]

It appears, moreover, that the success of using ISPs to block information depends upon the availability of alternatives. When The Pirate Bay was blocked by ISPs after court orders in the United Kingdom in 2012, this had little to no effect on the behaviour of consumers, who merely circumvented the ban.[103] A similar phenomenon was observed when a major piracy-linking site was blocked in Germany.[104] When nineteen additional sites were blocked in the United Kingdom, however, a meaningful reduction in total piracy was observed, and many users chose to rely on legal streaming services instead.[105] This result also seems to have been shaped by the availability of alternatives such as Netflix and Spotify, reinforcing the earlier point that users will always been drawn to the default of legality and convenience.[106] How successful ISP blocking would be in the blockchain context thus remains to be seen.

B. *Miners*

Miners, the nodes that add new data to a blockchain, are an additional potential regulatory access point.[107] Contrary to conventional assumptions, miners can be identified relatively easily. The nature of proof-of-work has created economies of scale (at least in Bitcoin), so that it has been a rational decision for miners to gather together in such conglomerates.[108] Given the extremely high consumption of electricity in proof-of-work-based systems, the location of these pools will often be well known.[109] Furthermore, when a new block is mined, newly generated coins are placed in the miner's address, allowing verification of the miner if they subsequently transact through an exchange or when addresses are repeatedly used and not changed for each coinbase transaction. ISPs might, moreover, be able to determine whether miners connect to nodes in their area, creating a presumption of

---

[102] Tim Wu, 'Cyberspace Sovereignty? The Internet and the International System' 10 Harvard Journal of Law and Technology 648, 652 (referring to the use of such techniques in relation to the Internet).

[103] Danaher et al., 'The Effect of Piracy Website Blocking' (n 90).

[104] Christian Peukert, Luis Aguiar and Jörg Claussen, 'Catch Me if You Can: Effectiveness and Consequences of Online Copyright Enforcement' (2018) Information Systems Research <https://papers.ssrn.com/sol3/papers.cfm?abstract_id=2604197> accessed 28 May 2018.

[105] Danaher et al., 'The Effect of Piracy Website Blocking' (n 90) 6.

[106] ibid.

[107] Depending on the consensus mechanism at issue miners can also carry different names such as 'validators' or 'stakers' (in a proof-of-stake system).

[108] 'How Bitcoin Mining Works' *The Economist* (20 January 2015) <www.economist.com/blogs/economist-explains/2015/01/economist-explains-11> accessed 28 February 2018.

[109] It is worth noting that if a government were to target miners for energy consumption and a high share thereof left the network for fear of repercussions, energy consumption in the network would go down dramatically, potentially leaving remaining miners safe from being discovered. This however also risks slowing down the network and causing an increase in transaction fees.

participating in blockchain governance. It has further been asserted that mining pools have been informal associations that can be seen as partnerships, a corporate form that would make it even easier to make them addressees of legal obligations.[110]

Miners are already subject to existing legal obligations, and it is possible that additional requirements will be imposed to directly shape the network.[111] Primavera De Filippi and Aaron Wright have envisaged distinct options for mining pool regulation. First, governments could compel mining pools to implement specific protocol changes or block applications, organizations, persons or devices.[112] Second, governments could provide miners with incentives, in the form of liability limitations or safe harbours as a reward for abiding by the law, or by processing only smart contracts that comply with legal requirements.[113] Finally, in order to dissuade miners from supporting illicit applications, governments could tax or penalize 'miners whenever they process transactions related to illegitimate blockchain-based systems or devices'.[114] These options underline not only that miners are access points for legal obligations but also that regulators have at their disposal a range of incentivizing mechanisms other than legislation, a point I return to in Chapter 6.

Chinese mining pools have been rumoured to have agreements with the government regarding electricity supply.[115] Depending on context, governments control the key resource (electricity) that miners rely on.[116] There is therefore reason to believe that, as long as proof-of-work is the predominant consensus algorithm, governments controlling electricity ultimately have the upper hand.[117] When governments have knowledge of the pools' location they may turn off power supply, confiscate hardware or exploit miners' governance role.[118] The degree to which a single state will be able to influence the network, though such radical steps depend

---

[110] 'Vermont Lawyer Warns of Legal Complications Ahead for Cryptocurrency Miners' (*Crypto Investor*, 12 February 2018) <https://bitcoinmagazine.com/articles/vermont-lawyer-warns-legal-complications-ahead-cryptocurrency-miners/> accessed 28 February 2018.

[111] For an analysis on whether they are caught by gambling law in Austria, see Tina Ehrke-Rabel, Iris Eisenberger, Elisabeth Hödl and Lily Zechner, 'Bitcoin-Miner Als Prosumer: Eine Frage Staatlicher Regulierung? Dargestellt Am Beispiel Des Glücksspielrechts (Legal and Regulatory Aspects of Bitcoin Mining as a Form of Prosuming)' (2017) 4 Austrian Law Journal 188.

[112] De Filippi and Wright, 'Blockchain and the Law' (n 1) 180.

[113] ibid.

[114] ibid.

[115] Eva Xiao, 'Cheap Electricity Made China the King of Bitcoin Mining. The Government's Stepping In' (*Medium*, 22 August 2017) <https://medium.com/@evawxiao/cheap-electricity-made-china-the-king-of-bitcoin-mining-the-governments-stepping-in-118c20725f7b> accessed 1 June 2018.

[116] 'Who Really Controls Bitcoin?' (*steemit*, 2017) <https://steemit.com/bitcoin/@dantheman/who-really-controls-bitcoin> accessed 28 February 2018.

[117] ibid.

[118] See further Chapter 7.

on the decentralization and resilience of the network: where pools are spread across a large number of jurisdictions not prone to cooperation, isolated events are unlikely to influence the network; where mining is geographically concentrated, the opposite is the case.

Miners have already been subject to regulatory control. In February 2018 the US Federal Communications Commission (FCC) notified a Brooklyn resident of harmful interference with a T-Mobile network.[119] The addressee's Bitcoin mining device emanated radio emissions that harmfully interfered with the network.[120] As a consequence, he was ordered to cease operating his device.[121] Here, the objective of regulatory control was not to affect the blockchain but, rather, to avoid interference with telecommunications networks. It nonetheless highlights that miners can be identified for law enforcement purposes. Under EU law, miners might, for example, have to comply with the intermediary liability specifications under the E-Commerce Directive.

Mining operations can, moreover, be targeted to unsettle a blockchain as such. China, which has long been the world capital of Bitcoin mining, was repeatedly rumoured to have outlawed Bitcoin mining to curb energy consumption and address the risks of cryptoasset speculation.[122] As a consequence of the changing climate of acceptance, local operators have relocated to friendlier jurisdictions, by setting up subsidiaries in Switzerland and moving mining operations to Quebec and Iceland, where electricity is cheap and the regulatory environment more welcoming.[123] Miners are highly mobile and likely to move to the most favourable jurisdiction. It is true that, where the energy-intensive proof-of-work consensus mechanism is used, relevant factors include not only regulation but also energy costs and climatic conditions (to lower cooling costs). These factors are likely to change with new consensus protocols, however.[124] Regulators' leeway over blockchain will be limited, moreover, by the fact that, unlike ISPs relying on deep

[119] Federal Communications Commission Enforcement Bureau Region One Letter to Victor Rosario, February 15, 2018, Case Number EB-FIELDNER-17-00025658 <https://apps.fcc.gov/edocs_public/attachmatch/DOC-349258A1.pdf>.

[120] Section 15.5(b) of the FCC rules.

[121] In accordance with Section 15.5(c) of the FCC rules.

[122] 'China Central Bank Can Tell Local Governments to Regulate Bitcoin Miners' Power Use: Source' (*Reuters*, 3 January 2018) <www.reuters.com/article/us-markets-bitcoin-china-mining/china-central-bank-can-tell-local-governments-to-regulate-bitcoin-miners-power-use-source-idUSKBN1ES0TD> accessed 28 February 2018.

[123] 'Bitcoin Miners Are Shifting Outside China Amid State Clampdown' (*Bloomberg*, 5 January 2018) <www.bloomberg.com/news/articles/2018-01-05/bitcoin-miners-are-shifting-outside-china-amid-state-clampdown> accessed 28 February 2018; Sara Hsu, 'China's Shutdown Of Bitcoin Miners Isn't Just About Electricity' (*Forbes*, 15 January 2015) <www.forbes.com/sites/sarahsu/2018/01/15/chinas-shutdown-of-bitcoin-miners-isnt-just-about-electricity/#6e03180a369b> accessed 28 February 2018.

[124] It is, however, unlikely that all miners of a given blockchain would establish in a single jurisdiction given that this would undermine the resilience of the chain.

packet inspection, miners may lack the capability to differentiate between lawful and unlawful transactions.[125] It is for this reason that other regulatory access points must also be considered.

C. *Core Software Developers*

The complex governance set-up of public permissionless blockchains, which is probed further in Chapter 7, includes core developer groups that decide on software upgrades. In the digital age, technology designers are not just software architects but also policy-makers shaping the world we live in. Groups of the most senior blockchain developers, such as Bitcoin Core or the Ethereum core developers, steer the network's evolution.[126] These decisions range from the rather mundane and technical to pivotal decisions that define the network. Considering permissionless blockchains' reliance on cryptoassets as an incentivizing mechanism, these decisions can be akin to monetary policy-making, such as in the case of decisions whether funds lost due to a software bug should be recovered.

Core developers suggest options regarding the functionality and underlining principles of the network that miners subsequently vote on.[127] Governments wishing to regulate DLT can leverage the malleability of code and impose legal obligations on core developers. They could compel developers to introduce specific features, such as government backdoors, into their systems. This approach also has shortcomings, however, including important security trade-offs. As the EU Security Commissioner recently recalled in another context, installing backdoors is undesirable because it weakens the overall security of the network, a consideration that should also apply in relation to blockchains.[128]

There are additional limitations that governments targeting core developers as access points will face. In some jurisdictions code benefits from free speech protection, limiting regulators' leeway for intrusiveness.[129] Software developers can, moreover, operate out of any jurisdiction, and one developer can quickly replace another

---

[125] De Filippi and Wright, 'Blockchain and the Law' (n 1) 181.

[126] <https://bitcoin.org/en/bitcoin-core/> accessed 28 February 2018.

[127] For a more detailed analysis of blockchain governance, refer to Chapter 7.

[128] Matthijs Koot, 'EU Commission Says It Does Not Seek Crypto Backdoors, Will Propose Legal Framework in Early 2018 for Member States to Help Each Other Access Encrypted Devices' (19 October 2017) <https://blog.cyberwar.nl/2017/10/eu-commission-says-it-no-longer-seeks-crypto-backdoors-will-propose-legal-framework-for-member-states-to-help-each-other-access-encrypted-devices/> accessed 28 February 2018.

[129] It appears that free speech protection for code is contingent on how 'expressive' code is. *Bernstein v Dept. of Justice*, 176 F.3d 1132 (9th Cir. 1999) (finding that 'encryption software, in its source code form and as employed by those in the field of cryptography, must be viewed as expressive for First Amendment purposes'.) See further Orin Kerr, 'Are We Overprotecting Code? Thoughts on First-Generation Internet Law' (2000) 57 Washington and Lee Law Review 1287; Tim Wu, 'Machine Speed' (2013) 161 University of Pennsylvania Law Review 1495.

that has been targeted by legal action.[130] In addition, Jonathan Zittrain has drawn attention to the 'generativity' of code, which allows it to overcome legal restrictions in quickly adapting to and outrunning the law.[131] Indeed, while the Napster case illustrated that online copyright infringement bears risks of legal repercussions, software developers never stopped successfully designing software to avoid digital rights management.

Nowadays core developers are, for the most part, publicly known, and some of them are pivotal voices in policy discussions surrounding blockchains, fulfilling an important educational function. Subjecting them to legal scrutiny may push some into anonymity, which in turn would discourage transparency in the governance of permissionless blockchains, as well as the important multilateral dialogues between industry insiders, regulators and experts.[132] Anonymity, or at least refuge in jurisdictional safe havens, will always be an option for core developers, highlighting potential limits in successfully leveraging access points. Circumstances need not be this adversarial, however. Core developers could accept the imposition of some regulatory requirements, or engage in private ordering through self-regulation. Although such moves doubtlessly limit core developers' freedom, they would also liberate them from current problems related to legal uncertainty.

D. *End Users*

In their current manifestations, permissionless blockchains are predominantly pseudonymous systems. While users cannot be identified immediately, they usually can when sufficient time and funds are made available, as deanonymization techniques relying on data mining and heuristic analytics enable the identification of users.[133] By and large, users can thus be identified for law enforcement purposes.

In his 1956 article 'A Pure Theory of Local Expenditure',[134] Charles Tiebout claimed that, in federal systems, citizens 'vote with their feet' by moving to communities providing a subjectively optimal bundle of taxes and public goods. Empirical analysis has proved the accuracy of this theory in some circumstances, but it has been shown to be limited in others.[135] Unlike miners and core developers, most

---

[130] See further Yochai Benkler and Helen Nissenbaum, 'Commons-based Peer Production and Virtue' (2006) 14 The Journal of Political Philospohy 394.
[131] Jonathan Zittrain, 'The Generative Internet' (2006) 119 Harvard Law Review 1974.
[132] See Chapter 6.
[133] See Chapter 4.
[134] Charles Tiebout, 'A Pure Theory of Local Expenditure' (1956) 64 The Journal of Political Economy 416.
[135] Economic analysis can confirm that people vote with their feet on air quality or welfare benefits by moving within the same jurisdiction. See Spencer Banzhaf and Randall Walsh, 'Do People Vote with Their Feet? An Empirical Test of Tiebout' (2008) 98 American Economic Review 843; Richard Cebula and Willie Belton, 'Voting with One's Feet' (1994) 53 The American Journal of Economics and Sociology 273.

users are not highly mobile, and are unlikely to vote with their feet by moving to the most blockchain-friendly jurisdiction. Every move entails moving costs, and it is safe to presume that, overall, users will not have sufficient incentives to use a blockchain or blockchain-based application to uproot their life. Individuals living in oppressive regimes are more likely to have these incentives, yet they also typically face the steepest burdens in emigrating, and migration and asylum law greatly limit inter-jurisdictional foot voting.[136]

End users' firm territorial grounding makes them an attractive access point. We could imagine future regulations that prevent users from uploading certain materials to a blockchain or use specific blockchain-based applications. Users are already subject to legal requirements. For instance, when a user adds defamatory content to a distributed ledger system, related criminal law principles apply. This is not to say that enforcing such principles will always be easy. Indeed, when regulators lean on ISPs as access points, there are few entities they must control for compliance. With end users, by contrast, enforcement may be much more burdensome in light of the sheer numbers. A further factor to consider is the evolution of social norms. Internet history suggests that, when social norms oppose a certain principle, enforcement becomes politically unwise. On the other hand, the mere existence of law, albeit hard to enforce, may be sufficient to steer a majority of citizens towards compliant behaviour through corresponding social norms.

Regular end users have little to no understanding of the underlying technology and related legal implications, however. In most scenarios they also have little leeway over the precise configurations of a given network. It follows that, while users should always be liable for their own actions (such as in the defamation example outlined above), they cannot easily be exploited to directly influence blockchain governance. Moreover, as outlined in further detail below, there are techniques that empower users to evade these legal obligations by opting into anonymity, which might hinder enforcement in future times.

It is worth noting that users cannot just be subjects of regulation; they are also enforcers of regulation. In early 2018 the US Commodity Futures Trading Commission (CFTC) advised customers to avoid so-called 'pump-and-dump' schemes for cryptoassets.[137] In addition to recalling that existing regulations on market manipulation apply to blockchain users, it designed an enforcement tactic through a whistle-blowing scheme. The scheme offers a monetary award of 10 to 30 per cent to those providing information that leads to a successful enforcement action

---

[136] Ilya Simon, 'Tiebout Goes Global: International Migration as Tool for Voting with your Feet' (2008) 73 Missouri Law Review 1247.

[137] In a pump-and-dump scheme, the price of a given asset is first artificially inflated in order to late sell at a higher price. In the cryptoasset space, these schemes are usually coordinated through social media.

resulting in sanctions of $1 million or more.[138] This not only discourages market manipulation but also creates incentives for user enforcement, which is probably more efficient than centralized state intervention.

E. *Old and New Intermediaries*

Blockchains are often considered to trigger broad disintermediation.[139] For the time being most established intermediaries persist, while new ones, such as cryptoasset exchanges, are emerging. Intermediaries, old and new, are attractive regulatory access points.[140] Examples of this can be pinpointed throughout the world in relation to Internet regulation. The controversial German Netzwerkdurchsetzungsgesetz (Network Enforcement Act, or NetzDG) obliges social networks to delete hate speech and fake news under certain conditions.[141] In Thailand, online intermediaries must prevent *lèse majesté*.[142] Search engines also enforce law on behalf of the state, as illustrated by their duty to apply the EU right to be forgotten.[143]

Intermediaries have already been used as regulatory access points in relation to DLT. The European Union has been quick to clarify that AML and know your customer (KYC) requirements apply to cryptoassets.[144] In the United States, tax authorities have summoned the Coinbase exchange to turn over information about customer accounts for the purposes of tax enforcement.[145] Established Internet intermediaries such as search engines could be ordered not to index blockchain-based

---

[138] CFTC, 'Costumer Advisory: Beware Virtual Currency Pump-and-Dump Schemes' <www.cftc.gov/idc/groups/public/@customerprotection/documents/file/customeradvisory_pumpdump0218.pdf> accessed 28 February 2018.

[139] There is no definition of an online intermediary that attracts consensus. The OECD defines online intermediaries as actors that 'bring together or facilitate transactions between third parties on the Internet. They give access to, host, transmit and index content, products and services originated by third parties on the Internet or provide Internet-based services to third parties.' See OECD, 'The Economic and Social Role of Online Intermediaries' (2010) 9.

[140] Giancarlo Frosio, 'Reforming Intermediary Liability in the Platform Economy: A European Digital Single Market Strategy' (2017) 112 Northwestern University Law Review 19. This is to be contrasted with an approach adopted since the mid-1990s to provide online intermediaries with exemptions from liability for wrongful activities committed by users of their services through safe harbour limitations.

[141] § 3 NetzDG (*Gesetz zur Verbesserung der Rechtsdurchsetzung in sozialen Netzwerken*).

[142] Pirongrong Ramasoota, 'Online Intermediaries Case Studies Series: Online Intermediary Liability in Thailand' (2015) The Global Network of Internet and Society Research Centers 4.

[143] Case C-131/12 *Google Spain* [2014] EU:C:2014:317.

[144] Francesco Guarascio, 'EU Agrees Clampdown on Bitcoin Platforms to Tackle Money Laundering' (*Reuters*, 15 December 2017) <www.reuters.com/article/uk-eu-moneylaundering/eu-agrees-clampdown-on-bitcoin-platforms-to-tackle-money-laundering-idUSKBN1E928M> accessed 28 February 2018.

[145] Matthew de Silva, 'Coinbase Sends IRS Summons Notification to 13–000 Customers' (*ethnews*, 24 February 2018) <www.ethnews.com/coinbase-sends-irs-summons-notification-to-13-000-customers?utm_source=ETHNews+-+NEWS&utm_campaign=ffedf7e295-Kodak+on+The+Comment%2C+Venezuela%2C+China%2C+Price&utm_medium=email&utm_term=0_1d28ae12bd-ffedf7e295-84349401> accessed 28 February 2018.

applications. Similarly, social networks could be required to block any blockchain-related content or prohibit advertisements related to such services.[146]

Although they are not strictly intermediaries, hardware producers could, moreover, be required to configure their products in a certain way, such as to prevent encryption techniques. The UK Investigatory Powers Act allows the government to serve a telecommunications operator a 'technical capability notice' (TCN) – in other words, a government backdoor that could be applied to blockchains.[147] As already seen, such techniques come at the cost of security, as these instruments can also be used by malicious attackers.

When targeting intermediaries as regulatory access points, governments must be wary of their choices. In South Korea, banks have been tasked to become cryptoasset exchanges and handle related AML and KYC requirements.[148] Banks might be familiar access points, and such an approach might heighten trust into cryptoassets. Yet it may also undercut innovation in allowing incumbents to benefit from the innovation created by market entrants. On the other hand, imposing hefty obligations on new players may also have that effect. To illustrate, the E-Commerce Directive created safe harbours to prevent the stifling of innovation through weighty enforcement duties.[149] Heavy compliance burdens may indeed take away focus and funding from the innovative process itself. In light of the varied outcomes, a case-by-case analysis of contextual factors is necessary whenever an intermediary is considered as an access point.

A further consideration must be that delegating enforcement priorities to online intermediaries reinforces the regulatory weight of the private sphere. The United Nations' Special Rapporteur of the Right to Freedom of Opinion and Expression indeed contended that an intermediary should not decide whether to remove content; this should be up to an independent court or independent body.[150] Rather than choosing to delegate such duties to various access points, governments may thus also decide to directly intervene in blockchain governance.

---

[146] As Facebook has already done in an effort to self-regulate. On this, see further Alex Hern, 'Facebook Bans Cryptocurrency Adverts Because So Many Are Scams' *The Guardian* (31 January 2018) <www.theguardian.com/technology/2018/jan/31/facebook-bans-ads-cryptocurren cies-scams> accessed 28 February 2018.

[147] Regulation of Investogatory Powers Act (2000). For a comment, see Asaf Lubin, 'The Investigatory Powers Act and International Law: Part I' (2016) UCL Journal of Law and Jurisprudence Blog <https://blogs.ucl.ac.uk/law-journal/2016/12/26/the-investigatory-powers-act-and-inter national-law-part-i/> accessed 28 February 2018.

[148] Kevin Helms, 'Korean Crypto Exchanges to Share Data with Banks in New Account System This Month' (*bitcoin*, 22 January 2018) <https://news.bitcoin.com/korean-crypto-exchanges-share-data-with-banks-new-account-system/> accessed 28 February 2018.

[149] Urs Gasser and Wolfgang Schulz, 'Governance of Online Intermediaries' (2015) Berkman Center Research Publication No 2015-5, 6.

[150] Frank La Rue, 'Report of the Special Rapporteur on the Promotion and Protection of the Right to Freedom of Opinion and Expression' (2013) United Nations Office of the High Commissioner of Human Rights.

F. *Governments as Blockchain Participants*

Governments may attempt to directly participate in blockchain governance to steer their development in serving as miners, nodes or developers. There is precedent of law enforcement agencies taking over technological systems such as darknet markets for enforcement purposes, and a similar approach could be envisaged with respect to blockchains.[151] It would be surprising if law enforcement agencies weren't already running nodes to gain access to transactions. Moreover, states that directly or indirectly control a majority of mining power could attempt to stage a 51 per cent attack on a proof-of-work-based blockchain.[152]

Alternatively, governments may create their own blockchains to offer the advantages promised by the technology, all the while making sure that these are delivered in accordance with their own preferences. Some related experiments are already under way. The European Union launched a call for a study on the feasibility of an EU blockchain infrastructure that could assist in implementing European services and policies in an optimized manner.[153] Sweden is conducting research into a digital currency that may or may not be blockchain-based, while similar efforts seem under way in China.[154] These projects could have effects well beyond the state's borders. The first widely deployed project might effectively become the new currency of the Internet, enabling micropayments that are not possible by relying on existing monetary instruments.

Alternatively, governments may tax mining rigs and pools, and the considerable gains for the public purse that could follow might create incentives to legitimize these business models. Such a strategy could also have ancillary effects, including the increase of network effects in the particular coin(s).[155] States can thus act to improve trust in the network and, by extension, innovation. Governments can also regulate a blockchain indirectly by interfering with its cryptoeconomic set-up. Market intervention has always been a mechanism enabling regulators to pursue their objectives. Well-known techniques include fiscal policy and the use of

---

[151] Martin Dittus, 'A Distributed Resilience Among Darknet Markets?' (*The policy and internet blog*, 9 November 2017) <http://blogs.oii.ox.ac.uk/policy/a-distributed-resilience-among-darknet-markets/> accessed 28 February 2018.

[152] A 51 per cent attack refers to the (until now hypothetical) attack by a group of miners controlling more than half of mining power to influence the network. Staging such an attack is extremely expensive.

[153] <https://ec.europa.eu/digital-single-market/en/news/study-opportunity-and-feasibility-eu-blockchain-infrastructure>.

[154] William Suberg, 'China: PBoC Head Says Digital Currency "Inevitable", Bitcoin "Not Accepted" as Payment' (*Cointelegraph*, 9 March 2018) <https://cointelegraph.com/news/china-pboc-head-says-digital-currency-inevitable-bitcoin-not-accepted-as-payment> accessed 1 June 2018.

[155] This also highlights that governments must exercise care when proceeding to such a move as they may be privileging particular projects over others.

subsidies or public procurement to encourage a desired outcome.[156] Commentators have noted that regulators may exploit blockchains' market dynamics 'to incentivize these systems to abide by the law by making it economically convenient for them to do so'.[157] We could, moreover, imagine blockchains with government access that are used to collect tax.

The availability of the various regulatory access points illustrated above has confirmed that blockchains are indeed a regulatable technology. Various access points enable policy-makers to influence blockchains and blockchain-based applications, and these access points have already been exploited to impose regulatory requirements. As the distributed ledger ecosystem matures we are likely to observe additional strides in this direction. Possible future technical developments may impede that strategy, however. Blockchain technology needs to develop further for large-scale deployment, yet the shape of related evolutions remains unknown. It is clear, though, that, depending on their specificities, future technical configurations may facilitate or hamper regulatory oversight. The subsequent section engages with some of the possible future evolutions in relation to DLT and explains how they could affect the availability of regulatory access points.

IV. THE DIFFICULTIES OF BLOCKCHAIN REGULATION

Observing that public and permissionless blockchains can be regulated does not imply that it will be straightforward to do so. Returning to the analogy between blockchain and Internet regulation, it is worthwhile stressing that, while the cyber-libertarian utopia never became a reality, regulation has been far from easy, as is evident from ongoing debates in relation to intermediary liability and IP protection.[158] The Internet challenged principles of territorial governance and generated new private regulators.[159] In a similar vein, we can already identify factors that may come to burden blockchain regulation. These elements include (i) their inherently transnational nature; (ii) their decentralized peer-to-peer set-up; (iii) steps towards stronger anonymity; and (iv) increased adoption and a related shift in social norms.

A. *Blockchains as Transnational Constructs*

Blockchains' constitutive attributes make regulatory intervention far from straightforward. The first element complicating regulation is their cross-jurisdictional

---

[156] On this, see for instance Christopher McCrudden, *Buying Social Justice* (Oxford University Press 2007).
[157] De Filippi and Wright, 'Blockchain and the Law' (n 1) 185.
[158] Werbach, 'The Song Remains the Same' (n 17).
[159] On the power of these actors, see further Orla Lynskey, 'Regulating "Platform Power"' (2017) LSE Legal Studies Working Paper No.1/2017 <https://papers.ssrn.com/sol3/papers.cfm? abstract_id=2921021> accessed 28 February 2018.

ambit. Unilateral state action powered by territorial jurisdiction has long been the key paradigm of regulatory competence. Under this competence archetype, effects remain largely confined to national territories. This allows mobile actors to game the system and relocate to a jurisdiction that matches their preferences. I have observed above that, while this is probably not an option for end users, it is for most nodes and miners, developers and new blockchain intermediaries, such as cryptoasset exchanges. There are already numerous examples illustrating how such actors are very willing to move, at least in these early stages of the technology. For example, the adoption of the BitLicence scheme in New York State prompted actors to relocate to other jurisdictions.[160]

In light of the resulting jurisdictional complications, multilateral cooperation will be called for to effectively regulate blockchains and their use cases.[161] Regulators are plainly aware of this reality. A board member of the German Bundesbank has affirmed that any regulation of Bitcoin must be global as 'the power of nation states is obviously limited'.[162] The UK Financial Conduct Authority (FCA) has likewise asserted the need for a global regulatory sandbox to better frame the cross-border operation of innovative technology-based business models.[163] In the United States, the various states are realizing the benefits of cross-jurisdictional cooperation on this matter, as the American Uniform Law Commission has passed a model act for digital currencies.[164] Enforcement is similarly burdensome in multijurisdictional settings, as 'courts may struggle to enforce rulings against distributed entities'.[165] Indeed, when a distributed entity 'spans the globe and operates on a consensus basis, an order from one jurisdiction may not be followed by nodes outside that jurisdiction'.[166]

In an ideal world, a global blockchain would be regulated by a global regulator. It is said that national law does not 'create effective solutions to prevent code-based

---

[160] See Chapter 6.

[161] For similar arguments in respect to Internet regulation, see Michael Geist, 'The Reality of Bytes: Regulating Economic Activity in the Age of the Internet' (1998) 73 Washington Law Review 521; Michael Spencer, 'Anonymous Internet Communication and the First Amendment: A Crack in the Dam of National Sovereignty' (1998) 3 Virginia Journal of Law and Technology 1, 36.

[162] 'Any Rule on Bitcoin Must Be Global, Germany's Central Bank Says' (*Reuters*, 15 January 2018) <www.reuters.com/article/us-bitcoin-regulations-germany/any-rule-on-bitcoin-must-be-global-germanys-central-bank-says-idUSKBN1F420E> accessed 28 February 2018.

[163] 'FCA Explores Creation of Global Sandbox' (*finextra*, 14 February 2018) <www.finextra.com/newsarticle/31677/fca-explores-creation-of-global-sandbox?utm_source=Weekly+FinTech+Pulse&utm_campaign=26914f2e6b-EMAIL_CAMPAIGN_2018_02_17&utm_medium=email&utm_term=0_ede4cf6fd3-26914f2e6b-87357703> accessed 28 February 2018.

[164] Peter van Valkenburg, 'The ULC's Model Act for Digital Currency Businesses has Passed' (*coincenter*, 19 July 2017) <https://coincenter.org/entry/the-ulc-s-model-act-for-digital-currency-businesses-has-passed-here-s-why-it-s-good-for-bitcoin> accessed 28 February 2018.

[165] Carla Reyes, Nizan Geslevich Packin and Benjamin Edwards, 'Distributed Governance' (2017) 59 William & Mary Law Review Online 1, 30.

[166] ibid.

problems', so a pooling of sovereignty is a better solution.[167] Short of such cooperation, rules will be fragmented and cooperation complicated. Yet few would believe that a global legal framework is a realistic option at this stage. More realistic solutions capable of pursuing the same objectives should thus be envisaged. These include transnational cooperation, dialogue and experience sharing. In the European Union there is an obvious potential for the European Commission to shepherd such efforts as part of the Digital Single Market project. The transnational nature of distributed ledgers is, of course, the result of its decentralized peer-to-peer nature, the element I now turn to.

B. *Decentralization*

Blockchains are decentralized networks, just like the Internet. As a matter of principle, nothing prevents blockchain regulation – just as Internet regulation has been possible in the past. There is, however, reason to contemplate whether blockchains will advance decentralization to a degree that will hamper regulatory oversight.

In fact, it has been possible to regulate the Internet in part because elements of centralization (the regulatory access points) have emerged over time from an originally decentralized structure. Although it was designed for geographically indifferent access, this later changed with the emergence of geolocation and the recreation of geographic origin and destination, which facilitated jurisdiction.[168] Today the Internet's global architecture may still be that of a distributed network, as a result of routers and distributed protocols, but 'the actually physical Internet is often centralised'.[169]

Whereas a similar evolution can be anticipated for blockchains, different scenarios are conceivable. Blockchains are a highly decentralized peer-to-peer technology, and we have just noted that multijurisdictional cooperation will be a prerequisite for successful regulation. Yet, even where applicable norms are determined through a collaborative effort, the enforcement challenge looms large. Viktor Mayer-Schönberger has speculated that peer-to-peer networks such as virtual worlds 'could eventually transmogrify into an unregulatable space that is both everywhere and nowhere'.[170] Satoshi Nakamoto has asserted that '[g]overnments are good at cutting off the heads of centrally controlled networks like Napster, but pure P2P networks like Gnutella and Tor seem to be holding their own'.[171] We have already observed that such peer-to-peer networks allow users to upload large quantities of

---

[167] Brown and Marsden, 'Regulating Code' (n 41) 6.
[168] Reidenberg, 'Technology and Internet Jurisdiction' (n 38) 1951.
[169] Andrés Guadamuz, *Networks, Complexity and Internet Regulation* (Edward Elgar 2011) 89.
[170] Mayer-Schönberger, 'Napster's Second Life' (n 86) 1824.
[171] <https://satoshi.nakamotoinstitute.org/emails/cryptography/4/> accessed 13 April 2018.

data, often copyrighted content, to a distributed network.[172] With Napster, users had to download the client and connect it to a central server. Newer structures have eliminated the centralized point of failure and spread the indexing duty evenly across the network.[173] These peer-to-peer networks 'provide stronger encryption and a more distributed system such that no central node could be found against which to pursue litigation'.[174] The Pirate Bay remains in operation despite legal challenges because enforcement against such distributed networks is burdensome.[175] This leaves us to wonder whether the same might be true for blockchains.[176]

Peer-to-peer systems have been shown to thrive when a number of conditions are present: first, they facilitate direct user-to-user interactions without a centralized point of failure; second, they are established in jurisdictions with lax legal frameworks and weak or underused enforcement mechanisms.[177] Blockchains can check both boxes, at least if developers are incentivized to relocate to jurisdictions with lenient legal frameworks (which there always will be). These factors may indeed burden legal enforcement, but may not render it impossible. Centralized servers and developers are definitely not the only access points available to regulators.[178]

The fact that BitTorrent and Bitcoin start with the same three letters might be no coincidence. Both peer-to-peer systems defy centralized points of failure and control to avoid outside interference with the network. While peer-to-peer file-sharing systems have been largely successful, this is due not only to technical sophistication but also to a lack of incentives for regulators to put their full weight behind enforcement. The pivotal question thus is whether blockchain and blockchain-based application will perfect decentralization to a degree that makes enforcement not just disfavoured but technically impossible. Numerous developments that are currently on the horizon might move blockchains further in the direction of decentralized file storage systems and decentralized exchanges.

Decentralized file storage solutions are, essentially, peer-to-peer storage platforms that rely on decentralized and redundant storage. The Interplanetary Files System

[172] Bryan Choi, 'The Grokster Dead-End' (2006) 19 Harvard Journal of Law and Technology 393, 403 (hereafter Choi, 'The Grokster Dead-End').

[173] Peer-to-peer networks have been defined as a network of equals (the peers) using appropriate ICT systems where two or more individuals can spontaneously collaborate without necessarily needing central coordination. Detlef Schoder and Kai Fischbach 'Core Concepts in Peer-to-Peer (P2P) Networking' in Ramesh Subramanian and Brian Goodman (eds) *Peer to Peer Computing: The Evolution of a Disruptive Technology* (Idea Group 2005) 21.

[174] Brown and Marsden, 'Regulating Code' (n 41) 25.

[175] See *Sweden v Neij & others*, Svea Hovrätt, No. B. 4041–09, 26 November 2011 and *Twentieth Century Fox & others v Sky & others* (2015) EWHC 1082 (Ch).

[176] Choi, 'The Grokster Dead-End' (n 172) 404.

[177] See further Smith Seagrumn, 'From Napster to Kazaa: The Battle over Peer-to-Peer Filesharing Goes International' (2003) 2 Duke Law & Technology Review 1.

[178] In a recent judgement, the European Court of Justice held that TPB can be held liable for copyright infringement. Case C-610/15 *Stichting Brein* [2017] EU:C:2017:456.

(IPFS) seeks to replace the Hypertext Transfer Protocol (HTTP) to remove the need to rely on central instances and URLs to retrieve data.[179] This could give rise to an 'uncensorable Wikipedia' curated by citizens – or, governments.[180] IPFS is considered 'similar to a single bittorrent swarm exchanging git objects', which could become a new major subsystem of the Internet.[181] Swarm, on the other hand, is presented as a censorship-resistant Dropbox, designed so that 'there is no way for a jurisdiction to take that down' in light of the obfuscation methods that are used.[182] By virtue of obfuscation, it is said that nodes can deny that they have the content, making the network essentially censorship-resistant.[183] Projects such as Storj and Sia split data to then encrypt and distribute it across the entire network.[184]

These projects not only replace the centralized point of failure with a peer-to-peer solution but also allow only owners to access and control files with their private key. Resilience and availability are increased in dividing and scattering files across multiple nodes. This renders the network more robust, yet also undermines the ease of regulatory enforcement, as it is unclear where a given file is located and how it can be accessed. Such storage solutions would raise the question of how defamatory content can be edited or how the law can be applied in a radically decentralized setting.

In the same vein, decentralized exchanges (DEXs) raise enforcement challenges. A DEX is a peer-to-peer network through which cryptoassets can be exchanged without the need to rely on the now prevailing online cryptoasset exchange platforms. There are currently many different DEX projects, none of which has made it past the proof-of-concept stage.[185] Although only time will unveil the precise configurations of an operable DEX, the absence of an obvious point of access may complicate enforcement. Currently centralized exchanges regulate the network in imposing KYC and AML duties, yet in a DEX scenario centralized actors may disappear. While, formally, these duties can be imposed on peers, the current system has not been designed to enable individuals to comply with these obligations.

We must again return to the scope of adoption. Regulators are unlikely to worry about these developments unless they are adopted in large numbers. When technical improvements in decentralization are coupled with widespread adoption and a resulting shift in social norms, however, these blockchain-based applications may

---

[179] Stefan Grasmann, 'FileCoin and IPFS – Reinventing Storage' (*Medium*, 17 December 2017) <https://medium.com/swlh/filecoin-and-ipfs-f5e84ae79afa> accessed 1 March 2018.
[180] <https://news.ycombinator.com/item?id=15367531> accessed 1 March 2018.
[181] Christian Lundkvist, 'An Introduction to IPFS' (*Medium*, 17 February 2016) <https://medium.com/@ConsenSys/an-introduction-to-ipfs-9bba4860abdo> accessed 1 March 2018.
[182] Rachel Rose O'Leary, 'Ethereum Storage Network Swarm Enters Next Test Phase' (*coindesk*, 2 November 2017) <www.coindesk.com/ethereum-storage-network-swarm-enters-next-test-phase/> accessed 1 March 2018.
[183] ibid.
[184] <https://storj.io/>; <https://blog.sia.tech/>.
[185] Projects include <https://github.com/nonamecoin/NonameCoin> accessed 1 March 2018.

become de facto unregulatable. While BitTorrent remains a solution adopted by the technologically savvy and ideologically motivated, most users have switched to more convenient and legal options. Blockchain-based decentralized services might not only be the objectively better option (for reasons of convenience and from an economic perspective) but also have a considerably improved user experience. In this case, the technologically savvy few (developers of blockchains and related applications) may render such services easily available to the many. This may then result in two alternative circumstances. First, we may imagine regulators resorting to brute force to maintain their influence over these systems. Alternatively, such attempts may not be politically feasible, rendering such applications de facto immune to regulation. This is a point I return to just below. Before venturing on to such analysis, I must first examine efforts to realize anonymous blockchains.

C. *Anonymity*

An additional factor that may burden regulatory oversight of DLT is increased anonymity. Most blockchains are currently pseudonymous networks the participants of which can be identified when sufficient time and resources are invested. There are technical developments on the horizon that may allow for more radical ano- nymity, however. Blockchains have roots in the cryptoanarchist community, the manifesto of which declares that combining cryptographic protocols and encryption would herald a socio-economic revolution and 'alter completely the nature of government regulation, the ability to tax and control economic interactions, the ability to keep information secret, and will even alter the nature of trust and reputation'.[186]

Thus far, users have had to use Tor or VPNs to maintain privacy. We might, however, imagine a future in which blockchain-based applications have built-in, universal privacy guarantees. Cryptocurrencies such as Zcash and Monero already lure users with higher anonymity. In particular, zero-knowledge proofs permit transactions in which both the public keys of the participants as well as the details of the transaction are hidden from public view.[187] Strong cryptographic privacy guarantees can enable blockchains designed for law avoidance. This becomes an even more pronounced problem when various intermediaries are eliminated through the decentralizing dynamics observed just above.

Regulators are faced with a dilemma when it comes to anonymous blockchains and blockchain-based applications. On the one hand, there are strong incentives for them to promote the development and application of anonymization techniques,

---

[186] Timothy May, 'The Crypto Anarchist Manifesto' (*activism,* 22 November 1992) <www.activ ism.net/cypherpunk/crypto-anarchy.html> accessed 1 March 2018.
[187] Christian Reitwiessner, 'zkSNARKs in a Nutshell' (*Ethereum Blog,* 5 December 2016) <https:// blog.ethereum.org/2016/12/05/zksnarks-in-a-nutshell/> accessed 1 March 2018.

particularly in the European Union. Chapter 4 highlights that blockchains are at present not sufficiently anonymous to meet the requirements of the General Data Protection Regulation, so blockchains and blockchain-based applications have incentives to adopt stronger privacy safeguards to ensure compliance. Privacy on blockchains is not, however, a zero-sum game. Protecting privacy can also mean facilitating money laundering and the financing of criminal activity. Greater anonymization may, moreover, burden legal enforcement, as it impairs users' function as regulatory access points. There is accordingly a desperate need to devise technical solutions that enable privacy without defeating the option of law enforcement.

D. *Increased Adoption*

The preceding three sections have highlighted how technical configurations may burden regulatory enforcement in relation to blockchains and blockchain-based applications. Arguably, however, the biggest factor affecting the regulatability of blockchains is user adoption.

When systems with regulation-defiant features are adopted on a large scale, social norms will shift to reject regulatory intervention. In such a setting regulation not only becomes hard from a technical perspective; it also becomes politically unattainable. Beyond feasibility, such developments would further raise the question of whether the enforcement of norms that no longer attract social consensus can be legitimate. On the one hand, large-scale adoption will increase regulators' incentives to become involved, simply because there are greater consequences. During Bitcoin's infancy years regulators hardly knew or cared about the phenomenon. This first changed with increased reliance on SilkRoad, and again as more and more individuals have invested significant sums in cryptoassets in recent years. With regard to the Internet, Joel Reidenberg has predicted that, as technology 'increases the points of involvement or attachment in various countries and at the user's location, each of these countries and the user's state has a greater interest in the Internet activity and a greater interest in applying its substantive law to that activity'.[188]

While arguments for regulatory intervention increase as the technology spreads, large-scale adoption may also make it more difficult for regulators to become involved. The history of the enforcement of copyright and obscenity legislation on the Internet has shown that, when technology is relied on to circumvent legal prescriptions, triggering a shift in social norms, enforcement becomes difficult. Outside cyberspace, there is also ample evidence that, as social norms change, it becomes increasingly difficult to enforce existing legal principles.[189] The scale of

---

[188] Reidenberg, 'Technology and Internet Jurisdiction' (n 38) 1963.
[189] The legalization of same-sex sexual intimacy, marriage and parenthood is a case in point.

adoption might accordingly come to be the biggest factor influencing whether, and, if so, how, blockchains can be regulated.

This confirms that blockchains are not immune to regulation. As long as access points to the blockchain can be grasped outside cryptospace, regulators can shape the development of distributed ledgers. Regulating blockchains may, nonetheless, be a case of 'easier said than done'. Leaving the colossal task of determining appropriate regulatory principles and techniques aside, the specific features of blockchains and blockchain-based applications might further complicate regulators' efforts. Specifically, blockchains' multijurisdictional nature, their peer-to-peer decentralized structure, increased privacy on blockchains and heightened adoption may limit governments' leeway to influence permissionless blockchains. Over time, special solutions such as the creation of safe harbour regimes for the infrastructure level may be discussed. Designing an appropriate regulatory response is, ultimately, context-specific, and will be highly dependent on future developments in this area. As these ecosystems evolve, further research will be needed to determine appropriate regulatory frameworks.

3

Blockchains as a Regulatory Technology

We were creating this new kind of legal system that was going to mean that, in the future, lawyers and programmers were going to be the same job.[1]

Blockchains are at once a regulatable and regulatory technology. There is no paradox in that statement. Whereas the preceding chapter underlined that access points to the protocol enable regulatory intervention, this chapter documents that the protocol itself is self-enforcing, regulating those who engage with it. Code truly is one of many forms of law. Technology's self-regulatory capacity extends to blockchain-based applications such as smart contracts. As such, distributed ledgers are one of many technologies that regulate those who engage with them. Code's regulatory potential, made explicit by Joel Reidenberg and Lawrence Lessig in the 1990s, has long materialized, as we've observed in the preceding chapter.[2] Here, I reflect on how code has become a source of regulation and what this may mean for blockchains and their future development – and also for law. It will be seen that they have an extraordinary potential to form a regulatory infrastructure governing humans and machines.

At first sight, law and code are noticeably distinct. Law is about intention, and thus deliberately vague, while code is about process, and must accordingly be specific. Software has a normative dimension, however, in that it governs the behaviour of those who engage with it. Whereas code is increasingly assuming the function of law, law growingly takes the form of code. In future times technical code might merge with legal code in giving expression to the normative objectives of its creators – whether these are public entities, such as the European Union and its

---

[1] Simpleweb, 'The Future of the Blockchain: Interview with Ethereum Co-founder Gavin Wood' (*simpleweb*, 18 September 2017) <https://simpleweb.co.uk/the-future-of-the-block chain-interview-with-ethereum-co-founder-gavin-wood/> accessed 24 April 2018.
[2] For example, online platforms have become regulatory agents of their own motion and also encouraged to assume such tasks by States and the European Union.

member states, or private actors, such as operators of online platforms or those in charge of blockchain governance.

This novel form of legal 'codification' should not come as a surprise, as technological change has always been a source of legal change. The invention of the printing press in the fourteenth century enabled the codification of law in the form of words written on paper. Over time, legislation, judicial decisions and constitutions were printed on paper, and the nineteenth century saw the emergence of the Napoleonic codes, which have considerably outlasted the related empire.

The age of digitalization and datafication has enabled new forms of creating, assessing and enforcing law. To illustrate, the online availability of legal texts and keyword searches has facilitated the daily tasks of many legal practitioners and students. Newer developments such as Legal Tech and RegTech are another step in the continuous transformation of law. Through Legal Tech, transactional lawyers can deliver legal services more efficiently. Current applications perform contract review and electronic discovery, as software is used to forecast litigation outcomes.[3] RegTech solutions are essentially technological tools that facilitate compliance with regulatory requirements. Applications include behavioural analytics, detecting unusual behaviour as a sign of misconduct, or tools that ensure regulatory compliance in respect of data management.[4] At the same time, as more and more human communication and transactions occur online, digital platforms have become regulators of our online and offline lives, as many transactions are governed by their terms of service and enforced through platform-based dispute resolution mechanisms divorced from ordinary courts. For example, around 60 million disputes per year are processed by eBay's dispute resolution mechanism alone.[5] These developments indicate that code has become a remarkably efficient regulatory tool, increasingly assuming the traditional function of law in shaping human behaviour.

Computer code has thus started to inaugurate a new era of legal codification. Blockchain technology could come to constitute an important building block of that evolution. Two main elements ground blockchains' potential as a regulatory technology. First, distributed ledgers' protocols enforce their creators' normative choices. Depending on their respective set-up, this could be leveraged by public and private actors alike to create an environment for transactions that adheres to specific rules, which may reflect applicable law, or not. Second, applications running on blockchains, most notably smart contracts, can be designed to be self-enforcing,

[3]   Edgar Rayo, 'AI in Law and Legal Practice – A Comprehensive View of 35 Current Applications' (*techemergence*, 29 November 2017) <www.techemergence.com/ai-in-law-legal-practice-current-applications/> accessed 24 April 2018.
[4]   Financial Conduct Authority, 'RegTech' (*FCA*, 12 September 2017) <www.fca.org.uk/firms/regtech> accessed 24 April 2018.
[5]   Arthur Pearlstein et al., 'ODR in North America' in Mohamed Wahab et al. (eds), *Online Dispute Resolution: Theory and Practice: a Treatise on Technology and Dispute Resolution* (Eleven International Publishing 2012) 457.

automating compliance with a predetermined rule set. As observed in the introductory chapter, smart contracts' execution cannot be stopped (unless this is explicitly indented from the beginning), leading to the automated enforcement of the encoded rule set.

My reflections on this new period of legal codification unfold as follows. I open with a cursory overview of the 'code as law' paradigm and subsequently evaluate blockchains' potential future impact. I then move on to examine the challenges created by using code as law, particularly with respect to distributed ledgers. In evaluating the complex relations between these systems I note that blockchains' impact on law is not limited to their ability to automate enforcement but also that we should be aware of its very potential to replace functions currently carried out by law. The analysis closes with the argument that, in spite of blockchains' theoretical potential to act as alternative legal systems, they will in practice be dependent on law for their successful deployment.

I. CODE AS LAW

In 1986 Langdon Winner wrote about the 'politics' of technology, highlighting that technological design choices become part of the wider framework for public order.[6] The past three decades have proved him right in many respects, as software is used for public and private ordering, expressing the normative objectives of its creators.

A. *Code as a Form of Private Ordering*

Normative choices embedded in code have come to determine many aspects of our online and offline lives. Code is a regulatory tool that expresses the objectives and preferences of its creators. More often than not, however, these creators are private actors. For example, digital platforms are 'increasingly undertaking regulatory and police functions, which are traditionally considered a matter of public law'.[7] These functions include the use of injunctions against third parties, as in *L'Oréal* v. *eBay*;[8] compelling private actors to implement the General Data Protection Regulation; and policing online hate speech, a matter delegated to platforms by the European Commission.[9] The Commission's encouragement that platforms assume such

---

[6] Langdon Winner, *The Whale and the Reactor* (University of Chicago Press 1986) 19–39.

[7] Luca Belli, Pedro Francisco and Nicolo Zingales, 'Law of the Land or Law of the Platform? Beware of the Privatisation of Regulation and Police' in Luca Belli and Nicolo Zingales (eds), *Platform Regulations: How Platforms are Regulated and How They Regulate Us* (FGV Direito Rio 2017) 41 (hereafter Belli et al., 'Law of the Land or Law of the Platform?').

[8] Case C-324/09 *L'Oréal SA and Others v eBay International AG and Others* [2011] EU:C:2011:474, paras 137–44.

[9] Belli et al., 'Law of the Land or Law of the Platform?' (n 7) 47–54.

functions is instructive, as public authorities have increasingly delegated enforcement tasks to private entities, while the latter are also self-appropriating such functions. This, it has been argued, has turned online platform intermediaries into 'private cyber-regulators and cyber-police'.[10]

Private sovereignty, exercised through terms of service, is replacing public sovereignty expressed through law. Digital platforms have become 'substitutes for state power – "adjudicating" speech rights under their own Community Guidelines, rather than law'.[11] To illustrate, code regulates the humans who are using digital platforms. Uber uses code to control its drivers. Its internal code of conduct is enforced through code, as non-observance thereof results in the automated delisting of the driver or rider.[12] The transportation platform, moreover, uses behavioural science to manipulate drivers through code-based psychological inducements.[13]

Beyond the platform context, code has become a form of private ordering in many other instances. Private companies are relying on big data and predictive algorithms to determine credit risk and decide on the professional promotions of their employees.[14] Digital rights management applies code to preclude the reproduction or modification of digital files. Although it was formally designed as a mechanism to avoid infringements of copyright law, DRM exhibits elements of private ordering, as exemptions and fair use requirements have not been incorporated into these systems.[15] Private code has turned these elements into a de facto dead letter, indicating that DRM is a 'private governance system' whereby computer code interprets legality differently from the state.[16] The past years have also witnessed the emergent use of algorithms as sentencing mechanisms, as AI assists in judicial decision-making in spite of the racial bias embedded in some of these systems.[17]

Code has thus doubtlessly become an important source of private ordering, an evolution that is not without problems. When code assumes this function, the primary source of rule-making is the technology developer.[18] Private ordering is

---

[10] ibid. 41.

[11] Daphne Keller, 'Introduction: Law, Borders, and Speech' in Daphne Keller (ed), 'Law, Borders, and Speech: Proceedings and Materials' (2017) iv <http://cyberlaw.stanford.edu/publications/proceedings-volume> accessed 10 April 2018.

[12] <www.uber.com/de/legal/community-guidelines/us-en/> accessed 28 March 2018.

[13] Noam Scheiber, 'How Uber Uses Psychological Tricks to Push Its Drivers' Buttons' *The New York Times* (2 April 2017) <www.nytimes.com/interactive/2017/04/02/technology/uber-drivers-psychological-tricks.html?_r=0> accessed 28 March 2018.

[14] Danielle Citron and Frank Pasquale, 'The Scored Society: Due Process for Automated Predictions' (2014) 89 Washington Law Review 1.

[15] Pamela Samuelson, 'Digital Rights Management (and, or, vs.) the law' (2003) 46 Communications of the ACM 41, 42.

[16] ibid. 42.

[17] Julia Angwin, Jeff Larson, Surya Mattu and Lauren Kirchner, 'Machine Bias' (*ProPublica*, 23 March 2016) <www.propublica.org/article/machine-bias-risk-assessments-in-criminal-sentencing> accessed 10 April 2018.

[18] Joel Reidenberg, 'Lex Informatica: The Formulation of Information Policy Rules Through Technology' (1998) 76 Texas Law Review 3, 552, 571 (hereafter Reidenberg, 'Lex Informatica').

not subject to the same checks and balances of law-making as public authorities are, however. The code that so often regulates us lacks transparency and escapes scrutiny, even more so when it benefits from trade secret protection.[19] This has led Frank Pasquale to refer to related algorithms as 'black boxes'.[20]

It is important to remember, however, that, when code acts as law, it is not acting in total isolation. Online policies, rather, are 'both shaped by and reshape existing laws, regulations and social mores'.[21] In recent years, though, increasing criticism has been voiced that law has not been able to stop the development of 'platform power' and the breach of fundamental human rights through code.[22] Standard content guidelines may not respect the principle of legality, as online codes of conduct prohibit content that is lawful under EU law.[23] This leads me to observe in Chapter 6 that, while there are convincing arguments why entities such as platforms should be able to leverage the regulatory power of code, we need to rethink the involvement of public authorities and the broader community in these processes to safeguard legitimacy. Indeed, important concerns arise when code is used as law in the absence of procedures that safeguard ideals of democracy, legitimacy, transparency and accountability. Code is not just an instrument of private but also of public ordering, however.

B. *Code as Public Ordering*

Public authorities progressively rely on code in their rule-making and enforcement responsibilities. Predictive technologies are increasingly informing the state in its legislative capacity while the automated enforcement of law is also on the horizon. Big data analytics, artificial intelligence (especially machine learning), blockchain technology and robotics are all tools capable of informing (legislative) decision-making to influence individual and collective behaviour. This computational turn

---

[19] A trade secret is in essence confidential commercial information that provides a firm with a competitive advantage (such as the Coca-Cola recipe) that benefits from special legal protection. In the EU, trade secrets are now governed by Directive (EU) 2016/943 of the European Parliament and of the Council of 8 June 2016 on the protection of undisclosed know-how and business information (trade secrets) against their unlawful acquisition, use and disclosure OJ L 157, 1–18.

[20] Frank Pasquale, *The Black Box Society* (Harvard University Press 2015).

[21] Ian Brown and Christopher Marsden, *Regulating Code* (MIT Press 2013) xii.

[22] On platform power, see Julie Cohen, 'The Regulatory State in the Information Age' (2016) 17 Theoretical Inquiries in Law 369 and Orla Lynskey, 'Regulating "Platform Power"' (2017) LSE Legal Studies Working Paper No. 1/2017 <https://papers.ssrn.com/sol3/papers.cfm?abstract_id=2921021> accessed 10 April 2018.

[23] Joe McNamee and Maryant Pérez, 'Fundamental Rights and Digital Platforms in the European Union: A Suggested Way Forward' in Belli et al., 'Law of the Land or Law of the Platform?' (n 7) 99.

in law has been portrayed as the source of a 'new system of social ordering known as algorithmic regulation'.[24] Karen Yeung has defined algorithmic regulation as

> decision-making systems that regulate a domain of activity in order to manage risk or alter behavior through continual computational generation of knowledge by systematically collecting data (in real time on a continuous basis) emitted directly from numerous dynamic components pertaining to the regulated environment in order to identify and, if necessary, automatically refine (or prompt refinement of) the system's operations to attain a pre-specified goal.[25]

Predictive technology can facilitate evidence-based law-making as sophisticated data analysis techniques help legislators 'predict which rules can precisely achieve a policy objective'.[26] AI and big data will, accordingly, alter how societies choose to govern behaviour. Technology bears the potential to support states and the European Union not just in their law-making function; a possibly even more transformative potential lies in technology's role in law enforcement. In the future, software could be used to provide evidence about the effects of existing legislation and insights about the need for and potential of planned legislation. At the same time, data analytics can detect unlawful behaviour and guide law enforcement. A UK government report highlights that 'public regulatory influence could be exerted through a combination of legal and technical code', a scenario in which technical code would ensure compliance with law.[27] Code has an extraordinary capacity to secure compliance as software enforces its own rules. For example, it has been used in border control to determine who is allowed to board a flight,[28] or, more generally, to quantify security risks.[29]

Anthony Casey and Anthony Niblett foresee a future of 'microdirectives', a predictive and communication technology that provides simple commands for all possible scenarios.[30] In each situation, a citizen would be instructed by a machine how to act to achieve legal compliance.[31] Already, at this stage, predictive policing algorithms are used to predict criminal activity before it happens (or, rather, is

---

[24] Karen Yeung, 'Algorithmic Regulation: A Critical Interrogation' (2017) TLI Think! Paper 62/2017, 1 <https://papers.ssrn.com/sol3/papers.cfm?abstract_id=2972505> accessed 10 April 2018.

[25] ibid.

[26] Anthony Casey and Anthony Niblett, 'The Death of Rules and Standards' (2017) 92 Indiana Law Journal 1401, 1410 (hereafter Casey and Niblett, 'The Death of Rules and Standards').

[27] Mark Walport, 'Executive Summary' in Government Office for Science, 'Distributed Ledger Technology: Beyond Block Chain. A Report by the UK Government Chief Scientific Adviser' 11–12 <www.gov.uk/government/uploads/system/uploads/attachment_data/file/492972/gs-16-1-distributed-ledger-technology.pdf> accessed 24 April 2018.

[28] Danielle Citron, 'Technological Due Process' (2008) 85 Washington University Law Review 1249, 1252.

[29] Frank Pasquale and Glyn Cashwell, 'Four Futures of Legal Automation' (2015) 63 UCLA Law Review Discourse 26, 37.

[30] Casey and Niblett, 'The Death of Rules and Standards' (n 26).

[31] ibid.

assumed to happen).[32] Algorithmic tools have been relied on to improve the predictive and decision-making abilities of police forces in the United Kingdom.[33] It is worth noting that EU law imposes some limits on automated decision-making, as the General Data Protection Regulation provides that data subjects have the right 'not to be subject to a decision based solely on automated processing, including profiling', when this produces legal effects or otherwise significantly affects the data subject.[34] When an option of human intervention is involved, however, systems such as those outlined above would probably not raise major concerns from a data protection perspective.

In acting as a form of public ordering, code can be used to increase state control. It would indeed be mistaken to believe that technological change necessarily is the source of deregulation, as cheaper sensors and cameras enable more surveillance, and connected devices will 'render ever more aspects of daily experience as pressure points for regulatory intervention'.[35] Tools such as RegTech have the potential to enable a 'close to real-time and proportionate regulatory regime that identifies and addresses risk while also facilitating far more efficient regulatory compliance'.[36] Technology thus has the capacity to enhance not only private but also public control over individuals.

Software, no doubt, is a powerful normative tool in the hands of those who operate it. It can be used as a means of public and private ordering. The lines between these dynamics are often fluid. Indeed, when the EU instructs platforms to monitor hate speech, this can be seen as ordering through code that has both a public and a private flavour. After this cursory overview of how code can act as a means of public and private ordering, I go on to examine the potential of blockchain technology in relation to these aspects.

II. BLOCKCHAIN CODE AS LAW

Blockchains are, essentially, software, a combination of code. Both the technology's specific features and its expected primary uses are indicative of its regulatory potential. Tamper evidence and the related guaranteed execution of blockchain-based applications such as smart contracts remove uncertainty as to whether rules

---

[32] Andrew Ferguson, 'Predictive Policing and Reasonable Suspicion' (2012) 62 Emory Law Journal 259.

[33] Marion Oswald et. al., 'Algorithmic Risk Assessment Policing Models: Lessons From the Durham HART Model and "Experimental" Proportionality' (2018) 27 Information and Communications Technology Law 223.

[34] Article 22(1) GDPR.

[35] Frank Pasquale and Glyn Cashwell, 'Four Futures of Legal Automation' (2015) 63 UCLA Law Review Discourse 26, 36.

[36] Douglas Arner, Jànos Barberis and Ross Buckley, 'FinTech, RegTech, and the Reconceptualization of Financial Regulation' (2017) 37 Northwestern Journal of International Law and Business 371.

that have been agreed upon by parties are in fact enforced. These features make distributed ledgers particularly amenable to act as regulatory constructs that enable original forms of normative ordering. Core use cases of the technology, such as record-keeping, the codification and enforcement of entitlements, property transfers and escrow, have an inherently regulatory dimension. This section surveys the regulatory nature of blockchains and blockchain-based applications in addressing claims that automated enforcement and customized legal orders make the technology a new form of law.

A. *The Emergence of a New Form of Law*

The parallels between code and law led Joel Reidenberg to craft the notion of *lex informatica*, a concept indicating that policy choices can be expressed through code.[37] Writing in 1998, Reidenberg examined these developments through the lens of the fast-paced (regulatory) innovations created by the Internet. His *lex informatica* is itself derived from the concept of *lex mercatoria*, the rules and principles defined in the Middle Ages to govern trade.[38] In analogy to these concepts, Primavera De Filippi and Aaron Wright have developed the concept of *lex cryptographia*. They predict the emergence of a new subset of law that consists of 'rules administered through self-executing smart contracts and decentralized (autonomous) organizations'.[39] Through *lex cryptographia*, they argue, the mainstream deployment and adoption of blockchains will 'require a shift in the way we perceive the role of law'.[40] For example, smart contracts may bypass property law, 'effectively turning property or even constitutional rights into a subset of contract law'.[41]

Carla Reyes agrees that DLT could have transformational effects on contemporary legal systems. She foresees the emergence of 'cryptolaw', a new jurisprudence in which law is delivered through smart contracts.[42] Blockchains are perceived to offer an opportunity to 'construct new legal structures which will give rise to new substantive legal issues and cause shifts in legal culture and legal structures'.[43] In the world of cryptolaw, law is first created through regulation or legislation and subsequently implemented through cryptographic smart-contracting

---

[37] Reidenberg, 'Lex Informatica' (n 18) 569.
[38] *Lex mercatoria* refers to the transnational body of rules observed by traders throughout Europe in medieval times, which still influences international commercial law today.
[39] Aaron Wright and Primavera De Filippi, 'Decentralized Blockchain Technology and The Rise of Lex Cryptographia' (2015) 1 <https://papers.ssrn.com/sol3/papers.cfm?abstract_id=2580664> accessed 28 February 2018 (hereafter Wright and De Filippi, 'Lex Cryptographia').
[40] ibid.
[41] ibid. 50.
[42] Carla Reyes, 'Conceptualizing Cryptolaw' (2017) 96 Nebraska Law Review 384.
[43] ibid. 387.

computer code.[44] This approach would leverage the ability of code to achieve compliance, a point indicated above that I return to in Chapter 6. Cryptolaw offers, moreover, the benefits of flexibility and rapid adaptability, so that the 'method and locus of creating crypto-legal structures' can be quickly adapted to the policy problem.[45] Through the combination of flexible adaptation and guaranteed execution, cryptolaw is anticipated to 'disrupt national legal systems at their very core elements' and alter how we study, think and talk about the law.[46]

These authors concur that the future will bring increased interconnection between code and law, with code acting as a means of delivering regulation that might diverge from state-sanctioned law. It is worth stressing that regulators are starting to think along the same lines. The Australian standards organization, which is shepherding the International Standards Organization's blockchain work, has suggested cultivating 'a regulatory framework that provides a mix of legal and technical rules'.[47] Indeed, as technological innovation progresses, standards are likely to take the place of law in many instances. The managing director of the International Monetary Fund (IMF), Christine Lagarde, believes that 'the same innovations that power crypto-assets can also help us regulate them'.[48] Considering that regulatory and supervisory technology can help shut criminals out of the crypto-world, she mentions two concrete examples. First, that DLT can be used to speed up information sharing between market participants and regulators.[49] The technology, which enables instant global transactions, could register customer records and digital signatures to reduce tax evasion. Second, she predicts that a combination of biometrics, artificial intelligence and cryptography could enhance digital security and 'identify suspicious transactions in close to real time'.[50] These features, she argues further, could be core elements of possible future central bank cryptocurrencies.[51]

Lex cryptographia and cryptolaw forecast that distributed ledgers will empower code, to the detriment of other forms of regulation. In 2001 Hans-Hermann Hoppe foresaw government-like organizations that enforce agreements among private parties, governments gradually becoming obsolete.[52] Combinations of smart contracts in the form of a DAO could be used to achieve that objective. Code, especially when tamper-proof, may thus come to trump other sources of normative influence

[44] ibid. 400.

[45] ibid. 400.

[46] ibid. 414.

[47] Standards Australia, 'Proposal for a New Field of Technical Activity' (2016) <www.jisc.go.jp/international/nwip/tsp258_Blockchain_and_electronic_distributed_ledger_technologies.pdf> accessed 28 March 2018.

[48] Christine Lagarde, 'Addressing the Dark Side of the Crypto World' (*IMFBlog*, 13 March 2018) <https://blogs.imf.org/2018/03/13/addressing-the-dark-side-of-the-crypto-world/> accessed 28 March 2018.

[49] ibid.

[50] ibid.

[51] ibid.

[52] Hans-Hermann Hoppe, *Democracy: The God that Failed* (Transaction Publisher 2001).

that guide human behaviour. There are two elements of blockchain technology that stand out in particular when assessing its potentially transformative impact on law: the self-executing nature of code and the possibility of customizing law.

1. Automated Enforcement

It has been suggested that 'the blockchain economy extends beyond the digital economy in that agreed-upon transactions are autonomously enforced, following rules defined in smart contracts'.[53] This evolution presents four distinct elements. First, automated execution is enabled by smart contracts. Second, automated enforcement can be used as a source of private ordering, and, third, as a source of public ordering. Fourth, this may unsettle some fundamentals of law as we know it, including with respect to law enforcement.

Lex cryptographia and cryptolaw assume that automatically executing code in the form of smart contracts is particularly revolutionary from a legal perspective. Although such software is neither smart (in the AI sense) nor a contract (in the legal sense), it may ultimately alter how we think of law. Kevin Werbach and Nicolas Cornell have suggested that these technical artefacts could 'displace the legal system's core function of enforcing agreements' as automated enforcement intrudes on law's historical province.[54] The option of automated and thus guaranteed enforcement explains why smart contracts are seen as 'one of the first truly disruptive technological advancements to the practice of law since the invention of the printing press'.[55]

Seen from this perspective, smart contracts are new regulatory agents. In traditional contractual arrangements, parties bear the risk of the counterparty not adhering to the agreement, and law provides remedies when this is the case. When smart contracts are used they ensure that aspects of an agreement are self-executing and remove such risk. For example, smart contracts could be used in supply chains to automatically execute payment when an oracle informs the software that a batch of goods has arrived at its destination. Similarly, in InsurTech, smart contracts could be relied on to speed up claims processes and automate financial payout to consumers when an oracle notifies occurrence of an insured event. The use of smart contracts to govern private relations is further explored in many other contexts, including testaments.[56]

---

[53] Roman Beck, Christoph Müller-Bloch and John King, 'Governance in the Blockchain Economy: A Framework and Research Agenda' (2018) 5 <www.researchgate.net/publication/323689461_Governance_in_the_Blockchain_Economy_A_Framework_and_Research_Agenda> accessed 3 April 2018.

[54] Kevin Werbach and Nicolas Cornell, 'Contracts Ex Machina' (2017) 76 Duke Law Journal 313, 314–15.

[55] Wright and De Filippi, 'Lex Cryptographia' (n 39) 11.

[56] Pabbaraja Sreehari et al., 'Smart Will Converting the Legal Testament into a Smart Contract' (2017) <http://ieeexplore.ieee.org/document/8076767/> accessed 3 April 2018.

Employed by the state, smart contracts can automatically levy fines when a red light is crossed or a car wrongly parked. Smart contracts have also been discussed as a method of ensuring tax compliance, to more efficiently enforce rules on value added tax (VAT).[57] Researchers are also currently experimenting with distributed ledgers to optimize financial regulation, specifically KYC processes.[58] The United Kingdom ran an experiment using blockchain technology to help benefits recipients better manage their money, amidst criticisms that using blockchain to do so could pose a serious threat to users' privacy.[59]

The technology can also be used to more tyrannical ends, however. When distributed ledgers are used as a means of public ordering, constraining regulatory and governance mechanisms are needed, as otherwise these systems can easily become mechanisms of control. By regulating code, the Internet has become at once a tool of freedom and oppression. Blockchains face the prospect of an identical future. Governments, it is feared, could use the technology to expand their own power, as the 'universal visibility of transaction on a distributed ledger is an authoritarian regime's dream'.[60]

Through automated execution, blockchains also become an option for law enforcement in relation to consumer contracts.[61] Today, even though consumers benefit from many mandatory rights, these are seldom enforced, due to limited knowledge regarding the existence of these rights and the high costs associated with enforcement actions. The resulting enforcement gap could be filled by smart contracting mechanisms. Martin Fries notes that, under existing Legal Tech solutions, responsibility often remains with the consumer, who has to actively search for and activate such mechanisms, and usually also pay a commission to the intermediary.[62] Smart contracts can automatically enforce contractual disputes. A smart contract could be fashioned to automatically refund money to the consumer in case of delay to enforce European passenger rights.[63] The potential of smart contracts in such scenarios has not gone unnoticed to regulators, as the German government seeks to determine the possibilities of using smart contracts in relation

---

57 Hissu Hyvärinen, Marten Risius and Gustav Friis, 'A Blockchain-Based Approach Towards Overcoming Financial Fraud in Public Sector Services' (2017) 59 Business & Information Systems Engineering 441; Richard Ainsworth and Andrew Shact, 'Blockchain Technology Might Solve VAT Fraud' (2016) 83 Tax Notes International 1165.

58 José Moyano and Omri Ross, 'KYC Optimization Using Distributed Ledger Technology' (2017) 59 Business & Information Systems Engineering 411.

59 Rory Cellan-Jones, 'Blockchain and Benefits - A Dangerous Mix?' *BBC News* (14 July 2016) <www.bbc.com/news/technology-36785872> accessed 10 April 2018.

60 Kevin Werbach, *The Blockchain and the New Architecture of Trust* (MIT Press 2018) 208.

61 Joshua Fairfield, 'Smart Contracts, Bitcoin Botsand Consumer Protection' (2014) 71 Washington and Lee Law Review Online 35.

62 Martin Fries, 'Law and Autonomous Systems Series: Smart consumer Contracts – The End of Civil Procedure?' (*Oxford Business Law Blog*, 29 March 2018) <www.law.ox.ac.uk/business-law-blog/blog/2018/03/smart-consumer-contracts-end-civil-procedure> accessed 10 April 2018.

63 ibid.

to consumer contracts over the coming years.[64] A careful evaluation of smart contracting techniques in such contexts is necessary, as the software could also be used to undermine, rather than empower, the weaker party. There is indeed a risk that smart contracts are applied to arbitrarily reinforce existing power imbalances, such as when a mortgage company uses smart logs to shut consumers in default of payment out of their house without considering contextual factors. To prevent reinforcing existing power imbalances, the benefits provided by autonomously operating software need to be encircled by legal principles protecting the weaker party.

Similar concerns have emerged in other domains, as it is feared that distributed ledgers may be wielded as unimpeachable ubiquitous personal surveillance networks that disclose the location and conduct and interactions of individuals to act 'as a powerful deterrent for those who might be tempted to commit violent interferences with the personal security and bodily integrity of others'.[65]

Blockchain technology has also been put forward as a novel method of enforcing competition law. At this stage, the implications of the technology from a competition standpoint cannot be comprehensively assessed considering that many markets have not yet formed. Many agree, however, that smart contracts could be an inventive means of coordinating collusion.[66] Research has suggested that, when this is the case, the technology itself should be employed to enforce existing prohibitions of anti-competitive conduct. When governments run a node the blockchains' real-time and tamper-proof records can enable more effortless detection and containment of market malfunctions at high frequency.[67]

Smart contracts' core value proposition of automated execution can accordingly be used as a mechanism of private or public ordering. When it is relied upon it forces us to reconsider some of the assumptions inherently enshrined in contemporary legal orders. In addition to triggering efficiency gains, smart contracts may cause changes to the nature of law. First, law is not automatically self-enforcing. Rather, it sets out behavioural specifications that parties are incentivized to comply with but have freedom to disregard and assume consequences, which are in turn administered by the legal system. When code is used, compliance is the only option, with the exception of those able to circumvent code. Second, when (smart contract) code is used to express legal obligations, law, in particular its ambiguity and flexibility,

---

[64] 'Koalitionsvertrag zwischen CDU, CSU und SPD' (2018) 124 <www.cdu.de/system/tdf/media/dokumente/koalitionsvertrag_2018.pdf?file=1> accessed 24 April 2018.

[65] Karen Yeung, 'Blockchain, Transactional Security and the Promise of Automated Law Enforcement: The Withering of Freedom Under Law?' (2017) TLI Think! Paper 58/2017, 3–4 <https://papers.ssrn.com/sol3/papers.cfm?abstract_id=2929266> accessed 3 April 2018 (hereafter Yeung, 'Blockchain, Transactional Security').

[66] Lin Cong and Zhiguo He, 'Blockchain Disruption and Smart Contracts' (2018) NBER Working Paper No. 24399, 1 <www.nber.org/papers/w24399> accessed 3 April 2018.

[67] ibid.

need to adapt to generate a kind of law that can more easily be translated into code. This would change legislative drafting, as language that can be translated into code has to be used, and, conversely, also change the process of legislative negotiation, which can include the intentional use of unclear language.

Smart contracts could further impact the status of ordinary courts of law, such as when built-in arbitration clauses are used. The need for such mechanisms results from the fact that, while the code executes in a pristine on-chain environment, it refers to facts that occur in the messy real world. Such mechanisms may thus be needed to resolve disputes that arise after a smart contract has been put on-chain, such as when concerns regarding the identity or capacity of an individual arise or when the code fails to operate as expected. Whereas the first point is a straightforward question of contract law, the second is not. Here, it may be necessary to involve specialized bodies that can adjudicate resulting disputes. This does not unavoidably imply a weakening of the state, as the state could be an oracle and, instead of a panel of arbitrators, in future times the judiciary could adjudicate the dispute at issue. As smart contract arbitration mechanisms are developed, the precise configuration thereof is not without broader consequences for the balance between public and private power. Next, I turn to outline how distributed ledgers may also alter our perception of law when they enable customized legal orders.

B. *Customized Legal Orders*

Law is impersonal, as it is not tailored to an individual's specific preferences. As a consequence of technological innovation, including big data analytics, more personalized rules are on the horizon. Digital footprints can be combined with machine-learning algorithms to offer personalized advertising and personalized pricing (also known as price discrimination).[68] The rise of big data could, equally, enable the creation and administration of personalized legal rules. According to Cass Sunstein, 'personalized default rules are the wave of the future; we should expect to see a significant increase in personalization as greater information becomes available about the informed choices of diverse people'.[69] Others agree that, with big data, 'implementing a personalized default rule regime is attainable,

---

[68] Ryan Calo, 'Digital Market Manipulation' (2014) 82 George Washington Law Review 995, 1016–18; Christopher Townley, Eric Morrison and Karen Yeung, 'Big Data and Personalised Price Discrimination in EU Competition Law' (2017) King's College London Law School Research Paper No. 2017–38 <https://papers.ssrn.com/sol3/papers.cfm?abstract_id=3048688> accessed 24 April 2018.

[69] Cass Sunstein, 'Impersonal Default Rules vs. Active Choices vs. Personalized Default Rules: A Triptych' (2012) Regulatory Policy Program RPP-2012–17, 25 <https://sites.hks.harvard.edu/m-rcbg/rpp/Working%20papers/RPP_2012_17_Sunstein.pdf> accessed 24 April 2018.

and personalized disclosures are within reach'.[70] The potential of machine learning to personalize law has also been debated.[71] Such developments should not be underestimated. The advent of modern technology could lead to the abandonment of the 'reasonable person' standard in tort law, which some argue should be replaced with a subjective analysis of individuals' inclination to create and reduce risk.[72]

One anticipated effect of blockchains' *lex cryptographia* is that smart contracts could 'make it easier for citizens to create custom legal systems, where people are free to choose and to implement their own rules within their own techno-legal framework'.[73] The individual customization of applicable norms would capacitate individuals to determine the rules applicable to them in line with their respective preferences and to switch between rule sets depending on time and circumstance. It has long been established that code is 'distinct from legal regulation because its mechanisms may implement customizations with minimal effort'.[74] This implies that anyone can be a regulator and engage in 'forum shopping', potentially weakening a state's territorial sovereignty and the rule of law.

Philipp Hacker has gone as far as to suggest that, when governments resort to personalized law, blockchain technology provides the ideal database for them to store related data in light of its tamper resistance and resilience, achieved through replication.[75] In a context of personalized law, distributed ledgers 'can be leveraged to create a decentralized, pseudonymous and dynamic government database which stores the relevant parameters for personalized law, such as the degrees of bounded rationality or specific personality traits of different persons'.[76] Accordingly, distributed ledgers can be used not only to more efficiently enforce law through automated execution but also to manage individual parameters to define individualized rights and obligations – not just in contractual settings but also by the state.

The ability of code to personalize law is not limited to smart contracts but constitutes a broader phenomenon. Cynics might object that these evolutions are nothing new, as, in ordinary legislative processes as well, legislation can be sold for 'campaign contributions, votes, implicit promises, and sometimes outright bribes'.[77]

---

[70] Ariel Porat and Lior Strahilevitz, 'Personalizing Default Rules and Disclosure with Big Data' (2013) Coase-Sandor Institute for Law & Economics Working Paper No. 634, 47 <https://chicagounbound.uchicago.edu/cgi/viewcontent.cgi?article=1365&context=law_and_economics> accessed 24 April 2018.

[71] For a critical appraisal, see <www.oii.ox.ac.uk/videos/oii-colloquia-whats-wrong-with-using-machine-learning-to-personalise-law/> accessed 10 April 2018.

[72] Omri Ben-Shahar and Ariel Porat, 'Personalizing Negligence Law' (2016) 91 New York University Law Review 627.

[73] Wright and De Filippi, 'Lex Cryptographia' (n 39) 40.

[74] Reidenberg, 'Lex Informatica' (n 18) 569, 580.

[75] Philipp Hacker, 'Personalizing EU Private Law. From Disclosures to Nudges and Mandates' (2017) 25 European Review of Private Law 651.

[76] ibid.

[77] William Landes and Richard Posner, 'The Independent Judiciary in an Interest-Group Perspective' (1975) 18 Journal of Law and Economics 875, 877.

Seen from this perspective, smart contracts simply lower entry costs to an already existing phenomenon. Yet, just because the real world doesn't always live up to its ideal, it doesn't mean that these ideals, including the rule of law, should be abandoned outright. While legislative processes, including the European Union's ordinary legislative procedure, are far from perfect, they nonetheless postulate salient guiding principles that fulfil important functions.[78] When code is used to personalize law, procedures must ensure that fundamental constitutional principles are upheld. This brings me to my next point. Whereas code assumes the function of law, it must be bridged with legal systems and their overarching ideals.

III. FROM LEGAL CODE TO TECHNICAL CODE

When code replaces law, challenges and opportunities arise. Regulation's computational turn has been illustrated through the example of blockchains above but is in no way limited to that technology. The future promises higher synergies between legal code and technical code. Developments in areas such as machine learning, big data and distributed ledgers offer the potential to reshape both the law-making process (through new means of information gathering) and legal enforcement (through more efficient means of enforcing legal obligations). This section provides a cursory overview of the implications of the stated shift in singling out ten developments that may come to characterize the turn to legal automation.

First, whereas legal code is based on the premise of *ex post* enforcement, technical code regulates in an *ex ante* fashion. Roger Brownsword and Han Somsen envisage a world in which regulation becomes 'technologically enabled to profile and to predict the actions of regulatees, to identify and to punish deviants, and even to preclude deviation'.[79] This has advantages and disadvantages, as there are stronger guarantees that laws are being complied with but, at the same time, human agency is subverted. *Ex ante* enforcement, as is the case with smart contracts, comes with the benefit of efficiency, as the only option is compliance, except for the technologically savvy, who can circumvent code with better code. In contrast, regular citizens lose their ability to disobey the law. At present legal norms are announced and individuals have the choice of compliance or non-compliance, with an associated risk of having to endure the resulting consequences. Removing human agency lessens individual freedom and may result in moral atrophy, as citizens would simply follow the law without being compelled to appreciate the moral choices that underline compliance.[80] Friedrich Hayek noted that there is a 'difference between

---

[78] Deirdre Curtin and Päivi Leino, 'In Search of Transparency for EU Law-making: Trilogues on the Cusp of Dawn' (2017) 54 Common Market Law Review 1673.

[79] Roger Brownsword and Han Somsen, 'Law, Innovation and Technology: Before We Fast Forward—A Forum for Debate' (2009) 1 Law, Innovation and Technology 1, 58.

[80] Anthony Casey and Anthony Niblett, 'Self-Driving Laws' (2016) 66 University of Toronto Law Journal 429, 438.

laying down a Rule of the Road, as in the Highway Code, and ordering people where to go'.[81] Whereas the first scenario provides direction, the latter amounts to coercion, as 'the individual is restrained from undertaking actions that do not comply with the law'.[82]

Second, reliance on technical code will change the nature of legal code. Natural language is ambiguous (and often intentionally so in legislative settings), whereas computer language knows only 1s and 0s. Law is typically drafted by humans for humans and its interpretation is subject to contextual appreciation. When legal code is translated into technical code, it becomes necessary to subscribe to novel legal drafting techniques so that law can be read by machines. Law is often designed to be flexible, to account for changing circumstances and to be applied on a case-by-case basis. Code relies on algorithms and mathematical models, however, and doesn't allow for such discretional application, at least not without much more sophisticated AI. At the same time, however, forcing law's translation into code might expose internal inconsistencies, and as a result improve the quality of law.

Third, the premises of law-making are altered through technology. When predictive analysis is used as an information-gathering tool for legislative purposes, the knowledge grounding legal change shifts from human observation, intuition and knowledge to machine knowledge. Big data is considered 'a game changer' for this process, as it 'implies another understanding of what counts as knowledge and creates different underpinnings for human, machine-to-machine and hybrid decision systems'.[83] This can be seen as an opportunity, as it increases the chances of successful evidence-based law-making, yet it is important to create the appropriate guiding principles that ensure that data is analysed, represented and interpreted objectively and that room for human assessment remains.

Fourth, code may undermine the role of law as the glue of societal relations. Karen Yeung fears that replacing legal with technological compulsion could erode 'the organic solidarity, the bond of trust between governors and the governed', that lies 'at the root of its social foundations, and with it, our cherished freedom under law'.[84] According to this vision, blockchains, portrayed as a new solution to the game-theoretic problem of cooperation, would threaten the very rule of law as the main framework that enables untrusting strangers to coexist and cooperate.[85] Even assuming that distributed ledgers are unlikely to *ex nihilo* replace the function of the rule of law, the mere provision of an alternative to state-sanctioned law may destabilize existing social bonds.

---

[81] Friedrich Hayek, *The Road to Serfdom* (Routledge 1944) 74.

[82] Casey and Niblett, 'The Death of Rules and Standards' (n 30) 440.

[83] Mireille Hildebrandt, 'Salves to Big Data. Or are We?' (2013) 17 Revista D'Internet, Dret I Política 27, 32.

[84] Yeung, 'Blockchain, Transactional Security' (n 65) 11.

[85] On the problem of cooperation, see further Chapter 1.

Fifth, we need to consider how safeguards of constitutional ideals such as transparency, accountability and legitimacy can be transplanted to a context in which law is expressed or enforced through code. In democratic societies, adherence to the rule of law requires authorization criteria for the use of technological enforcement instruments.[86] Through centuries of practical experience, procedures that (more or less) allow for the pursuit of these ideals in legislative procedures have been developed. As of yet, no similar mechanisms exist for code. This can be treacherous, as, devoid of public oversight, code risks increasing private power to the detriment of public power, or increase public power to the detriment of citizens. Mireille Hildebrandt warns that technological change risks draining 'the life from the law' in 'devouring the procedural kernel of the Rule of Law that enables people to stand up for their rights against big players, whether governmental or corporate or otherwise'.[87] Over time, safeguards must be determined that ensure that code doesn't remain the black box it is today but, rather, becomes amenable to public oversight.

Sixth, the transition from legal code to technical code doesn't just test procedural safeguards but also substantive principles. With respect to human rights, Giovanni Sartor notes that information technologies enhance human rights by offering opportunities for their realization that can be available to everybody.[88] At the same time, however, 'they put human rights at risk', because they provide potent means of interference.[89] Code should be utilized not to threaten established legal principles but, rather, as a more efficient means of achieving them. It is law's task to see to the realization of this objective, as '[t]he supremacy of law. . .must provide incentives for innovation and the development of technologies that can support public policy choices'.[90]

Seventh, the rise of regulatory technology will unsettle institutional power dynamics. When compliance becomes the sole option through automated enforcement, the judiciary will adjudge with fewer cases of alleged non-compliance, and, in turn, less opportunity to comment on the possible inadequacy of the law. Depending on domestic procedural arrangements, this may also deprive the judiciary of checking legislation against constitutional safeguards. These developments remove judicial enforcement's task of acting as a 'dynamic feedback loop' that enables the legal system to respond to socio-technological change and flag to law-makers when refinement and revision of existing legislation are required.[91] The weakened role

---

[86] Joel Reidenberg, 'Technology and Internet Jurisdiction' (2005) 153 University of Pennsylvania Law Review 1951, 1964 (hereafter Reidenberg, 'Technology and Internet Jurisdiction').

[87] Mireille Hildebrandt, 'Law as Information in the Era of Data-Driven Agency' (2016) 79 Modern Law Review 1, 2 (hereafter Hildebrandt, 'Law as Information').

[88] Giovanni Sartor, 'Human Rights and Information Technologies' in Roger Brownsword, Eloise Scotford and Karen Yeung (eds), *The Oxford Handbook of Law, Regulation and Technology* (Oxford University Press 2017) 424.

[89] ibid.

[90] Reidenberg, 'Technology and Internet Jurisdiction' (n 86) 1951, 1969.

[91] Yeung, 'Blockchain, Transactional Security' (n 65) 4.

of the judiciary will, in turn, empower the executive and legislative branches of government, and modify the existing separation of power and checks and balances arrangements.

Eighth, technology, including blockchain technology, will enable (almost) real-time governance and regulation. Data harvesting and analysis allow regulators to get real-time feedback, allowing them to react much more speedily.[92] Real-time analysis of data will, on the one hand, enable faster determination of the factual underpinnings of areas in which legal reform is debated (assuming the deliberative process is as fast as information collection can be). On the other hand, real-time data analysis can provide an immediate overview of where an algorithm thinks enforcement priorities should lie or where an instance of non-compliance has been detected.

Ninth, unlike law, code easily transcends jurisdictions. Its territoriality is not predefined. Where governments are able to influence code they can regulate with unprecedented territorial scope. Through the copyright regime developed by You-Tube, the platform has become a proxy for the global application of US copyright law.[93] Similarly, until recently Facebook users throughout the world (with the exception of Canada and the United States) were protected by the European Union's data protection regime, given that Facebook processed such data from its European headquarters in Dublin.[94] The non-territoriality of code also means that, in a data-driven economy, economic actors can more easily settle where they want. This explains the stark jurisdictional competition that is emerging in relation to blockchain-based ventures.[95] It also explains why Lithuania recently created a scheme that seems inspired by the Estonian E-residency programme. It allows for the creation of 'virtual limited liability companies' that can be created remotely and registered and managed through blockchain technology.[96] When business models centre on data and code, and teams are spread across jurisdictions, firms might simply incorporate where they receive the best deal.

Finally, legal automation through blockchain and beyond will alter how law is taught, learned and practised. This will challenge established practices but also provide opportunities to improve current processes. Legal Tech is already helping lawyers in transactional work, such as creating and executing legal agreements.[97] Increased interdisciplinarity is unavoidable to face these challenges. In her Chorley

---

[92] Wulf Kaal and Eric Vermeulen, 'How to Regulate Disruptive Innovation – From Facts to Data' (2017) 57 Jurimetrics 169.

[93] Belli et al., 'Law of the Land or Law of the Platform?' (n 7) 41.

[94] David Ingram, 'Exclusive: Facebook to Put 1.5 billion Users out of reach of New EU Privacy Law' (*Reuters*, 19 April 2018) <www.reuters.com/article/us-facebook-privacy-eu-exclusive/exclusive-face book-to-put-1-5-billion-users-out-of-reach-of-new-eu-privacy-law-idUSKBN1HQ00P?il=0> accessed 24 April 2018.

[95] See further Chapter 6.

[96] ibid.

[97] For an example, see OpenLaw, 'Introducing OpenLaw' (*MediaConsensys*, 25 July 2017) <https://media.consensys.net/introducing-openlaw-7a2ea410138b> accessed 21 March 2018.

lecture, Mireille Hildebrandt noted that lawyers should collaborate with computer scientists to 'sustain democratic participation in law-making, contestability of legal effect and transparency of how citizens may be manipulated by the invisible computational backbone of our rapidly and radically changing world'.[98] This is a task we must all yield to when teaching, learning and practising law.

The preceding analysis has established that, while code is law, law is also law. In light of increased legal automation, bridges are needed between both forms of normative constraints. It is also undeniable that code changes law, as revealed by the ten factors outlined above. Law will not be undermined by emerging technologies, however. Below, I introduce the need for bridges between blockchains and legal systems, and lay out an argument that blockchains are more likely to develop to become compliant with established legal systems than to provide alternatives thereto.

IV. THE NECESSARY INTEROPERABILITY OF ON-CHAIN AND OFF-CHAIN LAW

The above examination has concluded that blockchains have the potential to act as a regulatory technology that can be manoeuvred for public and private ordering. This, it has been seen, will force a reconsideration of numerous fundamental principles that contemporary legal orders rest on. The potential of technology, including blockchain technology, to act as a regulator has been understood by some as meaning that it has the capacity to replace law. Distributed ledgers, it has been put forward, are 'the strongest challenge ever posed to the monopoly of the state over the promulgation, formation, keeping and verification of institutions and the public record'.[99] It has been speculated that the technology may dethrone the state as the enforcer of agreements, a reserved state function as per social contract theories.[100]

At first glance, blockchain technology and state power expressed through law may appear radically incompatible. The 'trustless trust' that distributed ledgers rely on facilitates transactions between untrusting parties without necessary reliance on a third party. The state is a trusted intermediary, however, that has long served this function in providing for mechanisms such as contract law, international commercial or investment law to enable transactions in contexts devoid of trust, a function already performed by the *lex mercatoria* of the Middle Ages. The state and its legal system are thus exactly the kind of trusted intermediaries blockchains

---

[98] Hildebrandt, 'Law as Information' (n 87) 1.
[99] Brendan Markey-Towler, 'Anarchy, Blockchain and Utopia: A Theory of Political-Socioeconomic Systems Organised using Blockchain' (2018) 1 <https://papers.ssrn.com/sol3/papers.cfm?abstract_id=3095343> accessed 28 March 2018.
[100] Thomas Hobbes, *Leviathan* (1st edn 1651) ch. XIV, paras 18–19.

promise to render redundant. Does this mean that blockchains could or should replace the state in this function?

Any such radical assumption is misguided. Technological change forces law to adapt and change, and this is no different in relation to DLT. Although this process will not be free of friction, it will also not result in the replacement of law with code. Rather, code needs law to work as an instrument of regulation. In spite of their cypherpunk origins, blockchains depend on law for recognition, and, conversely, for large-scale adoption. The technology promises to be a new means of transferring data and value, benefits that cannot materialize in a meaningful manner unless such transfers are recognized by law. Indeed, what is the point of transferring ownership of a 'utility token' (a terminology many have suggested for cryptoassets that are avatars of real-world goods or services) on-chain if you cannot claim ownership of the corresponding good in real life? Similarly, smart-contract-based arbitration enforcement will usually be contingent on real-world enforcement for parties to willingly rely on it. Although some universities have started putting diplomas on the blockchain, this is sensible only when employers and public authorities recognize these diplomas as valid.[101] The success of blockchains is hence to no small degree contingent on recognition by the real world, and it simply cannot refuse to account for external legal requirements and systems.

It follows that blockchains cannot constitute regulatory systems divorced from the applicable law of the land but, rather, must reflect the latter. Systems such as Bitcoin can to some degree exist in isolation from these legal orders. The cryptoasset forms an artefact of its own system and the blockchain is the sole source of rights and obligations.[102] Its operation is heavily regulated by code, which has not been informed by law to secure compliance. Assets that are pure artefacts of the block-chain can ignore legal demands – at least to some degree.[103] Whenever there is a nexus between the on-chain and off-chain worlds, ignorance of law is not a tenable position. The conversion of Bitcoin into fiat currency has long been subject to detailed legal requirements. Further, while some couples have 'married on the blockchain', these marriages would be null and void from the perspective of many legal systems, which impose specific formal requirements for nuptials to be legally recognized.[104] Similarly, when an agreement is expressed in smart contract form, a plain-language version of the agreement may be needed for judges to evaluate in

---

[101] <www.unic.ac.cy/news/university-nicosia-first-university-world-publish-diplomas-all-graduating-students-blockchain> accessed 2 February 2018.

[102] Chris Reed et al., 'Beyond BitCoin – Legal Impurities and Off-Chain Assets' (2017) Queen Mary University of London, School of Legal Studies Research Paper No 260/2017, 18 <https://papers.ssrn.com/sol3/papers.cfm?abstract_id=3058945> accessed 10 April 2018, 4 (hereafter Reed et al., 'Beyond BitCoin').

[103] ibid. 5.

[104] Priyeshu Garg, 'Will You Marry Me, on the Blockchain?' (*btcManager*, 30 November 2017) <https://btcmanager.com/will-marry-blockchain/> accessed 10 April 2018.

case a dispute arises, and as a check whether the code represents what it was intended to represent.[105]

Compliance with existing legal systems is required if blockchain and blockchain-based applications are to have a real-world impact. Absolute tamper resistance is problematic from a legal perspective, as it stands in the way of amending records to reflect legal requirements or judicial decisions. What is thus needed are bridges that connect the technology and its opportunities with legal requirements. In the smart contract space, numerous attempts at creating interoperability between the on-chain and off-chain spheres can already be observed, such as projects to link the legal off-chain contract with the on-chain smart contract code or to provide for arbitration processes to resolve disputes.[106]

Some consider the blockchain to be more of an ideology as opposed to a technology, a preference for a world without institutions where trust is put into cryptography rather than the latter.[107] Right now, convergence between law and distributed ledgers is lacking. Despite blockchain's young age they raise numerous (potential) legal challenges. Digital currencies are not backed by states while smart contracts are designed to execute in isolation from human and institutional interference. If distributed ledgers' real value proposition is isolation from contemporary legal orders, they are unlikely to succeed. What is more likely is that technology and the law mutually adapt.[108]

The modalities of achieving this objective remain to be defined. It has been suggested that to accommodate legal obligations, such as the registration of a change in token ownership, there may be a need for a 'super-user'; a trusted person who 'has the power to modify the ledger'.[109] This, of course, can be seen to defeat the entire value proposition of a system that seeks to achieve trust through censorship resistance and disintermediation. These are challenging questions, which need to be addressed by future research that bridges computer science, law and governance theory.

History reliably repeats itself. In order to allow blockchains to provide recognized evidence about participants or entitlements, their structure needs to be (re)designed to incorporate law. Experience with *lex mercatoria* and *lex informatica* illustrates that

---

[105] It will make sense for such plain language contracts to be stored off-chain as on-chain storage is usually expensive and not sufficiently private.

[106] See, by way of example: <http://legalese.com/aboutus> and OpenLaw, 'Making Token Sales Smart' (*Media Consensys*, 24 August 2017) <https://media.consensys.net/making-token-sales-smart-28fe2011512f> accessed 24 April 2018.

[107] Michael Seemann, 'Digitaltechnologie Blockchain: Eine als Technik getarnte Ideologie'- *Deutschlandfunk Kultur* (15 March 2018) <www.deutschlandfunkkultur.de/digitaltechnolo gie-blockchain-eine-als-technik-getarnte.1005.de.html?dram:article_id=413022> accessed 3 April 2018.

[108] Arvind Narayanan, Kevin Werbach and James Grimmelmann, 'Why Porn on the Blockchain Won't Doom Bitcoin' (*wired*, 29 March 2018) <www.wired.com/story/why-porn-on-the-block chain-wont-doom-bitcoin/> accessed 10 April 2018.

[109] Reed at al., 'Beyond BitCoin' (n 102).

the emergence of a new subset of law, such as *lex cryptographia*, is less likely to uproot existing legal systems than to supplement them and develop in accordance with their overarching principles. This means that, rather than asking whether code will eclipse law or whether law will upstage code, the real question we need to be asking is how interoperability between these systems can be fashioned in a manner that allows us to reap the benefits of technological change while ensuring that it develops in line with our principles and ideals. I return to this theme in Chapter 6.

4

Blockchains and the General Data Protection Regulation

This is very sad. A potentially very useful service in the ethereum ecosystem discontinued due to GDPR issues.[1]

On 25 May 2018 the European Union's General Data Protection Regulation became binding.[2] DLT, as a new paradigm of data storage and management, stands in tension with this supranational legal framework.[3] Whereas the GDPR was fashioned for a world where data is centrally collected, stored and processed, blockchains decentralize these processes. Applying a legal framework constructed for a sphere of centralization to one of decentralization is thus not without difficulty. I map related complications and attempt to offer an optimistic perspective of their future interaction. I focus my analysis specifically at the infrastructure layer of public and permissionless ledgers. This is an important caveat, as applying the GDPR to blockchain-based applications or permissioned blockchains raises a different set of questions.

The data protection mechanisms developed for centralized data silos cannot be easily reconciled with a decentralized method of data storage, processing and collection. Herefrom results a risk that data protection legislation renders the operation of blockchains unlawful, hence asphyxiating the development of an innovative technology that the European Union is putting much hope into from a Digital Single Market perspective. My analysis documents the tension between the European Union's personal data law and this new technology. Whenever

---

[1] Vitalik Buterin [VitalikButerin] (18 May 2018) 'This is very sad. A potentially very useful service in the ethereum ecosystem discontinued due to GDPR issues.' [Tweet] <https://twitter.com/vitalikbuterin/status/997487947820740608?lang=en> accessed 1 June 2018.

[2] Regulation (EU) 2016/679 on the protection of natural persons with regard to the processing of personal data and on the free movement of such data [2016] OJ L 119/1.

[3] I first examined this tension in Michèle Finck, *Blockchains and Data Protection in the European Union* (2018) 4 European Data Protection Law Review 17–36.

technological change occurs this has a dual effect on legal frameworks. On the one hand, technological innovation can address the very market failures that once made law necessary, removing friction. Such innovations can also add friction, however, when new technology stands in tension with existing law. This is so because dated legislation was designed on the basis of factual assumptions that are simply no longer adequate. This is a broader challenge for the GDPR, highlighted by DLT, but also other forms of data storage and processing, such as big data and machine learning. What generally occurs in such scenarios is a process of mutual adaptation whereby law and technology approximate towards compatibility over time.

The GDPR's design as a technology-neutral and outcome- (rather than process-) orientated co-regulatory approach facilitates such developments. Whereas the incompatibility between public and permissionless blockchains and the GDPR draws a pessimistic image, the relationship between the technology and this legal framework is in reality more complex. EU regulators are committed to an innovation-friendly approach to technology in general and blockchains more specifically.[4] Added complexity stems from the fact that, while blockchains and related developments currently undermine privacy, they may come to further data protection and see the GDPR's objective of data sovereignty enhanced down the line. As a consequence, the tension between the GDPR and these decentralized databases also reveals a clash between two normative objectives of supranational law: fundamental rights protection and the promotion of innovation.

I will reflect on this complex relationship and highlight that legal interpretation techniques and technical solutions can facilitate an at least partial reconciliation of these apparently conflicting rationales. The chapter concludes in highlighting that, while at this stage blockchains are a technology that raises important challenges in relation to data protection, they might in the future achieve some of the objectives inherent in the GDPR through alternative technological means, albeit through mechanisms distinct from those envisaged by the legal framework itself.

My analysis unfolds in five steps. I first introduce the GDPR, before applying its legal principles to public and permissionless blockchains. This will establish that this technology, crafted to achieve decentralization, cannot be straightforwardly reconciled with a legal framework targeting centralized data silos. The implications of that finding are then evaluated. I conclude by arguing that a compromise is needed whereby the legal certainty of data protection in the European Union is reconciled with the desired promotion of innovation, and thus also alternative, and maybe more effective, means of data protection. To achieve this and ensure that the guarantees of data protection in the Union are respected, lawyers and technologists need to collaborate to craft technical solutions that are capable of furthering these aims.

---

[4] See further Chapter 6.

I. PERSONAL DATA ON BLOCKCHAINS

Before venturing on to examine the relation between distributed ledger technology and the GDPR, a refresher and a deepening of some concepts introduced in Chapter 1 are in order. On a blockchain, data is usually grouped into blocks that, upon reaching a certain size, are chained to the existing ledger through a hashing process. Through this process, data is chronologically ordered in a manner that makes it difficult to tamper with information without altering subsequent blocks.[5] Tamper evidence is indeed one of blockchains' most heralded features, and some would consider it its core value proposition. In this context, it is often stated that blockchains are 'immutable'. This terminology is misleading, because, even though it is very difficult to amend blockchains, it is far from impossible, as underlined by the The DAO hard fork (examined in Chapter 7).[6] Nonetheless, blockchains' append-only structure and their tamper evidence burden compliance with GDPR requirements, as we will observe below.

It is worth recalling that DLTs rely on a two-step verification process with asymmetric encryption. Every user has a public key (a string of letters and numbers representing the user), best thought of as an account number that is shared with others to enable transactions. In addition, each user holds a private key (also a string of letters and numbers), which is best thought of as a password that must never be shared with others. Both keys have a mathematical relationship by virtue of which the private key can decrypt data that is encrypted through the public key. Public keys thus hide the identity of the individual unless they are linked to additional identifiers.[7]

Data can be stored on a decentralized ledger in a variety of different forms. First, it is possible to store data, such as a document or digital art, on the ledger in plain text. This is problematic, however, for a number of reasons. On a permissionless blockchain, anyone can arbitrarily read such data, which is, of course, highly undesirable from a privacy perspective. Blocks have limited storage capacity, moreover, and storage is often expensive, so this would not be an economical solution. Rather than storing data in plain text, it is usually encrypted or hashed before it is added to a blockchain. Most DLTs contain two types of data: (i) the header, which includes the time stamp, the identity of the data's source, such as an address, and the previous block hash, whereas (ii) the block content (or payload) contains the data to be stored (on the Bitcoin blockchain this would be the

---

5   Whereas data stored on a blockchain is often described as 'immutable', this is not quite the case as such information can be modified in exceptional circumstances through human intervention, which however requires the collusion between a majority of the network's nodes.

6   See further Conte de Leon et al., 'Blockchain: Properties and Misconceptions' (2017) 11 Asia Pacific Journal of Innovation and Entrepreneurship 268.

7   See further Chapter 1.

relevant transactions as well as the Coinbase transaction).[8] Whereas the header is usually not encrypted, the payload normally is.

When data is encrypted, in principle, only a user in possession of the private key can decrypt the documents. On blockchains, asymmetric cryptography is used as a means to generate digital signatures. Encryption is a two-way function, meaning that, with the right cryptographic key, previously encrypted data can be 'unlocked' and reverted to its original state. This security technique renders data unintelligible to individuals without authorized access.[9] While data is in practice often encrypted, this is a completely optional process. The block header is usually[10] not encrypted, given that – for nodes to process a cryptoasset transaction – they need, for instance, to verify whether the relevant wallet holds the required funds.[11]

Data can also be hashed to a distributed ledger. The hashing process can register large amounts of data with a small digital fingerprint. Under the common SHA-256 hashing algorithm, any amount of data will be reduced to a thirty-two-byte hash value.[12] A cryptographic hash is a one-way function that cannot be reverse-engineered, meaning that there is no key that can unlock data that has been hashed.[13] Hashes allow for the verification of whether a certain document was stored in a database at a given time, as re-hashing the off-chain version of that document will produce the exact same hash.[14] I now turn to examine these technical characteristics from the perspective of the GDPR.

II. THE EUROPEAN UNION'S GENERAL DATA PROTECTION REGULATION

The GDPR pursues a twofold objective. It strives to facilitate the free movement of personal data between the European Union's various member states while providing a detailed framework to give effect to the fundamental right of data protection.[15] To pursue the dual objectives of data protection and the free movement of personal data in the internal market, the Union has opted for an ambitious data protection framework, the General Data Protection Regulation, which became binding on

[8] This refers to the transaction realizing the mining reward.
[9] Lawrence Lessig euphemistically declared it 'the most important technological breakthrough in the last one thousand years'. See Lawrence Lessig, *Code and Other Laws of Cyberspace* (Basic Books 1999) 35 (although cryptography has been used before).
[10] This is not always the case. Zcash for instance encrypts the sender and recipient as well as amount of data within single-signature transactions.
[11] This can all be a bit abstract. The following website provides live coverage of the Bitcoin blockchain and illustrates this further: <https://tradeblock.com/bitcoin>.
[12] SHA-256 is a hashing algorithm created by the NSA, which is considered particularly secure. It always generates a 32-byte hash value, notwithstanding the size of the original data.
[13] This, as many things, may change with quantum computing.
[14] This has enabled solutions that offer a timestamping service. See, by way of example: <www.bernstein.io/>.
[15] This right is enshrined in Article 8 of the Charter of Fundamental Rights.

25 May 2018, replacing Directive 95/46/EC.[16] Technological developments such as the rise of platform intermediaries have triggered new challenges for data protection, as the scale of data sharing and collection has steadily increased. In this context, a stronger and more coherent legal regime was deemed necessary.[17] This novel legal framework will apply to the personal data of natural persons that is wholly or partly automated or stored in a filing system.[18] Following the legal framework's recent entry into force, blockchain developers and entrepreneurs are now anxiously trying to determine whether the GDPR applies to their activities, for if this is the case their leeway for experimentation risks being considerably constrained. Bearing in mind the important distinctions between various forms of DLT and the corresponding need for a case-by-case analysis, I attempt here to provide a general overview of the application of the GDPR framework to DLTs, particularly public and permission-less blockchains, starting with the question of whether data related to a natural person stored on a decentralized ledger qualifies as personal data as a matter of EU law.

A. The GDPR's Material Scope: Does Data Stored on a Blockchain Qualify as Personal Data?

This section enquires whether public keys and other data stored on a distributed ledger fall within the scope of the GDPR. The regulation applies only to 'personal data', defined as 'any information relating to an identified or identifi-able natural person': the 'data subject'.[19] An 'identifiable person' is defined as a natural person who

> can be identified, directly or indirectly, in particular by reference to an identifier such as a name, an identification number, location data, an online identifier or to one or more factors specific to the physical, psychological, genetic, mental, economic, cultural or social identity of that natural person.[20]

When data is rendered completely anonymous it no longer amounts to personal data and thus falls outside the scope of the legal framework. When data is rendered pseudonymous, however, it continues to qualify as personal data, as the indirect identification of a natural person by an identifier remains possible. Two sets of data

---

[16] Directive 95/46/EC of the European Parliament and of the Council of 24 October 1995 on the protection of individuals with regard to the processing of personal data and on the free movement of such data [1995] OJ L 281/31.

[17] Recitals 6 and 7 GDPR.

[18] Articles 1 and 2 GDPR.

[19] Article 4(1) GDPR.

[20] ibid.

stored on blockchains can potentially be defined as personal data for the purposes of the GDPR: transactional data stored in the blocks and public keys.[21]

1. Personal Data Stored on a DLT

Depending on the respective DLT's use case, data stored in blocks may be data related to an identified or identifiable natural person. This includes data revealing individual behaviour in Internet of Things use cases; digital identities; and financial or medical data. To distinguish this data, which often contains personal information, from other data, such as personal keys, I will refer to it as 'transactional data'.[22]

Many current uses revolve around transactions, which usually contain specific information related to a person. We have already observed that this data can be stored on-chain in three alternative fashions: in plain text, in encrypted form or hashing it to the chain. This section evaluates whether these processes can sufficiently anonymize personal data to allow it to evade the GDPR's scope of application. It is worth noting that the distinction between personal and non-personal data is likely to vanish over time, as sophisticated machine-learning techniques enable the identification of individual characteristics and behaviour through non-personal data.[23]

The threshold for anonymization under the regulation is high, and results 'from processing personal data in order to *irreversibly prevent identification*'.[24] Personal data stored on a blockchain in plain text clearly remains personal data for the purposes of the GDPR, so this option does not merit any further analysis. When data is encrypted it can still be accessed with the correct keys, meaning that it is not irreversibly anonymized. For example, encrypted data can be connected to the data subject when transactions are effected for off-chain goods or when cryptoassets are converted into fiat currency through an exchange that performs KYC and AML duties. Encryption is indeed considered a method of pseudonymization under the EU data protection regime, given that the data subject can still be indirectly identified. As a consequence, it cannot, on its own, be considered an anonymization technique.[25] The conclusion that transactional data that has been encrypted remains personal data for the purposes of the GDPR is, accordingly, unavoidable.

Transactional data that has been subject to a hashing process also likely qualifies as personal data under the GDPR. Although a one-way hash function that cannot be reverse-engineered can offer stronger privacy guarantees than encryption, it will

---

[21] It is important to remember that there is a huge variance in blockchains and that the link between the encrypted data hashed to the chain and an individual will accordingly vary.

[22] Note, however, the different meaning of 'transaction' in law and computer science.

[23] Similarly data that is now anonymous may become personal data due to technological developments. On this, see further Chapter 5.

[24] Article 29 Working Party, Opinion 04/2014 on Anonymisation Techniques, 0829/14/EN, 20 (emphasis added) (hereafter Article 29 Working Party, 'Anonymisation Techniques').

[25] ibid.

usually not allow data to evade the qualification as personal data for GDPR purposes. The Article 29 Data Protection Working Party has stated that hashing constitutes a technique of pseudonymization, not anonymization, as it is still possible to link the dataset with the data subject.[26] This is so because, when the range of input values is known, they can be replayed through the hash function to derive the original data. Indeed, contrary to the widespread belief that the use of salted hashes (when a random value – the salt – is added to the attribute that is hashed) makes identification impossible, at least in theory it remains possible.[27] Whereas many have argued that hashes should in some circumstances qualify as anonymous data, there is currently no clear guidance as to whether, and if so under which circumstances, that would be the case. It follows that transactional data that is encrypted or has undergone a hashing process is likely personal data for the purposes of the GDPR. Whereas hashes may in some circumstances be anonymous data there is at present insufficient guidance on the relevant conditions.

The conclusion that transactional data stored on a blockchain is subject to GDPR requirements may be avoided in some scenarios. First, it is imaginable that, over time, some cryptographic processes or a combination thereof will be declared capable of anonymizing personal data.[28] The difficulty with hashing is that, depending on the specific process that is used (including the range of input values), it can either be very good for privacy, or not. A number of technical solutions are currently being developed that may prevent transactional data from being directly stored on the blockchain. Vitalik Buterin considers cryptographically secure obfuscation[29] as the 'Holy Grail' of privacy on blockchains but concedes that the tool isn't sufficiently developed to be used.[30] While this solution remains unavailable others can more readily be deployed.

Personal data could be stored off-chain and merely linked to the blockchain through a hash pointer.[31] In this scenario, on-chain data and likely also on-chain hashes of off-chain data would still qualify as personal data, yet it could be manipulated off-chain in line with GDPR requirements. In such a scenario, personal data can be recorded in a referenced, encrypted and modifiable database and not on the blockchain.[32] A number of data management and sovereignty solutions are further being developed that combine blockchain and off-chain storage to 'construct a

---

[26] ibid.

[27] ibid.

[28] If this is to be done such standards would require continued updating to account for evolutions in cryptography.

[29] Perfect cryptographically secure obfuscation is however mathematically impossible.

[30] Vitalik Buterin, 'Privacy on the Blockchain' (*Ethereum Blog*, 15 January 2016) <https://blog .ethereum.org/2016/01/15/privacy-on-the-blockchain/> (hereafter Buterin, 'Privacy on the Blockchain') accessed 13 April 2018.

[31] Note that this remains personal data that is put on the chain. What seems unclear for the time being is how this hash is to be interpreted once the underlying data has been manipulated, such as through erasure.

[32] We turn to this topic further below.

personal data management platform focused on privacy'.[33] Developers working on such solutions must be careful, however, to ensure that metadata is also treated appropriately, as it can reveal personal information even when personal data is not directly stored on-chain.[34] Off-chain storage solutions may further require the reintroduction of a trusted third party, which could then defeat the very motivation for relying on DLT as opposed to other forms of data storage. There are, moreover, attempts to design GDPR-compliant chains that hold data in a private store in which the blockchain merely holds proof that the data is valid.[35] It is further worth noting that, when off-chain data is also distributed, enforcing the GDPR in relation to that data becomes more burdensome.[36]

Jacob Eberhardt and Stefan Tai have designed a series of off-chain storage solutions that do not require the reintroduction of a trusted third party. These include challenge response patters; off-chain signature patterns; delegated computing patterns; low-contract footprint patterns; and content-addressable storage patterns.[37] The latter is particularly relevant for our purposes. Here, data is stored off-chain in a content-addressable storage system rather than on the blockchain. For example, a smart contract would merely contain the hash to said data rather than the data itself.[38] This pattern allows the 'trustless outsourcing of data to an off-chain storage system since a modification in the data would immediately change its address and with that invalidate its references'.[39] The benefits of this approach are not limited to data protection but also drastically limit an application's storage costs. Developers designing such a solution must be careful, however, that off-chain data doesn't become unavailable, as this would threaten the availability of the on-chain part of the application, and they must also avert data leaks, as leaked data can be immediately confirmed to be authentic by recalculating its address.[40]

Only time will reveal whether the Court of Justice of the European Union (CJEU) and the European Data Protection Board agree it seems safe to assume, for the time being, that solutions storing all personal data off-chain are the most important step, but developers must take to ensure GDPR compliance. Next, I evaluate whether a user's public key constitutes personal data under EU law.

---

[33] Guy Zyskind et al., 'Decentralizing Privacy: Using Blockchain to Protect Personal Data' IEEE Security and Privacy Workshops (2015) 180 <https://ieeexplore.ieee.org/document/7163223/> accessed 5 May 2018.

[34] James Smith et al., 'Applying Blockchain Technology in Global Data Infrastructure' (2016) Technical Report ODI-TR-2016-001, Open Data Institute.

[35] See further <http://news.sys-con.com/node/4080523> accessed 1 March 2018.

[36] A number of current projects such as Swarm, Storj and Filecoin are experimenting with such options.

[37] Jacob Eberhardt and Stefan Tai, 'On or Off the Blockchain' European Conference on Service-Oriented and Cloud Computing (2017) 3 <www.ise.tu-berlin.de/fileadmin/fg308/publications/2017/2017-eberhardt-tai-offchaining-patterns.pdf> accessed 20 February 2018.

[38] ibid. 10.

[39] ibid. 11.

[40] ibid.

2. Public Keys

Public keys are a string of letters and numbers that allow for the pseudonymous identification of a natural or legal person or a machine for transactional or communication purposes.[41] Satoshi Nakamoto considers that privacy is maintained not by encrypting data but, rather, by 'breaking the flow of information in another place: by keeping public keys anonymous'.[42] From a GDPR perspective, the pertinent question is whether public keys are really anonymous data. Article 4(5) of the GDPR defines pseudonymization as

> the processing of personal data in such a manner that the personal data can no longer be attributed to a specific data subject without the use of additional information, provided that such additional information is kept separately and is subject to technical and organizational measures to ensure that the personal data are not attributed to an identified or identifiable person.[43]

A public key is data that 'can no longer be attributed to a specific data subject' unless it is matched with 'additional information' such as a name or an address. When these two sets of information are combined, identification is plausible, explaining why public keys cannot qualify as anonymous data as a matter of EU law. We have already seen that, for data to qualify as being anonymous, identification must be irreversibly prevented.[44] Practice reveals that this cannot be the case in relation to public keys. DLTs' short history in fact testifies that, despite asymmetric encryption, identification remains possible. Connecting public keys with additional information permitting identification has been facilitated through users' voluntary release of such information, such as when they disclose their public key to receive funds; through illicit means; or when additional information is gathered in accordance with regulatory requirements, such as when cryptoasset exchanges perform KYC and AML duties.[45]

On the Bitcoin blockchain, encrypted data has been proved capable of revealing a user and transaction nexus that allows for transactions to be traced back to users.[46] Law enforcement agencies have, moreover, long developed forensic chain analysis techniques to identify suspected criminals on the basis of their public keys, and a range of

---

[41] Keys are technically always numbers, derived from large primes, that are however encoded alphanumerically to save space.

[42] Satoshi Nakamoto, 'Bitcoin: A Peer-to-Peer Electronic Cash System' (2009) <https://bitcoin .org/bitcoin.pdf.> accessed 20 March 2018.

[43] Article 4(5) GDPR.

[44] Emphasis added.

[45] Kelly Philipps Erb, 'IRS Tries Again To Make Coinbase Turn Over Customer Account Data' (*Forbes*, 20 March 2017) <www.forbes.com/sites/kellyphillipserb/2017/03/20/irs-tries-again-to-make-coinbase-turn-over-customer-account-data/#1841d9e5175e>.

[46] Fergal Reid and Martin Harrigan 'An Analysis of Anonymity in the Bitcoin System' (2012) <https://arxiv.org/abs/1107.4524> accessed 20 March 2018.

professional service providers performing related services have emerged.[47] Academic research has also shown that public keys can be traced back to IP addresses, aiding identification.[48] What is more, when users transmit a transaction to the network, they usually connect directly to the network and reveal their IP address. The GDPR leaves no doubt that personal data that has 'undergone pseudonymisation, which could be attributed to a natural person by the use of additional information', still qualifies as personal data.[49] To determine whether a person can be identified on the basis of pseudonymous data, account has to be taken of 'all the means reasonably likely to be used'.[50] Considering that public keys are in fact being used to identify individuals, they should be presumed to be a means 'reasonably likely to be used'.[51]

The CJEU's adjudicative practice reinforces the conclusion that public keys qualify as personal data. In *Patrick Breyer* v. *Germany*, it classified dynamic IP addresses as personal data.[52] The court ruled that IP addresses assigned to a computing device when connected to a network may constitute personal data even if a third party (such as an internet service provider) holds the data relevant to identify an individual. It is worth noting that this rationale was recently reaffirmed in *Nowak*. This situation is in many ways analogous to the information exchanges or other service providers that are legally obliged to collect data under KYC and AML requirements.

It follows that public keys are pseudonymous data caught by the EU data protection regime. Unlike transactional data, public keys cannot be moved off-chain to form part of a transaction's 'metadata' required for its validation. GDPR-compliant solutions that enable the required manipulation of data are, accordingly, more difficult to identify.

Some have suggested the use of a stealth address, which uses a one-time transaction that relies on hashed one-time keys. The cryptocurrency Monero, for example, hides the recipient of the transaction by generating a new dedicated address and a 'secret key'.[53] The use of one-time accounts for transactions requires that every transaction must completely empty at least one account and create one or multiple new accounts.[54] This so-called 'merge avoidance'[55] can be deployed on the Bitcoin blockchain, but some consider that, even when this is done, that system 'has proven

---

[47] Such as the appropriately named Chainalysis: <www.chainalysis.com/>.
[48] Biryukov et al., 'Denanonymisation of Clients in Bitcoin P2P Network' (2014) <https://arxiv.org/abs/1405.7418> accessed 20 March 2018.
[49] Recital 26 GDPR.
[50] ibid.
[51] ibid. (requiring that relevant factors are 'all objective factors, such as the costs of and the amount of time required for identification, taking into consideration the available technology at the time of the processing and technological developments').
[52] Case C-582/14 *Patrick Breyer* [2016] EU:C:2016:779.
[53] The cryptocurrency Monero uses stealth addresses to ensure privacy. See further <https://getmonero.org/resources/moneropedia/stealthaddress.html>.
[54] Buterin, 'Privacy on the Blockchain' (n 30).
[55] Mike Hearn, 'Merge Avoidance?' (*Medium*, 11 December 2013) <https://medium.com/@octsky ward/merge-avoidance-7f95a386692f> accessed 5 March 2018.

to be highly porous and heuristic, with nothing even close to approaching high guarantees' of privacy protection.[56]

The Bitcoin White Paper itself recommends that 'a new key pair should be used for each transaction to keep them from being linked to a common owner', while conceding that this is merely a security rather than an anonymization technique, as '[s]ome linking is still unavoidable with multi-input transactions, which necessarily reveal that their inputs were owned by the same owner. The risk is that if the owner of a key is revealed, linking could reveal all other transactions that belonged to the same owner.'[57]

Cryptographic research has moreover developed 'zero-knowledge proofs' that provide a binary true/false answer without providing access to the underlying data. For instance, the Zcash cryptocurrency relies on this process to ensure that, even though transactions are published on a public blockchain, its details (including the amount as well as its source and destination) remain hidden.[58] The ledger merely reveals whether a transaction has occurred, not which public key was used or what value (if any) was transferred. Other options that are currently being deployed involve state channels for two-party smart contracts that share information with outside parties only in the event of a dispute.[59] Ring signatures, on the other hand, hide transactions within other transactions by tying a single transaction to multiple private keys even though only one of them initiated the transaction.[60] The signature proves that 'the signer has a private key corresponding to one of a specific set of public keys, without revealing which one'.[61] Whether any of the above solutions can be considered to anonymize public keys remains to be seen. There is at present no legal certainty for developers wishing to handle public keys in a GDPR-compliant manner.

Another possible solution consists in adding 'noise' to the data.[62] Here, several transactions are grouped together so that, from the outside, it is impossible to discern the identity of the respective senders and recipients of a transaction. Algorithms similar to this model have already been defined for the Bitcoin[63] and Ethereum blockchains.[64] What is promising about this privacy technique is that the Article 29 Working Party has already recognized that, provided that the necessary safeguards are complied with, the addition of noise may be an acceptable anonymization

---

[56] See further Buterin, 'Privacy on the Blockchain' (n 30).

[57] Nakamoto, 'Bitcoin' (n 42).

[58] This solution is currently being relied on by Zcash. See <https://z.cash/technology/zksnarks.html>.

[59] Buterin, 'Privacy on the Blockchain' (n 30).

[60] See further <https://getmonero.org/resources/moneropedia/ringsignatures.html>.

[61] ibid.

[62] This has been explored by the MIT ENIGMA project and uses modified distributed hashables to store secret-shared data in combination with an external block chain for identity and access control.

[63] See further <https://sx.dyne.org/anontx/>.

[64] <https://gist.github.com/gavofyork/dee1f3b727f691b381dc>.

technique.[65] For this to be the case, it should be combined with additional privacy mechanisms, 'such as the removal of obvious attributes and quasi-identifiers'.[66]

It is, at this stage, difficult to predict whether any of these techniques is capable of anonymizing public keys for GDPR purposes. It is true that, for data to be considered anonymous, it need not be utterly impossible to link it to a natural person, as there is always a residual risk of identification.[67] Nonetheless, the standard of irreversibly preventing identification that applies under the framework is certainly a high one. The identified options require further observation and study to determine whether they can be considered suitable anonymization techniques. Regulatory guidance would be an important step providing legal certainty to the involved parties. As a consequence, public keys as well as the transactional data stored on blockchains will often qualify as personal data. When blockchain use cases are caught by the GDPR, its various substantive rights come to apply. The subsequent section investigates how these rights can be deployed on DLTs.

III. APPLYING THE GDPR TO BLOCKCHAINS

We have already seen that transactional data and public keys generally constitute personal data for the purposes of the EU data protection framework. To pinpoint the precise legal consequences flowing from this state of affairs, I now determine to whom the GDPR's obligations are addressed. I first evaluate who qualifies as the data controller on a decentralized ledger, given that this entity must enforce the GDPR's substantive rights, and then consider the territorial scope of the corresponding obligations.

A. *The Data Controller(s)*

Determining the data controller on a blockchain is highly contingent on the respective governance arrangements. The GDPR defines a data controller as any natural or legal person who 'determines the purposes and means of the processing of personal data'.[68] The use of the singular indicates that, in centralized data silos, there is often one legal entity that qualifies as a data controller. It is to them that the GDPR is addressed. The difficulty is that in DLT contexts, there usually isn't one entity that determines both the purposes and the means of data processing. When it comes to private blockchains, it might still be possible to identify a central intermediary that can qualify as *the* data controller, such as the systems operator, that will be the addressee of the data subject's claims. For other DLTs, there is no central point of control, as the network is operated by all nodes in a decentralized fashion.

---

[65] Article 29 Working Party, 'Anonymisation Techniques' (n 24) 12–13 (discussing the technique in general, not specifically with respect to blockchains).

[66] ibid. 12.

[67] ibid. 7.

[68] Article 4(7) GDPR.

Permissionless blockchains are distributed and decentralized peer-to-peer networks that everyone can participate in to interact with unknown or untrusted counterparties. Many consider nodes to be controllers. In such a setting, either no node qualifies as the data controller in the absence of independent determination of the means and purposes of processing, *every* node qualifies as a data controller. Nodes are indeed not subject to external instructions, autonomously decide whether to join the chain and pursue their own objectives. As a consequence, the regulation's legal obligations would rest on each node, meaning that data subjects can invoke claims via-à-vis each node independently. It is worth noting that this conclusion may be contingent on the view of nodes that is adopted. If we merely see nodes as machines plugged into the wall for economic ends, treating them as data controllers appears odd. If we consider that nodes are active governance participants that have a say in the software that is used, however, the conclusion is less surprising.

Nodes do not, in principle, qualify as 'joint controllers' under Article 26(1) of the GDPR as they do not 'jointly determine the purposes and means of processing'. This requires a clear and transparent allocation of responsibilities.[69] Nodes are free to determine whether to join the unpermissioned ledger and in what function (i.e. as a full or lightweight node). Nodes do not commonly determine applicable rules in the sense of Article 26; the system is, rather, shaped by the nodes' individual behaviour. Although a blockchain is fuelled by the interplay of various nodes, they don't determine the modalities of data processing of other nodes. Yet, depending on the relevant governance framework there may be joint control between miners and developers or users.

Determining that each node is a data controller raises considerable complications. The exact number, location and identity of nodes on a chain cannot be established without difficulty. What is more, nodes (i) see only the encrypted or hashed version of the data; and (ii) are unable to make any changes thereto. Nodes are thus decentralized entities that cannot respond to the tasks the GDPR requires of centralized agents in their capacity as data controllers.

The enforcement of obligations resting on nodes is thus burdened by significant difficulty. For the Bitcoin blockchain, there were in 2018 approximately 11,000 nodes around the planet, of which about 1,800 were in Germany and 800 in France.[70] The Ethereum blockchain counted around 19,000 nodes.[71] If one were to address each of these nodes, some of which may not be found in a single jurisdiction, this would create two sets of problems.[72] First, a large amount of nodes would need to be contacted and compelled to comply, as opposed to a single controller in a data silo scenario. Secondly, this might lead to forcing all nodes to stop running blockchain software when GDPR rights cannot be achieved through alternative means. This would result in a situation in which an entire blockchain would be taken down in

---

[69] Recital 79 GDPR.
[70] See further <https://bitnodes.earn.com/>.
[71] <www.ethernodes.org/network/1>.
[72] ibid. Through a getaddr message, nodes are asked for information about known active peers.

one jurisdiction for non-compliance with a single data subject's rights, which appears disproportionate. It is unclear, moreover, how fines will be calculated when a data controller on an unpermissioned blockchain has failed to comply with data protection requirements, given that Article 83 of the GDPR calculates them on the basis of annual worldwide turnover.[73] Besides the determination problem, further questions arise as to how ordinary nodes could pay the hefty fines associated with the GDPR.

It is also worth remembering that, through blockchains, data subjects can gain control over their own data through the private key, which triggers the question of whether the data subject herself can be considered a controller. Indeed, when an individual hashes personal information concerning herself to the blockchain, she is likely both the data subject and data controller. The 'means of processing' are determined by the software run by miners and nodes as well as the hardware they use.[74] The purposes of a data subject's reliance on a blockchain will vary, and we may thus also consider the data subject, at least in some instances, to be able to qualify as a data controller in adding personal data to a blockchain.

As stated above, my analysis engages with public and permissionless ledgers. If we examine blockchain-based applications, there is an argument to be made that these entities themselves should, rather, qualify as data controllers, as they largely determine the means and purposes of data processing. Indeed, if an ecosystem perspective is adopted, and in scenarios in which an individual doesn't engage with the network as such, nodes are maybe more adequately compared to analogous systems on the Internet. Whereas, in the early stages of the technology's development, many data subjects have directly engaged with the network itself, this may become exceptional in the future, as data subjects are more likely to communicate only with the application layer. This is easier for GDPR purposes, because it reintroduces the central entity the legislation was crafted for.

Similarly, with respect to private and permissioned blockchains, nodes are more likely to be qualified as data processors than as controllers.[75] For example, if a government relies on a blockchain the state itself may be considered the controller, and nodes the data processors. As a consequence, they are subject to the legal regime laid out by the GDPR in relation to data processors. There are probably other entities that qualify as data processors in the blockchain ecosystem. To illustrate, blockchain data is analysed by intermediaries, which could also be

---

[73] Fines for breaches of data protection requirements can be as high as 20 million Euro or 4 per cent of global turnover, whichever is higher.

[74] Miners cannot be considered controllers if we understand them purely as entities that hash new blocks to the chain. If we peek beyond their technical role and consider their role in governance then they may also be understood to contribute – to some degree – to the determination of the means and purposes of data processing on a blockchain.

[75] Article 4(8) GDPR defines a processor as 'a natural or legal person, public authority, agency or other body which processes personal data on behalf of the controller'.

considered to be data processors.[76] Ultimately, it is paramount to undertake a detailed analysis that considers a given distributed ledger's governance arrangements to determine the identity of the respective controllers and processors. A case-by-case analysis is needed that also considers whether there is actually the same controller for public keys and transactional data. Next I examine the regulation's territorial scope to specify which nodes are controllers under EU law.

B. *The GDPR's Territorial Scope*

Unpermissioned blockchains usually run on nodes located in various jurisdictions across the globe, leaving creators with no control over the geographic spread of the network. This makes those systems inherently transnational in nature, triggering a range of jurisdictional issues. The GDPR applies 'to the processing of personal data in the context of the activities of an establishment of a controller or processor in the European Union, regardless of whether the processing takes place in the Union or not'.[77] This establishment clause is designed to avoid firms escaping their obligations by simply outsourcing data processing out of the European Union. Pursuant to its Article 3(2), the GDPR also applies when the controller or processor are not established in the Union but when processing activities relate to either the offering of goods or services (paid or unpaid) to a data subject based in the Union[78] or when they monitor behaviour that takes place in the Union.[79] When a controller not established in the European Union processes personal data in a place where member state law applies by virtue of public international law, the GDPR also applies.[80] The GDPR's broad territorial scope probably entails that its obligations bind many blockchain-based applications with only an indirect link to the Union.

A further jurisdictional question relates to the application of EU data protection requirements to the transfer of data to third countries.[81] On permissionless ledgers we can presume that there is always an element of cross-border data processing. The GDPR provides that, whenever there is a 'transfer of personal data which are undergoing processing or are intended for processing after transfer to a third country or to an international organization', it is to occur only subject to a number of conditions.[82] The data stored in blocks is hashed to the chain by a miner that can be based anywhere. The ledger is subsequently updated on each node to reflect the addition of the new block. The conditions allowing such cross-border processing include the possibility of the Commission declaring a 'third country, a territory or

---

[76] See, by way of example, <www.blockchain.com/explorer>
[77] Article 3(1) GDPR.
[78] Article 3(2)(a) GDPR.
[79] Article 3(2)(b) GDPR.
[80] Article 3(3) GDPR.
[81] Articles 44–50 GDPR.
[82] Article 44 GDPR.

one or more specified sectors within a third country' or an international organization to ensure an adequate level of protection,[83] where the controller or processor provide appropriate safeguards and where 'enforceable data subject rights and effective legal remedies for data subjects are available'.[84] Competent supervisory authorities may, moreover, approve binding corporate rules governing data protection.[85] In theory, the chain's protocol could be designed to account for these concerns, yet, as seen below, the substantive requirements of data protection cannot easily be reconciled with DLT. A more realistic solution is enshrined in Article 49(1)(a) of the GDPR, which foresees the possibility of a data subject providing explicit consent for such a transfer, subject to being informed about possible risks. This could be easily implemented on a private blockchain where access is controlled and can be subject to terms and conditions, but it is not obvious how such consent could be acquired in a permissionless system.

It can be expected that courts will try to avoid such conclusions, when possible. In *Bodil Lindqvist*, the CJEU held that loading personal data onto an Internet page was not a transfer of that data to a third country for the purposes of the former Data Protection Directive, even though that data could be accessed worldwide.[86] The European Court of Justice opined that, in order to make that assessment, it was necessary to take into account the technical nature of the operations as well as the purpose and structure of the legal framework.[87] This was a means of avoiding an irreconcilable conflict between EU law and a new(ish) technology.

In attempting to determine the GDPR's personal, material and jurisdictional scope, we have seen that the European Union's data protection regime, fashioned for the centralized collection, storage and processing of data, cannot be easily transposed to decentralized digital ledgers. An analysis of the application of the regulation's substantive rights to distributed ledgers further validates this conclusion.

C. *Enforcing Substantive Data Protection Rights on Blockchains*

The GDPR creates a number of rights for data subjects with respect to their personal data. After having established that data stored on a distributed ledger and public keys constitute personal data, this section evaluates whether data subjects can invoke their rights vis-à-vis data controllers in a decentralized environment. Numerous frictions can be identified regarding data subjects' rights and the ability of nodes to respond to them. While from a legal perspective a data subject can invoke her rights vis-à-vis every single node, it is far from obvious how, from a technical perspective, nodes could implement related requests to correct, erase or restrict

---

[83] Article 45(1) GDPR.
[84] Article 46(1) GDPR.
[85] Article 47 GDPR.
[86] Case C-101/01 *Bodil Lindqvist* [2003] EU:C:2003:596.
[87] ibid. para 57.

data. Yet, as blockchain technology and literacy develop, technical solutions may provide relief. I limit my analysis to substantive rights. This does not mean that the GDPR's procedural obligations are any less problematic when applied to DLT. It indeed remains unclear what a suitable legal basis for data processing would be in the blockchain context.[88]

1. Data Minimization

The spirit of data minimization is profoundly at odds with data storage on a distributed ledger. The GDPR mandates that personal data be 'collected for specified, explicit and legitimate purposes and not further processed in a manner that is incompatible with those purposes'.[89] Data once added to a blockchain will perpetually remain part of the chain, given that it is an append-only database that continuously expands.[90] Distributed ledgers are, by definition, ever-growing creatures, which augment and accumulate further data with each additional block. What is more, integral copies are stored on each full node – quite the opposite of the data minimization spirit.

Once data has been added to the chain, it can in principle no longer be amended or deleted, which makes it difficult – not to say impossible – to implement the minimization principle and storage limitation requirements. It is worth recalling that the conflict between data minimization requirements and novel forms of data processing are by no means new and limited to the DLT context. Rather, they have also been stressed with respect to big data.[91]

A second look reveals, however, that technical solutions to these difficulties might be on the horizon. Transactional data that is stored off-chain can be modified and minimized in line with these legal requirements without touching the distributed ledger itself, though this solution may defeat the objective in using a ledger in the first place. The situation is more difficult in relation to the pseudonymous public keys, however, which cannot be retroactively removed from the ledger. A similar state of affairs exists in relation to the GDPR's right to amendment.

2. The Right to Amendment

The GDPR requires that personal data be accurate and up to date.[92] When this is not the case, 'every reasonable step must be taken to ensure that personal data that are

---

[88] Article 4(11) GDPR. Note that this is easier in private contexts.

[89] Article 5(1)(b) GDPR.

[90] Blockchains can however perish if nodes stop running them, which creates a whole range of different legal questions.

[91] Tal Zarsky, 'Incompatible: The GDPR in the Age of Big Data' (2017) 47 Seton Hall Law Review 995.

[92] Article 5(1)(d) GDPR.

inaccurate, having regard to the purposes for which they are processed, are erased or rectified without delay'.[93] Data subjects' rights under Article 16 of the GDPR include the right to obtain rectification from the controller without undue delay. This would mean that the data subject could address any or all nodes with a request to rectify personal data subject to the provided conditions. Two practical impasses arise in this context. First, a data subject cannot possibly identify any or all of a blockchain's full nodes.[94] Second, even if the data subject succeeds in addressing a claim under Article 16, nodes are simply unable to change any of the encrypted data stored in a block. Blockchains are branded as 'immutable' ledgers precisely because information can no longer be changed except in very exceptional circumstances.[95]

While it seems that, in principle, the right to modification cannot be implemented on blockchains, the provision explicitly provides that the principle of amendment must be applied with regard to the specific technology at stake. The purposes of the processing must be accounted for, and data can be rectified 'by means of providing a supplementary statement'.[96] This leaves us to wonder whether the addition of new data to the chain of blocks, which rectifies data previously added (without deleting the original entry, however), could fulfil the requirements of Article 16. This solution could be easily applied to an append-only ledger, yet doesn't lead to the modification of the problematic data itself. Transactional data could also be stored off-chain, so that it can be modified in line with data protection requirements without the need to touch the blockchain itself. Off-chain storage can, again, facilitate GDPR compliance in relation to transactional data but not public keys.

Article 19 of the GDPR, moreover, requires that the controller communicate any rectification or erasure of personal data to 'each recipient to whom the personal data have been disclosed'. This can be presumed not to apply to nodes, however, as the same provision clarifies that controllers are dispensed from said obligation when 'this provides impossible or involves disproportionate effort'. The application of the GDPR's right to access to a DLT is burdened by similar complications.

3. The Right to Access

In accordance with Article 15 of the GDPR, a data subject has the right to obtain confirmation from the controller whether or not her personal data is being processed.[97] When this is the case, she can request additional information, including but not limited to the purposes of such processing, the categories of personal data concerned, the recipients to whom the data will be disclosed, the duration of storage

---

[93] ibid.
[94] Reasons include that nodes may be online part time, may have closed ports or frequently change IP addresses.
[95] The Ethereum code was for instance changed to reverse an objectionable transaction in 2016.
[96] Article 16 GDPR.
[97] Article 15(1) GDPR.

and the existence of automated decision-making, including profiling.[98] Under Article 15(2), data subjects are moreover entitled to be informed about safeguards that apply where data is transferred to third countries – a pertinent question with regard to many blockchains' transnational nature.

Similarly to what we have already seen, Article 15 raises important questions in relation to its application to DLT, as controllers don't know which data stored on the blockchain handle the encrypted or hashed version thereof. Even if a data subject were successful in contacting a node, the latter would be incapable of verifying whether a data subject's personal data is being processed. The data subject could of course join an unpermissioned network and obtain a copy of all data, including her own, but it is questionable whether this would be regarded as a satisfactory solution. As a corollary of the right to access, Article 15(3) of the GDPR also entitles data subjects to obtain a copy of their personal data undergoing processing from controllers, which would be equally impossible when it has been cryptographically pseudonymized.[99] Again, storing personal data off-chain is to be preferred for transactional data but remains unfeasible for public keys. I now proceed to consider the GDPR's most famous provision: the right to be forgotten.

4. The Right to Be Forgotten

Article 17 of the GDPR mandates that the data subject has the right to obtain from the controller 'the erasure of personal data concerning him or her without undue delay'.[100] Controllers are obliged to delete personal data subject to a number of conditions, such as (i) that personal data is no longer necessary for the purposes it was collected or otherwise processed; (ii) that the data subject withdraws consent on which the processing is based or where there is no other ground for processing; (iii) that the data subject objects to the processing and that there are no overriding legitimate grounds for processing; (iv) that data has been unlawfully processed; (v) that personal data has to be erased for compliance with national or supranational law to which the controller is subject; or (vi) that personal data has been collected in relation to the offer of an information society service to a child under sixteen years of age.[101]

Tamper resistance is one of blockchains' most-heralded features. They are, by definition, unable to forget, as they were specifically designed to be censorship-resistant.[102] A straightforward application of the right to be forgotten to DLTs can thus be excluded. We again distinguish between transactional data and public keys.

---

[98] ibid.
[99] In this context it is worth recalling that encryption cannot be reverse-engineered.
[100] Article 17(1) GDPR.
[101] ibid. Additional limitations to the right to be forgotten that are not of specific interest in the context of blockchains, such as public policy reasons, can be found under Article 17(3) GDPR.
[102] Nakamoto, 'Bitcoin' (n 42).

With regard to transactional data, a number of possible solutions can be envisaged. When personal data is recorded in a referenced, encrypted and modifiable database, as opposed to the blockchain itself, it can be deleted in line with data protection requirements without the need to touch the blockchain. The status of the on-chain hash remains a subject of debate.

With regard to public keys or personal data stored on-chain, compliance is, again, more burdensome. First, it must be recalled that the right to be forgotten is not an absolute right. Article 17(2) provides, rather, that, when faced with a request for erasure, the data controller shall take 'account of available technology and the cost of implementation' when it has made data public and it is processed by other controllers. Here, the question arises as to whether the reference to 'available technology' could lead to an interpretation of the GDPR that was able to dispense with outright erasure (only for these other controllers!), in light of blockchains' technical limitations, in favour of an alternative solution. Further, one may wonder about the significance of Article 17(3) in relation to DLT. The provision specifies that the right to be forgotten does not apply when the continued processing of data is required to comply with legal obligation. This raises the question whether some transactions are legally qualified as financial data (as *Hedqvist* would indicate) and whether related obligations to store financial data could be applied in this context.

Some have suggested, moreover, that formalized procedures of transmitting a key to the data subject or deleting the private key in a supervised setting could amount to erasure for the purposes of the GDPR.[103] This doesn't imply, however, that the data is necessarily forgotten as it can still be accessed where prior to destruction someone writes down the private key or simply memorizes it. Unlike outright erasure, the encrypted data would remain on-chain but could be accessed only by the data subject (through her exclusive control of the private key), or simply no longer be accessed at all. This would not be erasure in the strict sense. Yet, it is widely accepted that the threshold of erasure under the GDPR can be met without erasure occurring in the literal sense, such as search index delisting where results are removed only from some domains, and only where the search entry corresponds to the data subject's name. Pruning could also be used to delete obsolete transactions in older blocks that are no longer necessary for the continuation of the chain, but the idea remains controversial.[104] A further option would be the use of chameleon hashes (which are non-interactive signatures based on a hash-and-sign paradigm) to rewrite the content of blocks by authorized authorities under specific

---

[103] For an overview of other techniques that can be used to employ privacy on blockchains, see Primavera De Filippi, 'The Interplay Between Decentralization and Privacy: The Case of Blockchain Technologies' (2016) 9 Journal of Peer Production 1 (hereafter De Filippi, 'The Interplay between Decentralization and Privacy').

[104] <www.diva-portal.org/smash/get/diva2:1130492/FULLTEXT01.pdf>.

constraints, and with full transparency and accountability.[105] There are a number of problems with this approach, however. First, if the lock key is destroyed or lost the chain reverts to being tamper-proof. This solution would, moreover, reintroduce the need for a trusted third party, such as special bodies or arbitrators, which some will find unacceptable given that it arguably defeats the very benefit of DLTs. Second, chameleon hashes can't eliminate old copies of the blockchain that will still contain the redacted information, and miners also have discretion as to whether to accept the changes or not.[106]

Whether any of these solutions can satisfy the requirements of Article 17 of the GDPR remains to be seen. I note that the precise meaning of 'erasure' is not defined in the GDPR, opening the door to interpretations other than absolute deletion.[107] Certain national 'implementing' laws have already directed themselves towards a softer version of the right to be forgotten.[108] The German framework accepts that data isn't deleted in instances of non-automated processing when the specific mode of storage makes this impossible.[109] In such circumstances an alternative solution of not deleting but merely limiting the processing of data is tolerated. This shows that the GDPR can be interpreted to combine its objectives with the respective technological characteristics of the instrument at issue. Further, this seems, at least as a matter of principle, to open the door for interpretations of the right to be forgotten that account for the ledger's tamper evidence and the need for alternative solutions. Other member states have not foreseen that option, however, which risks fragmenting applicable rules, which is precisely what the GDPR sought to eliminate.[110] Next, I look towards the GDPR's principles of data protection by design and data protection by default.

5. Data Protection by Design and Data Protection by Default

Data protection by design and data protection by default are two overarching guiding principles of the GDPR. Although they are not individual rights, I nonetheless briefly examine them, as they confirm the tension between blockchains' promises and perils for data protection. Under Article 25(1) of the GDPR,

the controller shall, both at the time of the determination of the means for processing and at the time of the processing itself, implement appropriate technical

---

[105] Giuseppe Ateniese et al., 'Redactable Blockchain – or – Rewriting History in Bitcoin and Friends' (2017) <http://ieeexplore.ieee.org/document/7961975/> 2, accessed 1 March 2018.
[106] ibid. 3.
[107] It is worth noting that the ECJ has accepted such techniques in other areas, such as search index delisting for search engines.
[108] While the GDPR is a regulation and does thus not require implementation under Article 288 TFEU, this is nonetheless possible through the existence of flexibility clauses.
[109] Article 35 of the Gesetz zur Anpassung des Datenschutzrechts an die Verordnung (EU) 2016/679 und zur Umsetzung der Richtlinie (EU) 2016/680.
[110] See, by way of example, Article 16 of the Luxembourg implementing legislation.

and organizational measures, such as pseudonymisation, which are designed to implement data-protection principles, such as data minimisation, in an effective manner and to integrate the necessary safeguards into the processing in order to meet the requirements of this Regulation and to protect the rights of data subjects.[111]

The above obligations are addressed to controllers, which must 'implement' such mechanisms defined by software developers.[112] Systems architects must from the beginning account for the GDPR's objectives, which should include 'minimising the processing of personal data, pseudonymising data as soon as possible, transparency with regard to the functions and processing of personal data, enabling the data subject to monitor the data processing, enabling the controller to create and improve security features'.[113] While data minimization will always be challenging on DLTs, Article 25(1) underlines that encryption can be a desirable feature, which may be a reason for regulators and courts to look favourably at the technology. This is an important point, which underlines that technology can be used to achieve legal objectives.

The minimizing of transactional data can be achieved by moving it, as far as possible, off-chain. The remaining question is whether the pseudonymization of public keys can be fashioned so as to be GDPR-compliant. The regulation considers that the pseudonymization of personal data 'can reduce the risks to the data subject concerned and help controllers and processors to meet their data-protection obligations'.[114] Data protection by design and default can be achieved in 'minimising the processing of personal data, pseudonymising personal data as soon as possible, transparency with regard to the functions and processing of personal data, enabling the data subject to monitor data processing, enabling the controller to create and improve security features'.[115] Article 32 of the GDPR obliges data controllers to adopt appropriate technical and organizational measures to ensure a level of security that is appropriate to the risk. Article 25(2), however, also requires the controller to implement 'appropriate technical and organisational measures for ensuring that, by default, only personal data which are necessary for each specific purpose of the processing are processed'.[116] This obligation applies to 'the amount of personal data that is collected, the extent of its processing as well as the period of storage and accessibility'.[117] Given that each full node holds a complete copy of each blockchain and that a new block is added to the complete preceding chain, this provision cannot easily be complied with. It appears that the only way to ensure compliance

---

[111] Article 25(1) GDPR.
[112] Whereas in a centralized setting the controller could determine and implement the principles.
[113] Recital 78 GDPR.
[114] Recital 28 GDPR.
[115] Recital 78 GDPR. On the desirability of pseudonymisation, see also Articles 6(4)(e), 31(1)(a) and 89(1) GDPR.
[116] Article 25(2) GDPR.
[117] ibid.

would be to recognize specific key-handling techniques, such as particularly strong encryption formulas or zero-knowledge proof, as GDPR-compliant.

The preceding analysis has revealed an undisputable lack of legal certainty when it comes to the application of the European Union's data protection framework to blockchains and other forms of distributed ledger technology.[118] Ultimately, the application of the GDPR to a specific blockchain or blockchain use case will come to be determined by the specific governance arrangements in practice. Only a close examination of these details on a case-by-case basis will allow for a determination of the respective data controller. It is obvious that the GDPR was designed for centralized models of data collection, storage and processing that cannot readily be transposed to decentralized and distributed databases. Only time will reveal how regulators and judges will approach the tension between the GDPR and DLT. In order to make sense of this tension we must consider it from a meta-perspective and evaluate the two conflicting normative objectives of EU law at play: fundamental rights protection, on the one hand, and the promotion of innovation, on the other.

IV. BLOCKCHAINS AS AN INNOVATION IN DATA PROTECTION?

Thus far, I have observed that distributed ledgers raise considerable challenges from a data protection perspective. At first sight, at least, it appears that the technology and the European Union's legal framework cannot be reconciled. Distributed ledgers pose threats other than to data protection, however. Rather, there is reason to believe that they could in fact be furthering the GDPR's underlying rationale in the future, as indicated in the introduction. Policy-makers are accordingly faced with the challenge of making sense of the current threat to data protection presented by DLT and their future promise of achieving the GDPR's underlying objectives.

A. Reconciling Fundamental Rights Protection and the Promotion of Innovation

Blockchains, in particular those of a public and permissionless character, and the European Union's data protection framework stand in tension. Whereas the GDPR was fashioned for an age of centralized data silos, blockchains promise a future of decentralized data management. This highlights that, even before the new supra-national data protection framework enters into force, it is already partly outdated, since it simply cannot account for the technology's characterizing features. Similar concerns have been voiced in relation to big data.[119] The law has always lagged behind

---

[118] Additional questions arise regarding the compatibility of the GDPR and blockchains, such as the application of Article 22(1) GDPR to smart contracts.

[119] Tal Zarsky, 'Incompatible: The GDPR in an Age of Big Data' (2017) 47 Seton Hall Law Review 995.

technological change, but this divide becomes more acute as the pace of innovation speeds up in the digital age. Specifically in respect of the GDPR, we have seen that pivotal features thereof, such as the rights to amendment and erasure, cannot be easily applied to new technologies for data storage and processing. We have also seen, however, that blockchains, if adequately designed, and the GDPR can share a common objective: giving a data subject more control over her data. This is the case, of course, only when blockchains are specifically fashioned to achieve that objective.

Others have warned that, if this isn't the case, these decentralized structures 'might turn out to be much more vulnerable to governmental or corporate surveillance than their centralized counterparts'.[120] The challenge thus lies in bringing law and technology together to ensure that law doesn't unnecessarily hinder technological progress but also that technology develops in a normatively desirable fashion. In this specific context, the challenge consists in applying the EU data protection framework in a manner that doesn't asphyxiate blockchains' innovative potential, yet at the same time ensures that data protection is guaranteed.

DLTs that store personal data are caught by the GDPR, which causes concern for many operators. The foolproof solution would be to simply refrain from storing such data on chains, which might be feasible for data itself, but not the keys and signatures without which these ledgers cannot function. Considering that both fundamental rights protection and the promotion of innovation are supranational objectives, a purposive interpretation of the GDPR should be adopted whenever possible. It is worth recalling that the GDPR is outcome- and not process-orientated. Blockchains indeed bear the promise of realizing the GDPR's objectives through technological means, and such techno-legal interoperability should not be stifled at inception. While we are used to seeing technology and privacy as antagonists, they don't have to be, as technology can help achieve the GDPR's objectives. A purposive approach would further reflect the need for legislation to be technology- and business-model-neutral, as a textual interpretation would risk disadvantaging blockchains over other technologies.[121]

The European Commission has stressed that the GDPR is technologically neutral legislation that will enable 'innovation to continue to thrive'.[122] Indeed, even the fiercest data protection proponents have argued that, although the GDPR will change 'nothing less than the world as we know it', it is also 'possible to achieve common action through a democratic process on the basis of high standards for citizens' and consumers' rights as well as a competitive and innovative single market'.[123]

[120] De Filippi, 'The Interplay between Decentralization and Privacy' (n 103) 1.
[121] See more generally Mireille Hildebrandt and Laura Tielemans, 'Data Protection by Design and Technology Neutral Law' (2013) 19 Computer & Security Review 509.
[122] European Commission, 'Questions and Answers – Data Protection Reform' (Press Release, 21 December 2015).
[123] Jan Philipp Albrecht, 'How the GDPR will Change the World' (2016) 2 European Data Protection Law Review 287, 289.

Blockchains can provide an alternative means of achieving the regulation's objective of allowing data subjects to control their own personal data, and bear much promise for the Single Digital Market.

The protection of natural persons in relation to the processing of personal data constitutes a fundamental right under Article 8(1) of the Charter of Fundamental Rights and Article 16(1) of the TFEU. Its importance can thus not be overstated. Innovation is also a normative objective of the European Union and its legal order, however. As per Article 173 of the TFEU, the European Union and its member states must work towards the Union's competitiveness, which includes the fostering of innovation and technological development. The 'Innovation Union', part of the Europe 2020 initiative, was designed to make the European Union an 'innovation-friendly environment that makes it easier for great ideas to be turned into products and services that will bring our economy growth and jobs'.[124] In competition law, agreements caught by the prohibition of illicit collusion in Article 101(1) of the TFEU may further be allowed to stand when, under Article 101(3), they contribute to 'promoting technical or economic progress'. In his 2017 State of the Union speech, the European Commission president, Jean-Claude Juncker, announced that the new EU Industrial Policy Strategy is designed to make European industries 'the number one in innovation'.[125] While 'innovation' is undoubtedly a term that is easy to use yet hard to define, there can be no doubt that the European Union currently considers it as a normatively desirable objective, just as it is hard to deny that DLTs are innovative technologies and that, despite numerous hiccups, blockchains promise to emerge as 'an important technological and economic phenomenon'.[126]

This is not to say that the promotion of innovation should outweigh fundamental rights protection. Rather than seeing these two objectives as antagonists, future blockchain development might reveal them be allies. If fashioned appropriately, DLT does not necessarily undermine the data protection objective but, rather, changes the means of its realization. The European Data Protection Supervisor recognizes that, even though 'advanced technologies increase the risk to privacy and data protection, they may also integrate technological solutions for better transparency and control for the persons whose data is processed'.[127] As a blockchain industry develops in the European Union, regulators must not shy away from using the variegated incentivizing mechanisms to ensure that the technology evolves in a normatively desirable manner.

The relationship between law and innovation is multifaceted, and stringent data protection requirements can work as an incentive to refine privacy-protecting

---

[124] See further <https://ec.europa.eu/research/innovation-union/index_en.cfm>.
[125] This speech is available online: <http://europa.eu/rapid/press-release_SPEECH-17-3165_en.htm> accessed 1 March 2018.
[126] Juho Lindman et al., 'Executive Summary' in Roman Beck et al., 'Opportunities and Risks of Blockchain Technologies' (2017) 7 Dagstuhl Reports 99, 102.
[127] See further <https://edps.europa.eu/data-protection/our-work/technology-monitoring_en>.

blockchain solutions and develop a corresponding industry in the Union. Provided that innovators are given the necessary flexibility, the GDPR could spur innovation to evolve in a direction compliant with these important public policy objectives. For this to materialize, discussion and mutual learning between the industry and policy-makers cannot be avoided.[128]

In this context, it is useful to remember that data protection operates in a wider context. The GDPR furthers two objectives: those of data protection and the free movement of data.[129] Data protection was 'designed to serve mankind'.[130] If we accept that innovation has also served mankind,[131] the conclusion that innovation is a consideration to be accounted for in interpreting the GDPR is reinforced. Data protection is not an absolute right but, rather, must 'be considered in relation to its function in society'.[132] The GDPR's pivotal principles of data protection by design and default even require technological innovation in mandating that new products and services account for data protection considerations.[133] It is encouraging in this respect that, in its 2016 *Annual Report*, the EDPS indicates that it is essential that data protection experts begin to examine the concepts behind blockchain technology and how it is implemented in order to better understand how data protection principles can be applied. An integral part of this process should be the development of a privacy-friendly blockchain technology, based on the principles of privacy by design.[134]

B. *Blockchains as a Mechanism of Data Sovereignty*

In their current state DLTs will in most, if not all, instances be incompatible with the GDPR as the specific requirements of the EU data protection framework cannot be easily applied to distributed ledgers. In the future, however, they could be compatible on a meta-level, as, if properly designed, blockchains could pursue the GDPR's underlying goal of giving a data subject more control over her data. In order to achieve the latter, we must be willing to adapt law to technological change and be accepting of greater techno-legal interoperability. This does not mean that data protection should be weakened but, rather, that it is worth exploring whether the

---

[128] On this, see further Michèle Finck, 'Blockchains: Regulating the Unknown' (2018), German Law Journal 665.

[129] Recital 13 GDPR ('The proper functioning of the internal market requires that the free movement of personal data within the Union is not restricted or prohibited for reasons connected with the protection of natural persons with regard to the processing of personal data').

[130] Recital 4 GDPR.

[131] The invention of sanitation should be an uncontroversial case in point.

[132] Recital 4 GDPR.

[133] Recital 78 GDPR.

[134] This Annual Report is available online: <https://edps.europa.eu/sites/edp/files/publication/17–04-27_annual_report_2016_en_1.pdf> accessed 1 December 2017.

GDPR's objectives can be achieved through means different from those originally envisaged. This does not mean either that blind trust should be placed in the technology, however. Blockchains by no means automatically support data sovereignty but, rather, must be purposefully designed to do so, as blockchains can also constitute a danger to data protection. Regulators must insist on the core of data protection regulations while also showing flexibility regarding the specific mechanisms employed and nudge blockchain developers to design their products in compliance with this important public policy objective.

Blockchains offer a record-keeping function that is said to dispense with the need for third-party intermediation and, by analogy, can decentralize the collection, storage and processing of data. This stands in sharp contrast with the current data economy, characterized by economic centralization in the form of 'platform power'.[135] Large intermediaries such as Google, Amazon, Apple and Facebook control how we search, shop and connect. They autonomously collect, store, process and monetize our data trails.[136] This, in turn, enables them to expand their position of power in building on the data mountains they sit on, for instance to train new algorithms. Such market power has caused concern from a competition policy perspective, because it hinders market entry by new players. The issues engendered by these circumstances are twofold, relating, on the one hand, to economic operators' market position and, on the other, to the protection of privacy.

Regarding the latter, blockchains offer the promise of the decentralized handling of data and data sovereignty, a concept that focuses on giving individuals control over their personal data and allowing them to share such information only with trusted parties.[137] The GDPR shares the data sovereignty objective, as it aims to give natural persons 'control over their own personal data'.[138] The right to data portability in Article 20 of the GDPR enshrines this objective in allowing a data subject to receive data from a controller in order to give it to another controller. The right to data portability is an emergent concept in EU law, the contours of which remain largely undefined.[139] There is no doubt, however, that it seeks to give data subjects more control over personal data. The Article 29 Working Party, for instance, considers that the 'primary aim of data portability is enhancing individuals' control over their personal data and making sure they play an active part in the data ecosystem'.[140]

---

[135] Orla Lynskey, 'Regulating "Platform Power"' (2017) LSE Legal Studies Working Paper 1/2017.
[136] Recital 6 GDPR.
[137] For an overview, see <https://blockchainhub.net/blog/blog/decentralized-identity-blockchain/> accessed 1 March 2018.
[138] Recital 7 GDPR.
[139] I have not examined the right to data portability in this chapter but it is worth noting that its application to blockchains is far from straightforward. I reflect further on this right in the next chapter.
[140] Article 29 Working Party, 'Guidelines on the Right to Data Portability' (2017) 16/EN WP 242, 4, note 1.

The precise meaning of the concepts of data portability and data sovereignty remains unsettled. Many predict that DLTs can be fashioned so that only the user has access to the public and private keys, deciding freely as to when she reveals her data with external parties.[141] Unlike ID cards or conventional medical records, blockchains promise selective data sharing through adequate applications, ensuring privacy and reducing the risk of identity theft.[142] Blockchains *could* thus facilitate new forms of identity management by enabling individuals 'to control access to their identity information and to create, manage and use a self-sovereign identity'.[143] Whether this will be the case, however, remains to be seen. It is true, for instance, that selective sharing is possible, yet what about the fact that, once data is revealed, those with access will generally be able to copy and extract data and store it perpetually?

While the promise of blockchain for data sovereignty should not be downplayed, it is also important to remain realistic and vigilant at a time when blockchain hype and hubris sometimes cloud rational judgement. Blockchains are authenticity solutions that do not, in themselves, provide any privacy guarantees, so that, for data sovereignty objectives to be achieved, they must be combined with additional mechanisms. Indeed, despite the technology's promises for data sovereignty, there are also perils, for, if the necessary safeguards are not implemented; blockchains can reveal any and all data stored on them. As a new technology, blockchains are malleable and can develop in a number of directions. It is here where law, technology and innovation must meet and where dialogue between innovators and regulators must occur to ensure that innovation can occur, yet in a fashion that is desirable for the public good. Much will thus depend on blockchains' design, which must reflect technological requirements as well as public policy considerations.

V. THE GDPR AND THE FUTURE OF BLOCKCHAIN TECHNOLOGY

New technology doesn't just change how we apply existing regulations to new facts; it may also profoundly unsettle the foundations upon which existing regulation rests. In the eyes of the GDPR, the onus of personal data stewardship rests on singular data controllers and processors that handle singular data silos. The technological innovation that brought us blockchains may, however, turn individuals into data

---

[141] Michael Mainelli, 'Blockchain Could Help Us Reclaim Control over our Personal Data' *Harvard Business Review* (5 October 2017) <https://hbr.org/2017/10/smart-ledgers-can-help-us-reclaim-control-of-our-personal-data> accessed 1 December 2017.

[142] Instead of having to show your ID at a supermarket to buy alcohol or reveal all medical data to a doctor to indicate prescription medicine currently used, these pieces of information could be revealed in isolation. For an example, see <https://shocard.com/>.

[143] Clare Sullivan and Eric Burger, 'E-Residency and Blockchain' (2017) 33 Computer Law & Security Review 460, 475.

sovereigns that can themselves, copy, change, share and move their data. It is now, in the still relatively early stages of blockchain technology, that appropriate data protection safeguards must be implemented and strongly encouraged by regulators.

While some degree of transparency on a DLT is unavoidable, to allow the network to reach decentralized consensus, transparency is unavoidable only at the ledger's most basic layer, which applies the consensus algorithm. Just as with the TCP/IP layer for the Internet, additional layers of encryption and obfuscation can be built on top to conceal personal data.[144] Only time will reveal whether blockchains' potential for data sovereignty is confirmed and whether the interpretation of the European Union's data protection framework allows such models to develop. In this context, those called upon to interpret and apply the GDPR should of course not blindly trust DLTs to, by definition, further data sovereignty. It is, rather, regulators' role as well to make sure that these considerations are incorporated into the software from the beginning.

---

[144] De Filippi, 'The Interplay between Decentralization and Privacy' (n 103).

5

Blockchains and the Idle Data Economy

I believe these marketplaces will transition us out of the current era of Web 2.0 data
monopolies into a Web 3.0 era of open competition for data and algorithms, where both
are directly monetized.[1]

In the above statement, Fred Ehrsam refers to blockchain-based machine-learning
marketplaces. Such marketplaces would be designed so that 'anyone can sell their
data and keep their data private, while developers can use incentives to attract the
best data for their algorithms'.[2] This revolutionary combination of private machine
learning (enabling analysis of sensitive data) and cryptoeconomics-based incentives
(to attract the best data and models) is seen as a crucial development in sophisticat-
ing AI, which currently suffers from the insufficient availability of data to train
existing algorithms.[3]

This idea may sound futuristic, yet, if it is successful, it could profoundly
alter how we think of data and its economic exploitation.[4] Over the past decades
data has become a decisive economic resource. It is the 'raw material' of the
Digital Single Market.[5] Only a miniscule share of all collected data is currently
subjected to data analytics, however, meaning that most data sits idle in databases.
This is problematic from an innovation perspective. To illustrate, the further
refinement of AI is contingent on making more data available to train existing

---

[1]   Fred Ehrsam, 'Blockchain-based Machine Learning Marketplaces' (*Medium*, 13 March 2018)
      <https://medium.com/@FEhrsam/blockchain-based-machine-learning-marketplaces-cb2d4
      dae2c17> accessed 3 April 2018 (hereafter Ehrsam, 'Blockchain-Based Marketplaces').
[2]   ibid.
[3]   Commission, 'Artificial Intelligence for Europe' (Communication) COM (2018) 237 final.
[4]   To date there is no general definition of 'data' under EU law.
[5]   European Commission, 'Towards a common European data space'(Communication) COM
      (2018) 232 final, 2.

algorithms.[6] Today a competitive edge in AI is not necessarily anchored in sophisticated models but, rather, the availability of huge volumes of quality data. This in turn is problematic from a competition perspective, as it reinforces the existing market power of data behemoths while encumbering market entry for others. It also makes it difficult to entertain university research in AI, including machine learning and deep learning, as researchers don't have the same access to data as powerful private firms.[7]

Despite its centrality to manifold business models and, increasingly, entire economies, current forms of exchanging data and the surrounding legal requirements remain riddled with uncertainties and complexities in the European Union. In order to leverage the full innovation potential of data, more mature and straightforward technical, economic and legal frameworks are required.

In this chapter, I survey the economic importance of (non-personal) data and outline current debates in the European Union as to whether legal reform is needed to unlock data's innovation potential. The European Commission has defined a need to facilitate access to data to promote the sharing of data between undertakings in the internal market. As a first step, the Commission considered the need for legal reform to encourage the private sector to increasingly share data. This included the suggestion of creating property rights in non-personal data in order to produce more legal certainty for undertakings, hoping that this would optimize data transactions. In April 2018 the European Commission abandoned such plans after extensive criticism from industry and academia, and changed its overall approach to achieving the formulated policy objective.

The Commission now looks towards extra-legal mechanisms to incentivize companies to open up their data treasures. This includes the encouragement of data marketplaces. This newly announced strategy then leads me to examine these statements in correlation with current suggestions regarding the development of blockchain-based data marketplaces. Blockchains may indeed have a unique potential in this respect, as they can be both a database and computational infrastructure. In doing so, I return to the theme developed in Chapter 3: technology's regulatory capacity. If blockchain-based data marketplaces develop in line with related promises, they could come to significantly further the normative objective of data sharing. It may be that, in this domain, code inspired by policy objectives is more efficient than law acting on its own. This does not erase the need for law, however, as law is still required to create incentives for such technology to develop in line with recognized policy objectives, including data protection.

---

[6] Cade Metz, 'Google Open-sourcing Tensorflow Shows AI's Future Is Data' (*wired*, 16 November 2015) <www.wired.com/2015/11/google-open-sourcing-tensorflow-shows-ais-future-is-data-not-code/> accessed 24 May 2018.

[7] ibid.

This confirms that blockchain technology, like most forms of technological change, creates challenges from the perspective of existing legal frameworks (as already observed in the preceding chapter), but that it can also help achieve the normative objectives underlying law in a more efficient manner. Indeed, while the preceding chapter underlined that technological change can create tensions with existing legal frameworks, this chapter emphasizes that innovations in database design and related cryptoeconomic incentive structures may remove the market failures (in this case, the insufficient sharing of data) that call for legal intervention. There is currently reason to speculate that blockchains might be able to pursue the policy-objectives identified by the Commission through technical and economic innovation. This does not negate the need for law, however, as normative principles can steer related developments in the desired direction.

I. IDLE DATA

In an economy that has been digitalized and datafied, data is a prime economic asset. The economic importance of data is now common ground and we know that, in the years to come, real-time data collection and analysis will profoundly impact all industries. There is no overstatement in claiming that unlocking the innovation potential of such data flows in a manner that accounts for normative imperatives will be one of the most eminent challenges of the twenty-first century.

Today data volume is continuously accelerating, and blockchains, as append-only data structures that incessantly accumulate data, exemplify this phenomenon. Blockchain infrastructure and decentralized applications will thus contribute to the ever-swelling data ocean.[8] More and more business models are nowadays anchored in the collection, processing and analysis of data. Digital datasets (often consisting of both personal and non-personal data) are a new asset, often used only in-house by the undertakings by which they are generated or collected. In a data-driven world, access to this resource is crucial, as data constitutes the 'raw material of future innovation'.[9] It is against this background that Tim Berners-Lee, the founder of the World Wide Web, has advocated making raw data publicly available.[10] The OECD similarly considers that open data can help stimulate innovation to promote economic development and the public good.[11]

---

[8] Rachel Wolfson, 'A Public Blockchain Aims to Secure Big Data Sharing' (*the merkle*, 23 March 2018) <https://themerkle.com/a-public-blockchain-aims-to-secure-big-data-sharing/> accessed 24 April 2018.

[9] Frank Pasquale, *The Black Box Society* (Harvard University Press 2015) 83.

[10] <www.ted.com/talks/tim_berners_lee_on_the_next_web#t-390833> accessed 19 April 2018.

[11] OECD, 'Data-Driven Innovation: Big Data for Growth and Well-Being' (2015) 195–98 <www.oecd.org/sti/data-driven-innovation-9789264229358-en.htm> accessed 24 April 2018.

The European Commission speaks of a 'data revolution', as '[d]ata has become an essential resource for economic growth, job creation and societal progress'.[12] Data, it has been argued, is 'a new factor of production, an asset, and in some transactions a new currency'.[13] Indeed, among the sixteen key actions of the European Union's Single Digital Market agenda there figures the 'building of a data economy', targeted at maximizing the growth potential of the digital economy.[14]

As myriads of data are being collected, stored, traded and analysed on a daily basis, the question of who owns and can access such data remains less than completely clear, leaving a considerable gap in the internal market legal framework. While one would presume that, in light of its economic magnitude, big data is governed by clear legal principles, this is not in fact the case. The resulting uncertainty risks generating deleterious effects, including not just the stifling of innovation but also the unregulated manipulation of data by actors that control it.

Although available data is continuously expanding, it largely sits idle. According to estimates, a meagre share of all data currently produced is analysed, leading to a massive unlocked innovation potential.[15] For example, the EU Council considers that, in the European Union, the development of digital health services is suffering from 'limited access and use of large databases for research and innovation purposes'.[16] This is a broader and problematic phenomenon, as the data economy cannot be fully realized so long as data is not more widely made accessible. In particular, real-time analysis of data can be an important source of more refined products.[17] For the time being data remains largely underutilized, as many companies hold data but are unable to easily monetize it. Data is largely non-rivalrous in nature, meaning that sharing data does not decrease its value, as the same data can be used for various purposes and applications. This matters, because, even though

---

[12] See European Commission, 'A Digital Single Market Strategy for Europe – Analysis and Evidence, Staff Working Document' SWD (2015) 100 final, 59 (hereafter European Commission, 'Staff Working Document').

[13] ibid. See also European Parliament, 'Proposal for a directive of the European Parliament and of the Council on certain aspects concerning contracts for the supply of digital content' COM (2015) 634 ('In the digital economy, digital content is often supplied without the payment of a price and suppliers use the consumer's personal data they have access to in the context of the supply of the digital content or digital service.').

[14] European Commission, 'Staff Working Document' (n 12) 59.

[15] James Manyika et al., 'Unlocking the Potential of the Internet of Things' (*McKinsey*, June 2015) <www.mckinsey.com/business-functions/digital-mckinsey/our-insights/the-internet-of-things-the-value-of-digitizing-the-physical-world> accessed 24 April 2018.

[16] General Secretariat of the Council, 'Draft Council conclusions on Health in the Digital Society – making progress in data-driven innovation in the field of health' (2017) 14076/17 SAN 398 TELECOM 271 Dataprotect 176, 2 <http://data.consilium.europa.eu/doc/document/ST-14078-2017-INIT/en/pdf> accessed 4 April 2018.

[17] Gintare Surblyte, 'Data as a Digital Resource' (2016) Max Planck Institute for Innovation and Competition Research Paper No. 16–12, 1 <https://papers.ssrn.com/sol3/papers.cfm?abstract_id=2849303> accessed 4 April 2018.

the economic potential of data can hardly be overstated, important knowledge gaps remain concerning the incentives for and technical means of its exchange.[18]

I take the insufficient sharing of data as a starting point to examine the legal regimes currently framing non-personal data in the European Union to observe that the current legal framework is not fit for purpose, as it mostly fails to provide adequate incentives and possibilities for more data sharing between undertakings (and the public sector). I then explore solutions proposed by the European Union to remedy that state of affairs. While such initiatives are important, they may be more efficient when they are complemented with technical infrastructure, such as block-chains, that facilitates data exchange and provides the often lacking economic incentives for vivid data markets. There is indeed growing awareness that the solution to the current state of data lock-up isn't just regulatory but also technical, highlighting that technology can sometimes complement law to achieve its under-lying objectives more efficiently.

II. THE LEGAL TREATMENT OF NON-PERSONAL DATA UNDER EU LAW

There is thus ample agreement that, in order to realize the Digital Single Market, data needs to be increasingly shared. This section briefly surveys the current state of the law applying to non-personal data in the European Union. We'll see that, unlike the *lex specialis* that exists in relation to personal data, there is currently no overarch-ing legal regime in relation to non-personal data. Rather, such data is subject to a mosaic of distinct frameworks. I briefly introduce relevant principles and conclude that none of them can be understood as providing overall incentives for more significant data sharing between undertakings.

A. *The Database Directive*

The 1996 Database Directive created a *sui generis* mode of property protection in the form of the database right long before the data economy took off in its present form.[19] The directive defines a database as 'a collection of independent works, data or other materials arranged in a systematic or methodological way and individually accessible by electronic or other means'.[20] Two modes of protection are available

---

[18] <http://datalandscape.eu/data-driven-stories/what-limits-data-sharing-europe> accessed 24 May 2018.

[19] Article 1(2) of the Council Directive 96/9/EC of the European Parliament and of the Council of 11 March 1996 on the legal protection of databases [1996] OJ L 77/20 (hereafter the Database Directive). For a detailed commentary, see Estelle Derclaye, 'The Database Directive' in Irini Stamatoudi and Paul Torremans (eds), *EU Copyright Law* (Edward Elgar 2014) (hereafter Derclaye, 'The Database Directive').

[20] Article 1(2) of the Database Directive (n 19).

under this legal regime: (i) copyright protection, which applies to creative databases;[21] and (ii) *sui generis* protection, for databases based on a substantial financial investment.[22]

Copyright protection applies when databases are 'the author's own intellectual creation'.[23] The directive states explicitly that copyright protection does not apply to the contents of a database, only to the software that is used.[24] *Sui generis* protection applies when the arrangement and storage of data are operated by 'electronic, electromagnetic or electro-optical processes'.[25] A collection of data can thus be presumed to normally amount to a database. The *sui generis* database right is triggered only when 'there has been qualitatively and/or quantitatively a substantial investment in the obtention, verification or presentation of the contents'.[26] These conditions have been interpreted restrictively, as the ECJ opines that the investment must relate to the 'resources used to seek out existing independent materials and collect them in the database, and not to the resources used for the creation as such of independent material'.[27] It considers that the directive's objective is to generate incentives for database creation but not for the accumulation of the data that feeds into the database.[28]

As a consequence, only the investment into the database – as opposed to the acquisition of data – falls within the directive's scope. *British Horseracing Board* confirmed that the objective of the *sui generis* right is to promote the storage and processing systems of data, not the creation thereof.[29] The substantial investment test was interpreted as not relating to the collection of data, which fell short of qualifying as creation, so that data cannot 'be taken into account in assessing whether the investment in the creation of the database was substantial'.[30] Data as such is, accordingly, not covered by this legal regime. This reflects the fact that, when this regime was initially designed, the database rather than its contents was considered to be the main economic asset – an assumption that has since become outdated.

This is an area of the law that suffers from uncertainties and paradoxes, which can be identified in the European Court of Justice's case law. *Ryanair* raised the

---

[21] ibid. Article 3.

[22] ibid. Article 7(1).

[23] ibid. Article 3(1). See also Case C-604/10 *Football Dataco v Yahoo! UK* [2012] EU:C:2012:115, para 38.

[24] Article 3(2) of the Database Directive (n 19).

[25] ibid. Recital 13.

[26] ibid. Article 7(1).

[27] Case C-203/02 *The British Horseracing Board Ltd and Others v William Hill Organization Ltd* [2004] EU:C:2004:695, para 31.

[28] ibid.

[29] ibid. para 42.

[30] ibid. paras 34–38. For a comment, see Stephen Kon and Thomas Heide, 'BHB/William Hill: Europe's Feist. Court of Appeal Confirmation Establishes Bright Lines' (2006) 28(1) EIPR 60; Tanya Aplin, 'The ECJ Elucidates the Database Right' (2005) 2 IPQ 204.

question of whether the practice of screen scraping is caught by the legal regime.[31] Screen scraping refers to the use of automated software or systems to extract data from a website.[32] A price comparison website had operated such practices with respect to data available on the flight operator's website. The ECJ determined that the database fulfilled the definition of a 'database' but fell short of protection under either of the two regimes. Given that the directive did not apply, Ryanair, the author of the database, was free to lay down contractual limitations on the use of the data by third parties.[33] This illustrates that owners of a dataset not caught by the directive can contractually limit third parties from the commercial use of such data.[34] This result, while true to the directive's wording, implies that an owner of a dataset not covered by the directive benefits from the more protective option of contractually prohibiting use of the database's contents. In the resulting paradoxical situation, those not qualified to invoke the directive's protective regime can benefit from stronger protection on the basis of contract law. This underlines that data sharing in the European Union is currently governed mainly by contract law in lieu of a specialized supranational regime.

The above analysis underlines that the Database Directive was not fashioned to deal with contemporary databases. It assumes that the economically most valuable aspect worthy of protection is the database itself rather than its content. In the face of the troubles inherent to this legal regime the European Commission has acknowledged that the scope of the *sui generis* right is unclear and that it may have failed to 'produce any measurable impact on European database protection'.[35] The objective underlying this legal regime was to boost the EU database industry vis-à-vis that of the United States, and it is unclear whether this has been achieved.[36] Furthermore, in 2016 two European Parliament committees called for the abolition of the directive, arguing that it constitutes an impediment to the development of the European data-driven economy.[37]

The Database Directive's regime accordingly doesn't encompass the sharing of non-personal data between various undertakings. As a consequence, parties are free to determine whether and how they want to make their data available to others. While this does not as such have a limiting effect on data sharing in the internal

---

[31] Case C-30/14 *Ryanair Ltd v PR Aviation BV* [2015] EU:C:2015:10.

[32] ibid. para 16.

[33] ibid. para 45.

[34] ibid. para 45.

[35] Commission of the European Communities, 'DG Internal Market and Services Working Paper: First Evaluation of Directive 96/9/EC on the legal protection of databases' (2005) 23 <http://ec.europa.eu/internal_market/copyright/docs/databases/evaluation_report_en.pdf> accessed 24 April 2018.

[36] Derclaye, 'The Database Directive' (n 19) 9; Recitals 11 and 12 of the Database Directive (n 19).

[37] Committee on Industry, Research and Energy, Committee on the Internal Market and Consumer Protection, 'Motion for a European Parliament Resolution on Towards a Digital Single Market Act' (2015/2147(INI)) 108.

market, the regime has also failed to provide incentives for parties to unlock the potential of idle data in the internal market. In contrast, the essential facilities doctrine compels undertakings to make their data available to others, but only in extraordinary circumstances.

B. *The Essential Facilities Doctrine*

The optimal allocation of resources has always been a key concern for competition law. In exceptional cases, competition law serves as an instrument providing access to data if an undertaking has abused its dominant market position.[38] Under the doctrine of essential facilities, intellectual property rights holders are compelled to compulsorily license exclusive rights to competitors under certain conditions and in very select contexts.

The essential facilities doctrine can be triggered only under Article 102 of the TFEU, which requires not just that the undertaking holds a dominant position but also that it has abused its dominance, a notion that is attracting increasing controversy when applied to the digital economy.[39] The European Court of Justice has applied the doctrine of essential facilities in a few select cases to hold that intellectual property rights can be compulsorily licensed. In *Magill*, access was granted to dynamic data in the form of television listings; in *IMS Health*, access was granted to a database containing information on regional pharmaceutical sales; and, in *Microsoft*, access was granted to interoperability information.[40] In such circumstances, compulsory licences awarded to other market players can open up the market and enhance innovation by increasing competition.

There are considerable limitations, however, to applying this regime to further access to data. First, compulsory access is granted only in exceptional circumstances when access to such data is indispensable; competition in a related market will probably be eliminated; the absence of access hinders the appearance of a new product or technical development and the conduct of refusal cannot be objectively justified.[41] Second, there are difficulties in establishing that market dominance is the result of control over data, how markets for datasets can be considered to be substitutable and how abuses in relation to refusals to grant access to data can

---

[38] Article 102 TFEU.

[39] United Brands has defined a dominant position as follows: 'a position of economic strength enjoyed by an undertaking which enables it to prevent effective competition being maintained on the relevant market by giving it the power to behave to an appreciable extent independently of its competitors, customers and ultimately of its consumers.' Case C-27/67 *United Brands* [1978] EU:C:1978:22, para 65.

[40] See, by way of example, Joined Cases C-241/91 and C-242/91 *Magill* [1995] EU:C:1995:98 (hereafter *Magill*); Case C-418/01 *IMS Health GmbH* [2004] EU:C:2004:257 (hereafter *IMS Health*); Case T-201/04 *Microsoft* [2007] ECR II-3601 (hereafter *Microsoft*).

[41] *Magill*, paras 53–56; *IMS Health* para 52; *Microsoft* para 291.

be established.[42] Third, competition law provides an *ex post* remedy rather than an *ex ante* incentive. While this can lead to concrete results in a specific case it has proved unsuitable as a systemic instrument of economic policy. In light of the above, the essential facilities doctrine cannot be considered as a general access regime to non-personal data but, rather, as a regime that applies in exceptional cases only.

C. *Sector-Specific Solutions*

Ad hoc solutions in the form of sector-specific instruments have been devised to regulate access to privately held non-personal data.[43] In these instances, data does not have to be provided for free but, instead, under a regulated system. For instance, the REACH Regulation obliges private operators to make data from animal testing public to limit the repetitive testing of chemical substances on animals.[44] Regulation 715/2007 obliges car manufacturers to provide unrestricted and standardized access to vehicle repair and maintenance information to create a level playing field between independent and authorized dealers and repairers.[45]

The second Payment Services Directive (PSD2) obliges banks to provide access to certain information in order to facilitate the operation of new payment solutions.[46] The PSD2's access-to-account rule compels providers of payment initiation services and account information services to grant free access to a user's account data (if consent is provided and the information is available online).[47] The objective is

---

[42] Josef Drexl et al., 'Data Ownership and Access to Data – Position Statement of the Max Planck Institute for Innovation and Competition of 16 August 2016 on the Current European Debate' (2016) Max Planck Institute for Innovation & Competition Research Paper No. 16–10, 10 <https://papers.ssrn.com/sol3/papers.cfm?abstract_id=2833165> accessed 4 April 2018 (hereafter Drexl et al., 'Data Ownership').

[43] Council Regulation (EC) 715/2007 of the European Parliament and of the Council of 20 June 2007 on type approval of motor vehicles with respect to emissions from light passenger and commercial vehicles (Euro 5 and Euro 6) and on access to vehicle repair and maintenance information [2007] OJ L 171/1; Council Directive 2010/40/EC on the framework for the development of Intelligent Transport Systems in the field of road transport and for interfaces with other modes of transport [2010] OJ L 207/1.

[44] Articles 17 and 30 of the Council Regulation (EC) 1907/2006 of the European Parliament and of the Council of 18 December 2006 concerning the Registration, Evaluation, Authorisation and Restriction of Chemicals (REACH) [2006] OJ L 396/1.

[45] Recital 8 and Articles 6–9 of the Council Regulation (EC) 715/2007 on type approval of motor vehicles with respect to emissions from light passenger and commercial vehicles (Euro 5 and Euro 6) and on access to vehicle repair and maintenance information [2007] OJ L 171/1.

[46] Council Directive 2015/2366/EC of the European Parliament and of the Council of 25 November 2015 on payment services in the internal market [2015] OJ L 337/35.

[47] ibid. Articles 35 and 36.

to support innovation in financial technology (fintech) services such as mobile and Internet payments by allowing market entrants to use data held by incumbents. A similar regime exists under the Universal Service Directive, which allows for the porting of telephone numbers.[48]

Beyond the private sector, EU law has adopted a specific legal regime governing access to data held by the public sector. Indeed, although there is no legal framework that incentivizes data sharing between private companies, the directive on the reuse of public sector information (the PSI Directive) provides a common legal framework for an EU-wide market for government-held data.[49] It applies to all levels of government, state agencies and organizations funded for the most part by or under the control of public authorities.[50]

Under the directive, member states are encouraged to make as much information available for reuse as possible. The European Union Open Data Portal constitutes a single point of access for data from the bodies and institutions of the Union, which makes data available for free to use and reuse for commercial and non-commercial purposes.[51] Numerous member states have created similar websites,[52] as have local and regional authorities.[53] In addition to this overarching regime, the European Union has also adopted access-to-data schemes regarding specific initiatives. For example, the Copernicus programme makes Earth observation information collected by the European Union available through a free and open data policy while the INSPIRE Directive facilitates access to geospatial data.[54]

These sector-specific regimes provide important obligations for actors of the public and private sectors to share data with others. The effect of such initiatives remains limited, however, as they do not constitute a *lex specialis* encouraging data sharing that would create the required incentives for the private sector.

---

[48] Directive 2002/22/EC of the European Parliament and of the Council of 7 March 2002 on universal service and users' rights relating to electronic communications networks and services (Universal Service Directive).

[49] European Commission, 'European legislation on the re-use of public sector information' (7 November 2013) <https://ec.europa.eu/digital-single-market/en/european-legislation-reuse-public-sector-information> accessed 24 May 2018.

[50] Note that there is an ongoing revision process in relation to this legislation. On this, see further <https://ec.europa.eu/digital-single-market/en/european-legislation-reuse-public-sector-information>.

[51] <https://data.europa.eu/euodp/en/data/> accessed 19 April 2018.

[52] See, by way of example: <https://data.gov.be/en>; <www.govdata.de/>; <http://opendata.ee/>; <https://data.gov.ie/>; <http://opendata.gov.lt/index.php?vars=/public/public/search>; <https://data.public.lu/fr/>; <www.data.gv.at/>.

[53] <http://opendata.paris.fr/>; <www.dati.piemonte.it/>.

[54] <www.copernicus.eu/>; Council Directive 2007/2/EC of the European Parliament and of the Council of 14 March 2007 establishing an Infrastructure for Spatial Information in the European Community [2007] OJ L 108/1.

D. *The General Data Protection Regulation as a General Data Law?*

In the preceding chapter we noted the tension between blockchains as a decentralized paradigm of data management and the European Union's General Data Protection Regulation, which was crafted with centralized data silos in mind. Here I return to this *lex specialis* of personal data protection to ponder its impact on the sharing of datasets, which are conventionally comprised of both personal and non-personal data. Below, I introduce the GDPR's right to data portability, which allows a data subject to port data from one provider to another. Thereafter I turn to the European Union's regulatory approach of distinguishing between personal and non-personal data, concluding that the lines between the two categories are increasingly elusive.

1. Data Portability

The novel right to data portability, one of the GDPR's few genuine novelties compared to the previous legal data protection regime, could serve as a mechanism promoting the free flow of data in the European Union. In accordance with Article 20 of the GDPR, a data subject has a qualified right to 'receive the personal data concerning him or her, which he or she has provided to a controller, in a structured, commonly used and machine-readable format'. This should empower the data subject to 'transmit those data to another controller without hindrance from the controller to which the personal data have been provided'.[55]

Data portability is, accordingly, a tool enabling a data subject to keep her 'digital personality' when switching from one provider to another.[56] The purpose of this new right is to support 'user choice, user control and user empowerment'.[57] This links to the GDPR's overarching objective of giving data subjects more control over their personal data. Even though the right to data portability embodies many objectives, its primary aim has been defined as 'enhancing and individual's control over their personal data and making sure they play an active role in the data ecosystem'.[58] The data subject's right to port data to another controller is without prejudice to other rights, so that, even after Article 20 of the GDPR has been invoked, the data subject remains entitled to continue using the controller's services.[59] In the same vein, data portability does not automatically trigger the erasure of data; when a data subject

---

[55] Article 20(1) GDPR.
[56] Gabriela Zanfir, 'The Right to Data Portability in the Context of the EU Data Protection Reform' (2012) 2 International Data Privacy Law 149, 151.
[57] Article 29 Data Protection Working Party, 'Guidelines on the Right to Data Portability' 16/EN WP 242 (2017) 3 (hereafter A29WP, 'Guidelines on Data Portability').
[58] ibid. 4 (note 1).
[59] ibid. 7.

wishes to achieve that goal, a separate request for erasure ought to be made.[60] In order to allow such switching, the data provided by data controllers needs to be in a structured, commonly used and readable format.[61]

The precise contours of data portability will be defined by future case law. The GDPR itself recognizes that the right to port data is a qualified right and that controllers need to comply only 'when [it is] technically feasible'.[62] The Article 29 Working Party has clarified that technical feasibility is to be assessed on a case-by-case basis.[63] It has also been noted that the portability right needs to be balanced against the rights of others, including intellectual property rights and trade secrets.[64] What this entails and who qualifies as an 'other' remains unclear. It is, for instance, still to be determined whether a data processor could invoke the Database Directive regime in this regard. According to the regulation, the right should also create no obligation for controllers to adopt or maintain technically compatible processing systems.[65] It remains to be seen whether this will allow for a circumvention of the right to data portability in the blockchain context. Nonetheless, the Article 29 Working Party has encouraged self-regulation on this point, calling on industry stakeholders and trade associations to define 'a common set of interoperable standards and formats to deliver the requirements of the right to data portability'.[66]

Whereas the right to data portability is explicitly fashioned as a fundamental right, it has clear analogies to a competition law remedy, which leaves us to wonder whether it could be a broader tool for unlocking data's competitive potential. Pursuant to the European Data Protection Supervisor, data portability could release synergies in data protection and competition law in preventing exclusionary or exploitative abuses of dominance and consumer lock-in, in addition to empowering consumers 'to take advantage of value-added services from third parties while facilitating greater access to the market by competitors'.[67] Article 20 of the GDPR also presents analogies to the PSD2's access-to-account rule, as both aim to give the data subject more control over her data. The underlying rationales are partly overlapping (in the sense that both can further competition and innovation) yet also clearly distinct. The GDPR right is a fundamental right whereas the PDS2 instrument was fashioned largely to increase competition in the financial services

---

[60] A29WP, 'Guidelines on Data Portability' (n 57) 7.
[61] Article 20(1) GDPR.
[62] Article 20(2) GDPR.
[63] A29WP, 'Guidelines on Data Portability' (n 57) 16.
[64] Inge Graef, Martin Husovec and Nadezhda Purtova, 'Data Portability and Data Control: Lessons for an Emerging Concept in EU Law' (2017) Tilburg Law School Research Paper 2017/22 <https://papers.ssrn.com/sol3/papers.cfm?abstract_id=3071875> accessed 24 May 2018.
[65] Recital 68 of the GDPR.
[66] A29WP, 'Guidelines on Data Portability' (n 57) 3.
[67] Preliminary Opinion of the European Data Protection Supervisor, 'Privacy and Competitiveness in the Age of Big Data: The Interplay between Data Protection, Competition Law and Consumer Protection in the Digital Economy' (2014) 36 <https://edps.europa.eu/sites/edp/files/publication/14–03–26_competitition_law_big_data_en.pdf> accessed 4 April 2018.

sector in lowering switching costs and reducing barriers to entry. It is very much expected that, when users can switch between different service providers, new services will be developed.[68]

The right to data portability is, moreover, limited to data that is provided by the data subject herself, and can be exercised no matter the circumstances, even when competition has not been restricted.[69] The fact that portability applies only where the data subject herself has provided the data excludes important sources of data such as online reviews, which is problematic in sectors such as the gig economy, where such reviews are crucial and might lock in users to a specific platform only. As an access regime, it will undoubtedly promote data sharing between various undertakings, but it should not be misunderstood as a general tool of economic policy. Framed as a fundamental right, access to data is granted exclusively at the data subject's request. Its macroeconomic value is limited, as data is 'unlocked' only as a consequence of a data subject invoking her GDPR right. What is more, Article 20 of the GDPR applies only when data is processed on the basis of consent or contract. Although the data protection framework's right to data portability certainly illustrates and supports the desire to create more data sharing between economic operators, it can achieve this purpose in very specific circumstances only and should not be misunderstood as a general data-sharing regime. It constitutes an important innovation from the perspective of personal data sovereignty, but it is unable to serve as an instrument of general economic policy capable of facilitating data sharing in business-to-business contexts. While examining data sharing through the lens of Article 20 of the GDPR underlines that this legal regime may to some extent contribute to that objective, overall the GDPR may have limiting effects on data sharing.

2. The GDPR as the European Union's General Data Law?

The GDPR was fashioned as a *lex specialis*, covering only personal data. The dividing lines between personal and non-personal data are increasingly hard to draw, however. Already, at this stage, it is difficult to distinguish between different categories in relation to datasets that conventionally encompass personal and non-personal data. In the future advanced methods of data analytics may turn all data into personal data.

Data that does not seemingly relate to a data subject can be processed in a manner that subsequently allows the inference of personal information about that individual. Further, when machine-learning algorithms self-learn and upgrade, their operation and usage of data might move beyond human comprehension,

---

[68] A29WP, 'Guidelines on Data Portability' (n 57) 3.
[69] Orla Lynskey, 'Aligning Data Protection Rights with Competition Law Remedies? The GDPR Right to Data Portability' (2017) 42 European Law Review 793.

making it challenging to establish whether data that has been used is personal or non-personal as a matter of EU law.[70] This calls into question any attempt to devise a legal framework designed to apply solely to non-personal data, such as the European Union's proposal for a regulation on a framework for the free flow of non-personal data in the Union that 'concerns data other than personal data'.[71] This recently announced proposal seeks to remove data localization requirements within member states in order to promote the free movement of data across the bloc.[72]

What is more, the same data can be personal or non-personal depending on context. Advocate general Kokott recently acknowledged the dynamic nature of data in *Nowak*.[73] Data is indeed dynamic, to the extent that it can 'relate' to a person (in the sense of Article 4(1) of the GDPR) without being directly about her.[74] The Article 29 Working Party concurs that the nature of data must be determined in light of the relevant context.[75] While the same data can be personal in one context, it can be non-personal in another context.[76] This may discourage those in control of datasets to share them with others, afraid that the data protection may come to apply even when they assume it does not.

As a consequence, any regime that applies different rules to personal and non-personal data is complicated, as the point at which non-personal data becomes personal data, and vice versa, has to be established. This tipping point changes as data analytics tools become more sophisticated, so that something that doesn't qualify as personal data today may qualify as personal data tomorrow. Acknowledging that the lines between personal and non-personal data are becoming increasingly blurred we must wonder whether data portability will in the future be a concept of general significance in the European Union, not limited to personal data. If so, it becomes increasingly difficult to draw dividing lines between the GDPR fundamental right and a general competition law remedy.

The above analysis has underlined that a patchwork of provisions with different rationales currently applies to non-personal data in the EU context. As a consequence of the resulting uncertainties, it has been suggested that a generalized overhaul of the current system may be required, in the form of the vesting of

---

[70] Nadezhda Purtova, 'The Law of Everything. Broad Concept of personal Data and Future of EU Data Protection Law' (2018) 10/1 Law, Innovation and Technology <www.tandfonline .com/doi/abs/10.1080/17579961.2018.1452176> accessed 24 May 2018.

[71] European Commission, Staff Working Document, 'Impact Assessment', SWD (2017) 304 final Part 1/2.

[72] As per Recital 3 of the proposed Regulation, this 'free movement of data' derives from the freedom of establishment and the freedom to provide services.

[73] Case C-434/16 *Nowak* [2017] EU:C:2017:582, Opinion of AG Kokott.

[74] See also Article 29 Working Party, Opinion 4/2007 on the concept of personal data, 01248/07/ EN, 11.

[75] ibid.

[76] To determine whether data is personal or not the possibility of identification, not actual identification, taking into account the means reasonably likely to be used are to be considered under Recital 26 GDPR.

personal property rights in non-personal data. Next, I turn to introduce that suggestion and appraisals that have been made thereof.

E. *Property Rights in Data*

In its report 'Building a European Data Economy', the European Commission observed that public and private players in the data market need access to large and diverse datasets.[77] To achieve this objective, the Commission ponders the introduction of a 'data producer's right' – essentially, a proprietary right that would provide a clear legal framework for such data – in the hope of authorizing the use of non-personal data and unlocking machine-generated data.[78] Some academic voices agreed that vesting property rights in non-personal data may be a suitable manner of facilitating data sharing between economic operators.[79] The main benefit of such an approach would be to provide an 'effective legal tool to enforce individual control over his or her personal data'.[80] Despite these expected benefits, however, the approach suffers from severe shortcomings.

It must be stressed that, in itself, the creation of a data producer's right does not allow others to access the data; it merely reinforces exclusive control.[81] While it is hoped that a property law regime will provide legal certainty in relation to data's legal status and the attached rights of those who produce or control it, we simply cannot be sure whether this policy would in fact constitute an incentive for parties to exchange such data. Further, there is a considerable risk that property rights in data strengthen 'existing data power and the creation of new market power derived from data' and would go counter to the principle of a 'public domain of free information'.[82]

What is more, the dynamic nature of data explains why the same piece of data can be personal or non-personal depending on the specific context. This characteristic of data triggers its own set of complications. To start, there is uncertainty as to whether property rights can be vested in personal data, considering that data protection is enshrined in Article 8 of the Charter of Fundamental Rights, and fundamental rights are widely considered to be unalienable rights.[83] Moreover, property rights in

---

[77] European Commission, 'Building a European Data Economy' (Communication) COM(2017) 9 final, 4.

[78] ibid. 13.

[79] Herbert Zech, 'Information as Property' (2015) JIPITEC 6 (3)/2015, 192 <https://papers.ssrn.com/sol3/papers.cfm?abstract_id=2731076> accessed 24 May 2018.

[80] Nadezhda Purtova, 'Do Property Rights in Personal Data Make Sense after the Big Data Turn?' (2017) 10 Journal of Law and Economic Regulation 208 (hereafter Purtova, 'Do Property Rights Make Sense?').

[81] Drexl et al., 'Data Ownership' (n 42) 8.

[82] ibid. 2.

[83] For a discussion, see Orla Lynskey, *The Foundations of EU Data Protection Law* (Oxford University Press 2015) 242–44.

personal data would be onerous to enforce. As Nadezhda Purtova has highlighted, 'data processing resulting from a decision of one person will inevitably have spill-over effects on others'.[84] In the absence of singular ownership, as is the case with genetic data, property rights will be futile, as enforcement will hinge on consent by another individual or group of individuals. Furthermore, in light of the dynamic and contextual nature of data, according to which the same data can be personal and non-personal, one must wonder how a property right would be practicable, con-sidering that it would apply only in the specific context of the data being non-personal.

Establishing who holds property rights in data is even more troublesome than establishing who controls a given dataset. The smart city context underlines these complications. The concept of a smart city refers to urban systems 'characterized by new forms of developing and managing urban technologies and infrastructures that provide efficient and effective solutions to a great many challenges of modern life'.[85] In smart cities, sensors on bins alert collection teams that it is time for a pick-up, while smart traffic sensors allow cities to manage transportation flows and smart water meters detect leaks. Numerous cities have installed technology that gathers GPS data in real time from vehicles, which is in high demand for app developers as it allows them to communicate predicted, rather than scheduled, vehicle arrival times.[86] A smart city accordingly generates vast amounts of data, which is expected to enable better decision-making. It is entirely unclear, however, which entity would be considered the data producer in such contexts. To illustrate, imagine the situation of a private company installing sensors on a transit system to collect and process data. Who owns this data? The city that has taken the initiative for such collection or the company that carries it out? Alternatively, should it be the citizens, without whom no such data can be collected, collectively or individually, who own the data? Amidst such uncertainty and interconnection a firm property law regime seems misguided.

The above overview has illustrated that multiple legal regimes indirectly relate to data access in the Digital Single Market. None of these regimes can be considered to provide a general framework that would have the effect of promoting access to non-personal data on a broad scale, however. More recently the European Com-mission itself has recognized that 'there is no comprehensive legislative framework on what rights can be exercised with respect to access to such data, in particular with respect to data created by computer processes or collected by sensors processing

---

[84] Purtova, 'Do Property Rights Make Sense?' (n 80) 208.
[85] Andrea Caragliu et al., 'Smart Cities' in James Wright (ed), *International Encyclopedia of the Social & Behavioral Sciences* (2nd edn, Elsevier Science 2015) 113.
[86] See Teresa Scassa and Alexandra Diebel, 'Open or Closed? Open Licensing of Real-Time Public Sector Transit Data' (2016) 8 Journal of E-Democracy 1.

information from equipment, machines or software or in respect to the conditions under which such rights can be exercised'.[87]

The Commission's suggestion that property rights should be vested in non-personal data to promote data sharing has been rejected as a suitable general regime. With that move, the institution also more generally rejected the possibility of law as a suitable means of achieving its stated objective of furthering data sharing in the Digital Single Market. Indeed, the Commission now considers that a preferable approach consists in using alternative behaviour-inducing mechanisms. Below, I survey the related policy initiatives and illustrate that these may work best when complemented by technology.

III. ACCESS OVER OWNERSHIP

It follows from the above that, in the European Union, there is currently no general legal regime that would create the necessary incentives for parties to more readily share their data. While there are a number of legal frameworks that indirectly touch this matter, law has thus far been unable to trigger broader data sharing within the internal market. Nonetheless, consensus remains that it must be more common and easy for economic actors to access non-personal data controlled by others in order to realize the Digital Single Market objective.

At present there remain important limitations to achieving the data-sharing objective. These include cultural and organizational limitations, including a lack of awareness of potential benefits, as well as a lack of trust and a fear of competition.[88] Further, legal and regulatory barriers persist in the form of restrictions on data location and uncertainties of data ownership and access.[89] In addition, technical and operational barriers include an absence of interoperability between datasets, a lack of standards and the high costs of data curation necessary to adapt it for sharing.[90]

In order to achieve its aim of stimulating access to data in the Union, the European Commission at first envisaged a legal solution to this problem in the form of property rights. After extensive criticism, this option was abandoned, as illustrated above.[91] The Commission's new proposal focuses on access rather than ownership. Indeed, more recently it has considered that, in order to achieve its stated objective, voluntary data trading in business-to-business contexts ought to be

---

[87] European Commission, 'Commission Staff Working Document on the free flow of data and emerging issues of the European data economy' (Commission Staff Working Document) SWD (2017) 2 final, 22.

[88] <http://datalandscape.eu/data-driven-stories/what-limits-data-sharing-europe> accessed 24 May 2018.

[89] ibid.

[90] ibid.

[91] Drexl et al., 'Data Ownership' (n 42).

considered the best-suited solution. This should be achieved in relying on the freedom of contract principle as opposed to an obligation to licence.[92]

Notably, the Commission is striving to achieve this objective through non-regulatory measures. The suggestions put forward include using the regulatory potential of code by relying on data marketplaces designed to facilitate data sharing. The Commission considers that fostering the use of application programming interfaces (APIs) and the development of recommended contract terms is a more suitable measure.[93] In order to support these objectives, the Commission has announced the creation of a 'Support Centre for data sharing' under the Connecting Europe Facility work programme, which will provide information on the sharing of public and private sector data by offering know-how and assistance.[94]

The Commission has accordingly chosen a non-regulatory approach that promotes technical solutions by the private sector, including the creation of data marketplaces. Below, I outline that the normative data-sharing objective may be efficiently implemented by blockchain-based data marketplaces that combine technical sophistication with cryptoeconomic incentive mechanisms to further data sharing.

IV. BLOCKCHAINS AS A TECHNICAL SOLUTION TO THE DATA ACCESS PROBLEM?

There is growing awareness that technical infrastructure may be a valuable component in achieving the European Union's data-sharing objective. The EU Council has suggested that, to improve the quality, interoperability and comparability of data, 'common data structures, coding systems and terminologies' should be used.[95] Elsewhere, the same idea has been voiced. For example, in order to make increased data available for AI development, China's Next Generation AI Development Plan seeks to build data-sharing exchanges.[96] In its April 2018 'data package', the European Commission has provided further detail on its own approach. It considers that the economic value of data may be unlocked through the use of data marketplaces.

---

[92] European Commission, 'Commission Staff Working Document on the free flow of data and emerging issues of the European data economy' (Commission Staff Working Document) SWD (2017) 2 final, 12.

[93] Commission, 'Towards a common European data space' (Communication) COM (2018) 232 final, 10.

[94] <https://eur-lex.europa.eu/legal-content/EN/TXT/?uri=COM:2018:232:FIN>, 11 accessed 3 May 2018.

[95] General Secretariat of the Council, 'Draft Council conclusions on Health in the Digital Society – making progress in data-driven innovation in the field of health' (2017) 14076/17 SAN 398 TELECOM 271 Dataprotect 176, 5 <http://data.consilium.europa.eu/doc/document/ST-14078-2017-INIT/en/pdf> accessed 4 April 2018.

[96] Elsa Kania, 'China's AI Agenda Advances' *The Diplomat* (14 February 2018) <https://thediplomat.com/2018/02/chinas-ai-agenda-advances/> accessed 24 April 2018.

A data marketplace has been defined as an electronic marketplace where data is traded as a commodity.[97] There are currently data marketplaces in existence, such as those offering personal data for marketing purposes or marketplaces for very specialized data.[98] There are few examples of general-purpose marketplaces, however.[99] In the vast majority of cases, data is still generated in-house and then analysed by the company or a subcontractor.[100] This limits innovation, as undertakings generally innovate only on the basis of their own data, as opposed to including that of others. Some are now suggesting that blockchain technology could improve the current status quo in enabling broader access to data through blockchain-based data marketplaces.

The Commission had already indicated in 2017 that 'data marketplaces will give organisations, in particular smaller ones who have datasets to sell, additional routes to market as well as easier billing and subscription mechanisms'.[101] In its guidance on sharing private sector data in the European data economy, the Commission lists three distinct options of increasing business-to-business data sharing. First, it mentions the open data approach, whereby data is made available to an open range of users through APIs.[102] Second, it suggests the use of data marketplaces, an approach in which the marketplace serves as an intermediary to create bilateral contracts against remuneration.[103] Third, it adds the possibility of using data exchanges in a closed platform, such that data is supplied against remuneration or added-value services.[104]

This approach indicates that, in order for the normative objective of data sharing in the European Union to be promoted, technology can help. Interestingly, the European Commission itself has noted the potential of blockchain technology in this respect. It has referred to the Dawex data-sharing platform as an example of how a data marketplace can promote access to data. Dawex uses blockchain and smart contracts to guarantee the licence contracts generated between the data buyer and supplier during a transaction that governs terms of use.[105] In considering data sharing via technical enablers, the Commission moreover explicitly notes

---

[97] Lara Vomfell et al., 'A Classification Framework for Data Marketplaces' (2015) ERCIS – European Research Center for Information Systems, No. 23 <www.econstor.eu/handle/10419/118643> accessed 24 April 2018.

[98] European Commission, 'Commission Staff Working Document on the free flow of data and emerging issues of the European data economy' (Commission Staff Working Document) SWD (2017) 2 final, 13.

[99] ibid. 13.

[100] ibid. 15.

[101] ibid. 13.

[102] European Commission Staff Working Document, 'Guidance on sharing private sector data in the European data economy', SWD (2018) 125 final, 5.

[103] ibid. 5.

[104] ibid. 5.

[105] See further <www.dawex.com/en/news/20170419-blockchain-contract-security-dawex/> accessed 5 March 2018.

that blockchain technology could fulfil a valuable role in logging data access and processing actions.[106]

Blockchains offer distinct advantages for data marketplace solutions. Blockchain-based systems, at least in theory, (i) enable data sharing without mutual trust created through the existence of a trusted third party; (ii) create more transparency as to who can access data; (iii) secure data when encryption is used and when data cannot be downloaded (the idea being that the data provider holds the private key, and thus exercises control over the data); and (iv) automate the sale and sharing of data through smart contracts, making this a more attractive option thanks to reduced transaction costs. Further, blockchains' cryptoeconomic incentive structure could enable entirely new data markets, in which data is tokenized so that it can be traded in new ways.

Depending on how they are designed, such models could also radically alter the political economy of data. In the smart city context highlighted above, blockchain-based data marketplaces could 'meaningfully enable user participation and data sovereignty', and, depending on how access is managed, also allow citizens to use data for their own purposes.[107] It is also worth noting that the European Commission has identified the absence of trust as a factor that currently limits data sharing in the European Union, which is problematic because trust is 'indispensable when sharing data'.[108] This lack of trust has been defined as consisting of data availability for regulators, sovereignty and compliance concerns, cyber-security concerns and comparability of security levels.[109] Blockchain protocol's trustless trust premise could provide some relief in this regard. Indeed, the Commission highlights that one aspect of building trust is 'transparency on how data will be stored, processed and for what purposes they will be used'.[110] If properly configured, distributed ledgers could fulfil that objective.

The solution recommended by the Commission is already being avidly explored in research and industry. Multiple research projects and business ventures currently experiment with data marketplaces based on distributed ledgers. For example, research has considered the potential of creating a big data-sharing solution combined with smart contracts to enable the safe sharing of data.[111] This is based on the presumption that there is currently a lack of trust between parties that prevents data

---

[106] European Commission Staff Working Document, 'Guidance on sharing private sector data in the European data economy', SWD (2018) 125 final, 11.

[107] Jason Potts, Ellie Rennie and Jake Goldenfein, 'Blockchains and the Crypto-City' (2017) 5 <https://papers.ssrn.com/sol3/papers.cfm?abstract_id=2982885> accessed 3 April 2018.

[108] 'Synopsis Report', 5 <https://ec.europa.eu/digital-single-market/en/news/synopsis-report-public-consultation-building-european-data-economy> (hereafter 'Synopsis Report').

[109] European Commission Staff Working Document, 'Impact Assessment', SWD (2017) 304 final Part 1/2, 7.

[110] 'Synopsis Report' (n 108) 5.

[111] Li Yue et al., 'Big Data Model of Security Sharing Based on Blockchain' (2017) 117 <https://ieeexplore.ieee.org/document/8113055/> accessed 24 April 2018.

sharing, which could be resolved through DLT's trustless trust architecture.[112] The expectation is that distributed ledgers' traceability and tamper resistance, coupled with the automatic execution of smart contracts, could establish a 'reliable big data distribution system without trusting third parties'.[113] In this context, storage and query data requests would be administered through smart contracts.[114]

Blockchain-based data sharing is considered in a particularly prominent form in the health sector.[115] Here, research projects seek to develop self-sovereign data-sharing solutions based on DLT designed specifically for health data.[116] In this context, the role of the blockchain is to (i) secure uploaded data, (ii) use a decentralized permission management protocol to manage access to the data and (iii) record all access activity.[117] Patientory uses distributed ledgers to encrypt and shred medical records to prevent data breaches.[118] MedRec uses smart contracts as a record management system for electronic medical records in multi-institutional settings.[119]

In the United States, five leading healthcare organizations are collaborating on a pilot project that explores how data can be shared through DLT to improve data quality and reduce administrative costs.[120] Another project encourages breast cancer victims to use a distributed ledger to share medical data with researchers.[121] The objective is to train AI algorithms to detect cancer on mammograms while giving patients the option to revoke access to their data.[122] Further, MyHealthMyData is a project funded under the EU Horizon 2020 scheme that uses blockchain technology to create a structure whereby data subjects can allow, refuse and withdraw access to their data according to different cases of potential use.[123] Smart contracts are used to implement such choices with a view to advancing data sovereignty.[124] This also underlines a point made in the preceding chapter, namely that in the long run

---

[112] ibid.
[113] ibid.
[114] ibid.
[115] Robert Pearl, 'Blockchain, Bitcoin And The Electronic Health Record' (*Forbes*, 10 April 2018) <www.forbes.com/sites/robertpearl/2018/04/10/blockchain-bitcoin-ehr/#43c3545d79e7> accessed 24 April 2018.
[116] Xueping Liang et al., 'Integrating Blockchain for Data Sharing and Collaboration in Mobile Healthcare Applications' (2017) <https://ieeexplore.ieee.org/document/8292361/> accessed 24 April 2018. This project uses the permissioned Hyperledger blockchain.
[117] ibid.
[118] <https://patientory.com/our-solution/>.
[119] See <https://medrec.media.mit.edu/>.
[120] United Health Group, 'Humana, MultiPlan, Optum, Quest Diagnostics and UnitedHealthcare Launch Blockchain-Driven Effort to Tackle Care Provider Data Issues' (*United Health Group*, 2 April 2018) <www.unitedhealthgroup.com/Newsroom/Articles/Feed/Optum/2018/0402HumanaMultiplanOptumUHCBlockchain.aspx> accessed 19 April 2018.
[121] Amy Maxmen, 'AI Researchers Embrace Bitcoin Technology to Share Medical Data' (*nature*, 9 March 2018) <www.nature.com/articles/d41586-018-02641-7> accessed 24 April 2018.
[122] ibid.
[123] <www.myhealthmydata.eu/>.
[124] Rocco Panetta and Lorenzo Cristofaro, 'A Closer Look at the EU-funded My Health My Data project' (2017) 4 Digital Health Legal 10.

DLT, if properly designed, might come to further the GDPR's objective of giving data subjects more control over their data.

In addition to these specific projects, general-purpose data marketplaces based on blockchain technology are being developed. For example, Enigma seeks to create a safe and open data marketplace through an open-source protocol whereby data can be openly exchanged.[125] OpenMined enables entities to run AI models on user data without users losing control over that data.[126] Elsewhere, researchers are working on global exchanges that everyone can contribute computation and data to in order to train machine-learning applications.[127] In order to incentivize users to make data and/or computing power available, a dividend is paid to a contributor whenever her hardware or data is used to train a machine-learning model.[128] The Ocean Protocol was designed specifically to unlock data for AI.[129] Streamr and IOTA develop solutions designed to facilitate machine-to-machine data exchanges and payments in the IoT context.[130] The Weeve platform strives to create a global network of IoT devices that can autonomously buy and sell their data.[131] Morpheo is a machine-learning platform that collects and analyses large datasets to build prediction models, allowing only the owner and the algorithm to read the data.[132] Datum develops a blockchain-based marketplace on which users can sell or share data on their own terms.[133] Researchers have also explored blockchains as a solution to enable data sharing in the context of intelligent vehicles.[134]

There is accordingly a wide diversity of projects that seek to harness the technical infrastructure and cryptoeconomic incentive mechanisms of distributed ledgers to further data sharing in the European Union. The World Economic Forum is also exploring DLT to facilitate data sharing. Its Earth Bank of Codes maps the genetic sequences of the biodiversity of the Amazon by registering biological and biomimetic IP assets on a distributed ledger to record the rights and obligations associated with natural assets and track their provenance and use. When value is created from accessing these assets, smart contracts automate the sharing of benefits to custodians.

---

[125] Enigma Project, 'Beyond Catalyst: Enigma's Vision for the Future of Data' (*Blog Enigma*, 1 August 2017) <https://blog.enigma.co/beyond-catalyst-enigmas-vision-for-the-future-of-data-22fbb5845556> accessed 24 April 2018.

[126] <https://hackernoon.com/the-amazing-tech-stack-of-openmined-a4a0b208d62e>.

[127] David Dao, Dan Alistarh, Claudiu Musat and Ce Zhang, 'DataBright: Towards a Global Exchange for Decentralized Data Ownership and Trusted Computation' (2018) 1 <https://arxiv.org/pdf/1802.04780.pdf> accessed 24 April 2018.

[128] ibid.

[129] <https://oceanprotocol.com/>.

[130] <www.streamr.com/#howItWorks>.

[131] <https://weeve.network/>.

[132] Mathieu Galtier and Camille Marini, 'Morpheo: Traceable Machine Learning on Hidden Data' (2017) <https://arxiv.org/abs/1704.05017> accessed 24 April 2018.

[133] <https://datum.org/>.

[134] Singh Madhusudan and Kim Shiho, 'Blockchain Based Intelligent Vehicle Data sharing Framework' (2017) <https://arxiv.org/pdf/1708.09721.pdf> accessed 24 April 2018.

The hope behind this initiative is that it may unlock a new bio-economy for the Amazon basin that provides income for local communities and creates incentives to maintain the ecosystem.[135] It would function as a one-stop shop that innovators worldwide could tap into for research and to provide a technical means of implementing the Convention on Biological Diversity Nagoya Protocol's goal of eliminating bio-piracy.[136] If the project succeeds it will be an illustration of technology stepping in when regulation on its own has fallen short. It is important to stress that this does *not* undermine the value of regulation but, rather, reveals that in some instances technology can help achieve its underlying normative objectives.

What these projects, which are all still being refined, have in common is that they embody a twofold promise. First, blockchain technology would create a decentralized mode of data sharing that generates a large data pool. Second, blockchains' own incentivizing mechanisms would encourage more active data sharing than is currently the case. Of course, DLT should not be considered as an omnipotent panacea in this respect. It must be remembered that all these projects remain in the very early stages of development. Further, we must be careful as to what these projects actually promise. Their purpose can be undermined when data escapes are possible. A data escape occurs when data is sold once and the buyer can then resell or manipulate the dataset at will. When data is to be downloaded from the ledger, most of the benefits of using distributed ledgers to initially store and sell it are lost. While some solutions are designed to counteract this problem by doing privacy-preserving computations to ensure that data is not downloaded and remains anonymous, little information is available about other projects.[137]

In order to address the issue of data leaks, the idea of 'moving the algorithm to the data' rather than bringing data to the algorithm deserves to be explored in greater detail.[138] For this to happen, data providers could stake data and make it available to algorithms. In such a scenario, the algorithm is brought to the data, as opposed to data being brought to the algorithm. This has the pivotal advantage of training models through a secure computation method in which there is no need to reveal the underlying data.[139] To achieve this, secure computation methods need to be used, such as homomorphic encryption, secure multi-party computation or zero-knowledge proofs.[140] All these methods are slow and need to be further developed.

---

[135] World Economic Forum, 'Harnessing the Fourth Industrial Revolution for Life and on Land' (2018) <www3.weforum.org/docs/WEF_Harnessing_4IR_Life_on_Land.pdf> accessed 24 April 2018.

[136] Nagoya Protocol on Access to Genetic Resources and the Fair and Equitable Sharing of Benefits Arising from their Utilization to the Convention on Biological Diversity.

[137] Enigma Project, 'Why Enigma's Privacy Protocol Will Power Our Decentralized Future' (*Blog Enigma*, 13 December 2017) <https://blog.enigma.co/why-enigmas-privacy-protocol-will-power-our-decentralized-future-aedb8c9ee2f6> accessed 24 April 2018.

[138] See further <www.trust.mit.edu/projects/>.

[139] Ehrsam, 'Blockchain-Based Marketplaces' (n 1).

[140] ibid.

The European Commission recently confirmed that the 'bringing the algorithm to the data' model could address many current security and data protection challenges.[141] It also emphasized that privacy-preserving computation (such as secure multi-party computation), which was developed to perform operations on confidential data (as the extraction of the desired output information is allowed without the input data being disclosed) should be considered in the data marketplace context.[142] We could thus be moving into an age when the debate about sharing data is altogether replaced by one about sharing computation.

V. BLOCKCHAINS AS A TOOL OF DATA GOVERNANCE

The preceding chapter made the point that technological change can be the source of friction with established legal frameworks. In contrast, the present chapter makes the argument that these developments may also remove friction in remedying market failures. Current developments in research and industry indicate that blockchain-based data markets could provide a novel means of incentivizing and operationalizing data sharing, in a context in which greater access to data has been identified as a key requisite to further stimulate innovation in the Digital Single Market.

Law acting in isolation has thus far not been able to create the necessary incentives to encourage undertakings to more widely share their data. Distributed ledgers could provide a more sophisticated technical infrastructure to allow parties to both share data and run data analysis in a more secure and privacy-protecting fashion. In addition, DLT could furnish cryptoeconomic incentives through a token structure to incentivize data sharing via the provision of monetary rewards for high-quality datasets. In the future a combination of law and technology could effectively pursue the supranational objective.

Active regulatory stewardship could nudge technologists to fashion their technology in a way that achieves these objectives. Indeed, even when technology advances to remedy market failures such as the current lack of incentives to share data, there remains a role for law. In this context, regulation would serve to provide the normative framework that encourages such development, create the required legal certainty and makes sure marketplaces respect normative postulates, including data protection. Indeed, law is a necessary guiding principle directing data marketplaces in a direction that complies with established fundamental rights guarantees. To illustrate, it was revealed in early 2018 that Cambridge Analytica intended to create a marketplace for personal data, which some argued would inflict government and

---

[141] European Commission Staff Working Document, 'Guidance on sharing private sector data in the European data economy', SWD (2018) 125 final, 17; accessed 24 May 2018.
[142] ibid.

private corporate control over individuals – a dystopian vision that can hopefully be avoided through the application of a legal framework such as the GDPR.[143]

Law can create and moderate data markets, generate certainty, which encourages experimentation and innovation, and minimize risks for market participants. These attempts are futile, however, when there are no technical means to achieve these objectives. Whether current proposals will ever reach fruition is still to be seen. Their success will be contingent not only on technical developments and the suitability of surrounding legal frameworks but also on adoption. It is still unclear whether the incentives for sharing that can be created through a token structure will achieve their stated objective. Indeed, although they can make data sharing more attractive through financial rewards, such rewards may simply be insufficient, such as when an undertaking fears that sharing its data will empower competitors or lead to the development of business models that will make it the victim of Schumpeterian creative destruction.

[143] Nathaniel Popper and Nicholas Confessore, 'Inside Cambridge Analytica's Virtual Currency Plans' *The New York Times* (17 April 2018) <www.nytimes.com/2018/04/17/technology/cambridge-analytica-initial-coin-offering.html> accessed 19 April 2018.

6

Blockchains, Law and Technological Innovation

If facts are changing, law is changing, law cannot be static. So-called immutable principles must accommodate themselves to the facts of life, for facts are stubborn and will not yield.[1]

The term 'blockchain' is increasingly being referred to as a metaphor for broader technological innovation, as opposed to a precise reference to the technology itself. Such usages connote the perception that we're in the midst of a phase of consequential technological and socio-economic transformation. There is currently a widely shared feeling that profound technological transmutation will trigger pronounced economic, social and political change. In this chapter I outline the challenges regulators face in dealing with such developments, and argue that technological innovation calls for legal innovation that is able to safeguard established public policy objectives.

During the first few years of its existence blockchain technology seemed of little interest. As an emerging technology with few use cases beyond cryptocurrencies perceived as having any real-world significance, there was no reason why policymakers should carefully engage with related developments.[2] More recently, however, blockchain could no longer be ignored, as interest, experimentation, hype and speculation spread. Beyond, there is wide agreement that DLT might come to profoundly impact the public and private sector as firms and governments are testing the technology for their own usages.[3] In light of its potential future importance,

---

[1] Felix Frankfurter, *The Zeitgeist and the Judiciary in Law and Politics: Occasional Papers of Felix Frankfurter* (Harcourt, Brace and Company 1913–38) 6.

[2] Blockchains had however become noticed by law enforcement, as in the case of Silk Road.

[3] An indication of the speed with which this domain evolves is the increasing number of patents filed in relation to blockchain technology, including by established institutional actors. See, by way of example, Wolfie Zhao, 'Bank of America Files for 3 New Blockchain Patents' (*coindesk*, 1 August 2017) <www.coindesk.com/bank-america-files-3-new-blockchain-patents/> accessed 20 March 2018.

steep jurisdictional competition has emerged as some governments have adopted a strategy of legislative marketing, in designing legislation primarily to attract blockchain ventures to their territory, while others are trying to dominate the standardization process.[4]

Blockchain technology may thus be profoundly disruptive, triggering a new technological revolution.[5] It may also come to not have any such effects at all. The course of history is impossible to predict, and a complex combination of technological, economic, political and societal factors will be the judge of the technology's future. Regulators are thus torn between voices prophesying a blockchain future and those denying that distributed ledgers are anything beyond scams and hype. In this context, adequate public policy approaches are hard to craft. On the one hand, caution is mandated, as public resources should not be deployed to engage with a technology that might never materialize, to the detriment of the vast domains that already call for such engagement. On the other hand, governments that fail to be proactive risk missing out on reaping the socio-economic and geopolitical fruits of related innovations.

Today there is a growing determination that policy must be innovation-friendly. In the European Union, Commissioner Valdis Dombrovskis recently remarked in relation to blockchains, 'To remain competitive, Europe must embrace this innovation.'[6] Innovation is a free-standing normative objective in the supranational context. Article 173 of the TFEU determines that the European Union and its member states must work towards the Union's competitiveness, which includes the fostering of innovation and technological development. The 'Innovation Union', part of the Europe 2020 initiative, was designed to make the European Union an 'innovation-friendly environment that makes it easier for great ideas to be turned into products and services that will bring our economy growth and jobs'.[7] In his 2017 State of the Union speech, Commission president Juncker announced that the Union's new Industrial Policy Strategy is designed to make European industries 'the number one in innovation'.[8] What exactly this innovation means remains to be seen, as, generally, although 'there is widespread agreement in policy circles that

---

4   Nathaniel Popper, 'Blockchain will be Theirs, Russian Spy Boasted at Conference' *New York Times* (29 April 2018) <www.nytimes.com/2018/04/29/technology/blockchain-iso-russian-spies .html> accessed 3 May 2018.
5   Carlota Perez, *Technological Revolutions and Financial Capital* (Edward Elgar 2002).
6   European Commission, 'Remarks by Vice-President Dombrovskis at the Roundtable on Cryptocurrencies' (Speech) <http://europa.eu/rapid/press-release_SPEECH-18-1242_en.htm> accessed 28 March 2018 (hereafter European Commission, 'Remarks by Vice-President Dombrovskis').
7   See further <https://ec.europa.eu/research/innovation-union/index_en.cfm> accessed 14 March 2018.
8   European Commission, 'President Jean-Claude Juncker's State of the Union Address 2017' <http://europa.eu/rapid/press-release_SPEECH-17-3165_en.htm> accessed 13 March 2018.

fostering innovation should be a priority, there is far less consensus on what this entails and how to achieve this objective'.[9]

Distributed ledgers promise to emerge as 'an important technological and economic phenomenon'.[10] They thus call for the innovation-friendly approach targeted by EU institutions. Innovation friendliness must also be combined with respect for public policy objectives, however. While openness to new technologies is paramount, policy-makers must look beyond innovation narratives and engage critically with actual developments. This is easier said than done, especially in light of the manifold possible uses of DLT. The decisions to be made are much more complex than the dichotomy between 'banning' or 'allowing' use cases of the technology. Rather, sensible regulatory frameworks that balance innovation and public policy must be designed. This difficult task requires an in-depth understanding of the technology and the specific context within which it operates.

Despite blockchains' young age, the time to start asking related questions is now. Budding technologies are malleable technologies. In providing direction for their development, regulators can shape the technology's future, which becomes much more burdensome at a later stage.[11] Indeed, although the first 'blockchain laws' have emerged, many of these texts pursue but one goal: to attract related capital and industry to the jurisdiction. In a context of regulatory competition and arbitrage, these strategies may be short-sighted. Such signalling alone will not allow a jurisdiction to attract a *sustainable* blockchain ecosystem. This can be achieved only through well-considered and appropriate efforts, based on a solid understanding of the technology and the law. In this chapter, I strive to combine insights from regulatory theory and the literatures on law and technology and law and innovation to devise guiding principles for regulators seeking to develop a sustainable approach towards distributed ledger technology, and, more generally, any technological development that promises to have profound impacts on current paradigms.

I will argue that, amidst dynamic change, regulation cannot be static and top-down. Rather, alternative strategies that focus on dialogue, principles and incentives must be devised. Policy-makers must consider how applicable legal and regulatory frameworks should adapt in light of rapid paradigm changes. With this in mind, I introduce the concept of polycentric co-regulation, an approach focused on collaboration between public authorities, industry and other stakeholders to regulate private activity while accounting for technological requirements and safeguarding

---

9   Anna Butenko and Pierre Larouche, 'Regulation for Innovativeness or Regulation of Innovation?' (2015) TILEC Discussion Paper DP 2015–007, 2 <https://papers.ssrn.com/sol3/papers.cfm?abstract_id=2584863> accessed 10 April 2018.

10 Juho Lindman et al., 'Executive Summary' in Roman Beck et al. (eds), 'Opportunities and Risks of Blockchain Technologies' (2017) 7 Dagstuhl Reports 99, 102.

11 For an account of the pitfalls of delayed regulatory intervention, see Frank Pasquale, *The Black Box Society: The Secret Algorithms That Control Money and Information* (Harvard University Press 2015).

public policy objectives. A framework of this kind formally acknowledges that law must adapt to the changing context in which it operates. It does not, however, unduly delegate regulatory authority to the private sector and abandon public policy objectives. My argument unfolds in three parts. I first consider public authorities' role in technological innovation, before venturing on to determine how regulators have approached blockchain to date and stressing related problems. My analysis concludes by introducing the general framework of polycentric co-regulation as a more suitable alternative for regulation in the age of data.

I. REGULATION, INNOVATION AND TECHNOLOGY

The complex interaction of law, innovation and technology is at the crux of current debates concerning the regulation of distributed ledgers, as it is in other areas also, such as big data analysis, AI and biotechnology. In areas of rapid technological change, 'the contours of legal and regulatory action are not obvious, nor are the frames for analysis'.[12] I thus start by presenting my understanding of the involved concepts.

Regulation has been defined by Julia Black as 'the intentional use of authority to affect behaviour of a different party according to set standards, involving instruments of information-gathering and behaviour modification'.[13] Regulation thus essentially refers to constraints that shape individual behaviour, which can take various forms, including law, social norms, market forces and technical code.[14] This wide definition of regulation is warranted, as the pure study of law provides an incomplete picture of the norms shaping the human condition.[15] Regulation has numerous objectives, including addressing market failures and furthering normative objectives, but also the promotion of innovation.

Innovation refers to 'the ability of individuals, companies and entire nations to continuously create their desired future'.[16] It denotes humans' drive to improve their current condition. The OECD adopts a stricter definition, referring to innovation as 'the implementation of a new or significantly improved product (good or service), process, a new marketing method, or a new organizational method in business practices, workplace organization or external relations'.[17] An idea in itself doesn't constitute innovation in the absence of concrete effects. This underlines regulators'

---

12 Roger Brownsword, Eloise Scotford and Karen Yeung, 'Introduction' in Roger Brownsword, Eloise Scotford and Karen Yeung (eds), *The Oxford Handbook of Law, Regulation and Technology* (Oxford University Press 2017) 4.

13 Julia Black, 'Critical Reflections on Regulation' (2002) 27 Australian Journal of Legal Philosophy 1, 1.

14 Lawrence Lessig, *Code and Other Laws of Cyberspace* (Basic Books 1999).

15 See also Robert Ellickson, *Order Without Law: How Neighbors Settle Disputes* (Harvard University Press 1991) 16–32.

16 John Kao, *Innovation Nation* (Free Press 2007) 19.

17 OECD, *The OEDC Innovation Strategy: Getting A Head Start on Tomorrow* (OECD 2010).

defiance of having to adopt an innovation-friendly approach without knowing whether (desirable) innovation will materialize. Predicting innovation has always proved onerous. The flying cars many saw coming remain science fiction while social networks and their effect on democratic processes and human psychology took us by surprise.

Technology has been defined as 'any tool or technique, any product or process, any physical equipment or method of doing or making, by which human capability is extended'.[18] Matching this with the definition of innovation above, technology emerges as a tool of innovation designed to improve the human condition. It permeates all areas of life. In this sense, almost any debate about law and innovation is also one about technology, and any debate about technology is also one about innovation.

There is hence significant overlap between the above concepts. Most innovation has a technological component, while regulation can be considered as a form of technology, and technology is a form of regulation.[19] What is more, technological change impacts law and may question its legitimacy. This in turn creates uncertainty in relation to the path of a new technology, regulatory options and their legitimacy.[20] It is this *uncertainty*, rather than technology itself, that complicates regulators' task. As Lyria Bennett Moses has shown, technology qua technology is not what is challenging for regulators; it is, rather, its tendency to evolve, as law must continuously adapt to the socio-technical landscape that surrounds it.[21] The relevant question to ask is thus not whether something qualifies as an innovative technology but, rather, what its implications are. Indeed, change is itself challenging to regulatory paradigms, even if not triggered by technology, as in the case of socio-cultural and climate change.[22] With this in mind, I now turn to examine the role of public authorities in relation to (technological) innovation.

A. Public Authorities as Participants in the Innovation Process

Innovation is often framed as a one-point event; a spontaneous idea occurring to a single individual that is then rapidly deployed and immediately produces significant disruption. The truth is often different. Innovators stand on the shoulders of other

[18] Donald Schön, *Technology and Change: The New Heraclitus* (Dell Publishing Company 1967) 1.

[19] Robert Baldwin, Martin Cave and Martin Lodge, *Understanding Regulation: Theory, Strategy and Practice* (2nd edn, Oxford University Press 2010).

[20] Gregory Mandel, 'Legal Evolution in Response to Technological Change' in Roger Brownsword, Eloise Scotford and Karen Yeung (eds), *The Oxford Handbook of Law, Regulation and Technology* (Oxford University Press 2017) 225 (hereafter Mandel, 'Legal Evolution in Response to Technological Change').

[21] Lyria Bennett Moses, 'Regulating in the Face of Sociotechnical Change' in Roger Brownsword, Eloise Scotford and Karen Yeung (eds), *The Oxford Handbook of Law, Regulation and Technology* (Oxford University Press 2017) 577 (hereafter Moses, 'Regulating the Face of Sociotechnical Change').

[22] Elizabeth Fisher, Eloise Scotford and Emily Barrit, 'The Legally Disruptive Nature of Climate Change' (2017) 80 Modern Law Review 173–201.

giants. Satoshi Nakamoto's invention is transformative but, essentially, a combination of others' prior ideas.[23] Innovation is, accordingly, a convoluted process that involves many actors.[24] Importantly, the state is one of these actors. Public authorities are often conceived of as outsiders to the innovation process, as a bureaucracy captured by special interests intent on slowing down innovation. The state has an image problem in this respect, as it is in reality often a pivotal actor that stimulates, guides and supports successful innovation processes. Below, I introduce several mechanisms available to public authorities to steer the course of innovation processes, which include but are not limited to law.

1. Research Finance and Investments

Mariana Mazzucato leaves no doubt that, through the funding of basic research, states have been instrumental in triggering significant innovation, including the Internet.[25] Financing innovation through public research not only helps develop a given technology but, further, creates a pool of independent experts not reliant on industry money who can objectively evaluate developments and provide independent information to the State and the public. In the past years, however, public funding has too often been limited as a consequence of state budget austerity programmes.[26]

States have always relied on economic policy to encourage a particular variant of innovation, such as strategic investments or long-term investments, which often lack appeal for the private sector. To illustrate, the Prussia Railway Fund was designed to promote the construction of militarily critical lines that would not have been commercially viable.[27] Public authorities also finance innovation through subsidies (within the limits of the EU state aid provisions), strategic public procurement and fiscal policy.[28] In making such expenses, they should strive to support long-term

---

[23] Arvind Narayanan and Jeremy Clark, 'Bitcoin's Academic Pedigree' (2017) 60 Communications of the ACM 36.

[24] See generally Robert Atkinson and Stephen Ezell, *Innovation Economics: The Race for Global Advantage* (Yale University Press 2012).

[25] Mariana Mazzucato, *The Entrepreneurial State: Debunking Public vs. Private Sector Myths* (Public Affairs 2015) (hereafter Mazzucato, 'The Entrepreneurial State').

[26] Pēteris Zilgalvis, 'The Need for an Innovation Principle in Regulatory Impact Assessment: The Case of Finance and Innovation in Europe' (2014) 6 Policy and Internet 377, 380.

[27] See Braden Allenby, 'Governance and Technology Systems: The Challenge of Emerging Technologies' in Gary Marchant et al. (eds), *The Growing Gap Between Emerging Technologies and Legal-Ethical Oversight* (Springer 2011) 7 The International Library of Ethics, Law and Technology, 3.

[28] Arthur Cockfield, 'Tax Law and Technological Change' in Roger Brownsword, Eloise Scotford and Karen Yeung (eds), *The Oxford Handbook of Law, Regulation and Technology* (Oxford University Press 2017) 563 ('Tax laws at times seek to promote technological change, or at least the location of innovative activities, primarily by offering tax incentives for research and development.').

investments and focus on 'making things happen that otherwise would not. And making sure those things are things we need.'[29]

At present blockchain development is funded by a variety of sources, including corporate capital[30] and new actors that raise funds through venture capital and/or ICOs. Bitcoin's academic pedigree demonstrates, however, that even crypto-anarchic innovation can benefit from public funding. Going forward, public authorities are targeting funds specifically at DLT as the European Union allocates €340 million for blockchain research[31] and €5 million in prize money for research exploring how blockchains may be used for social good.[32] Further to financing sustainable innovation, public authorities can encourage such innovation in becoming early adopters.

2. Early Adoption

The public sector can support innovation through adoption. Many public authorities have embraced this strategy in relation to blockchains. Sweden is experimenting with distributed ledgers for land registries after Georgia became the first country to register land titles using the technology.[33] Ukraine has partnered with Bitfury to put government data on a blockchain with the hope of addressing concerns over transparency and accountability.[34] The Singapore Smart Nation project uses a distributed ledger to handle domestic interbank payments.[35] The Dubai 2020 initiative plans to move all government documents and systems onto a blockchain by 2020.[36] Most of these projects will be qualified by limited success, and some, such as the Honduras land title registry experiment, have already failed because of disputes with local officials.[37]

[29] Mazzucato, 'The Entrepreneurial State' (n 25) 209.
[30] See, by way of example: <www.research.ibm.com/blockchain/> accessed 28 March 2018.
[31] European Commission, 'Blockchain Technologies' (2017) <https://ec.europa.eu/digital-single-market/en/blockchain-technologies> accessed 28 March 2018.
[32] Committee of the Regions, 'Blockchains for Social Goods' (2016) <https://ec.europa.eu/digital-single-market/en/news/blockchains-social-good> accessed 28 March 2018.
[33] Jonathan Keane, 'Sweden Moves to Next Stage with Blockchain Land Registry' (*coindesk*, 30 March 2017) <www.coindesk.com/sweden-moves-next-stage-blockchain-land-registry/> accessed 13 March 2018.
[34] Gertrude Chavez-Dreyfuss, 'Ukraine Launches Big Blockchain Deal with Tech Firm Bitfury' (*Reuters*, 13 April 2017) <www.reuters.com/article/us-ukraine-bitfury-blockchain-idUSKBN17F0N2> accessed 13 March 2018.
[35] See <www.mas.gov.sg/Singapore-Financial-Centre/Smart-Financial-Centre/Project-Ubin.aspx> accessed 13 March 2018.
[36] Nikhil Lohade, 'Dubai Aims to Be a City Built on Blockchain' (*Wall Street Journal*, 24 April 2017) <www.wsj.com/articles/dubai-aims-to-be-a-city-built-on-blockchain-1493086080> accessed 13 March 2018; see also <www.dubaifuture.gov.ae/our-initiatives/global-blockchain-council/> accessed 13 March 2018.
[37] Pete Rizzo, 'Blockchain Land Title Project "Stalls" in Honduras' (*coindesk*, 26 December 2015) <www.coindesk.com/debate-factom-land-title-honduras/> accessed 28 March 2018.

It can be tricky to differentiate between pure marketing and genuine experimentation in relation to such strategies. Nevertheless, the early adoption of a new technology has numerous benefits. First, it enables learning and experimentation, which must be the first steps in engaging with new technology. The Swedish land registry project is openly framed as an 'innovation' project, the goal of which is not so much to disrupt current database processes as to learn about blockchains' potential *and* limitations first-hand.[38] Second, experimentation with new approaches bears the potential of rendering existing processes more efficient and transparent, thus improving public administrations and services. Third, such projects give rise to dialogue between governments and external experts, which allows both sides to reach a common understanding of their respective needs and areas where a new technology promises to be most beneficial. Fourth, early adoption by public authorities lends credibility to the technology and generates trust, a crucial factor in large-scale adoption.

Typically, the national level is framed as the appropriate scale of experimentation. In reality, variance has benefits. A UK report has encouraged the establishment of blockchain demonstrators at city level, an approach that can be particularly warranted in the smart city context.[39] For larger projects, the European Union can be an appropriate actor. In 2017 the Commission indeed issued a call for tenders for a study on the feasibility of an EU blockchain infrastructure, to determine when and how blockchain may help deliver supranational services and implement policies more efficiently.[40] Another important facet of states' role in the innovation process lies in their capacity as information providers.

3. The Provision of Information

The role of the state in relation to technological innovation is also informational. Public authorities must provide information to their citizens as a means of managing risk. This approach has already been adopted by public authorities in relation to DLT. For example, Commissioner Dombrovskis has noted in relation to cryptoasset speculation that 'warnings about these risks to consumers and investors are important: these must be clear, frequent and across all jurisdictions'.[41]

---

[38] <http://ica-it.org/pdf/Blockchain_Landregistry_Report.pdf> accessed 28 March 2018. Insights based on private correspondance (on file with author).

[39] Government Office for Science, 'Distributed Ledger Technology: Beyond Block Chain. A Report by the UK Government Chief Scientific Adviser' 11 <www.gov.uk/government/uploads/system/uploads/attachment_data/file/492972/gs-16-1-distributed-ledger-technology.pdf> accessed 3 April 2018.

[40] European Commission, 'Study on opportunity and feasibility of a EU blockchain infrastructure' (2017) <https://ec.europa.eu/digital-single-market/en/news/study-opportunity-and-feasibility-eu-blockchain-infrastructure> accessed 28 March 2018.

[41] European Commission, 'Remarks by Vice-President Dombrovskis' (n 6).

Similarly, many national authorities have issued warnings in this respect. The German BaFin, the Federal Financial Supervisory Authority, has warned consumers of the high risks involved in cryptoasset speculation.[42] Many others, including the Dutch Authority for the Financial Markets and the Luxembourg Financial Supervisory Authority, have similarly called for caution.[43] Such information campaigns matter, because, especially amidst novelty and hype, it can be extremely difficult for citizens to identify objective and reliable information – a need public authorities can tackle, as they are usually trusted information intermediaries. States can also encourage innovation through regulation. Below, I review a number of ways through which law can achieve that objective.

B. *Regulation as a Motor of Innovation*

In addition to the above techniques, regulation can be used as an innovation-promoting tool. Regulation can provide stimulus for innovation in numerous ways. For example, the Porter hypothesis assumes that strict environmental regulation encourages innovation and efficiency and improves competition.[44] The European Union is plainly aware that its legislative decisions impact innovation in the internal market. To illustrate, the eIDAS Regulation announces that, given the 'pace of technological change', its text should 'adopt an approach which is open to innovation'.[45] Below, I consider various avenues how this can occur.

1. Promoting Legal Certainty

Innovation can be promoted through legal certainty. As per Jeremy Bentham, '[t]he grand utility of the law is certainty'.[46] It is a mistake to believe that industry necessarily dislikes regulation, as it can furnish the necessary certainty for operation and planning, with regard both to a firm's own actions and to those of competitors. Legal uncertainty, on the other hand, discourages entrepreneurial resolve for fear of legal repercussions. It further increases compliance costs, as entrepreneurs must go to great lengths to clarify their legal situation.

---

[42] 'Initial Coin Offerings: Hohe Risiken für Verbraucher' (*BaFin*, 15 November 2017) <www .bafin.de/SharedDocs/Veroeffentlichungen/DE/Fachartikel/2017/fa_bj_1711_ICO.html> accessed 3 May 2018.

[43] <www.afm.nl/en/professionals/onderwerpen/ico> accessed 3 May 2018; <www.cssf.lu/filead min/files/Protection_consommateurs/Avertissements/A_ICOS_140318.pdf> accessed 3 May 2018.

[44] Michael Porter and Claas van der Linde, 'Toward a New Conception of the Environment-Competitiveness Relationship' (1995) 9 Journal of Economic Perspectives, 97.

[45] Recitals 16 and 26 of Regulation 910/2014 on electronic identification and trust services for electronic transactions in the internal market and repealing Directive 1999/93/EC (2014) OJ L 257/73.

[46] Jeremy Bentham, *The Works of Jeremy Bentham: Now First Collected* (William Tait, 1838–43) vol 3, 206.

Worries around legal liability make for hesitant innovators, shy about realizing their vision, or driven to flee their jurisdiction to establish themselves elsewhere. This is particularly problematic for small players and non-profits that cannot afford extensive legal advice. Legal uncertainty also increases litigation risks, swells legal costs and creates delay in the clarification of legal obligations. Uniformity is sacrificed, as obligations are determined on a case-by-case basis. Prolonged uncertainty is thus to be avoided, as consumers are exposed to risk and innovators to unintended liability, and a jurisdiction may see an exodus of important innovations.[47]

2. Creating a Market for a New Technology

If law doesn't require technology to develop in line with specific normative requirements and, instead, 'accepts technological attacks', there 'is little incentive for technical developers to innovate in ways that support public values'.[48] Regulation may be used to create a market for a new technology that corresponds to such values.

The GDPR provides an elucidating example of how law can be wielded as an incentive for innovation. Its right to data portability, the legal framework's main substantive innovation, has triggered the emergence of a range of new personal data services designed to empower consumers.[49] The European Union, with its large internal market, is particularly well placed to take such initiatives. Anu Bradford has documented the 'Brussels effect', according to which manufacturers worldwide create products compliant with European regulations in order to access the internal market.[50] GDPR standards are designed as global standards, a strategy that has been critiqued as 'data imperialism'.[51] In light of the tensions between the GDPR and blockchains documented in Chapter 4, there have been discussions as to whether the technology should be exempted from the legal framework.[52] This would be misguided. Not only would this be problematic from a rule of law perspective, it would additionally remove incentives for developers to design products furthering the strong privacy regime the GDPR set out to create. This is particularly impactful at an early stage of a technology's development, as a malleable technology more easily adapts to regulatory requirements than a matured technology.

[47] Mandel, 'Legal Evolution in Response to Technological Change' (n 20) 225.
[48] Joel Reidenberg, 'Technology and Internet Jurisdiction' (2005) 153 University of Pennsylvania Law Review 1951, 1973.
[49] Brian Hills, 'Five Ways GDPR Will Drive Innovation' (*DataLab*, 26 July 2017) <www.thedata lab.com/news/2017/five-ways-gdpr-will-drive-innovation> accessed 28 March 2018.
[50] Anu Bradford, 'The Brussels Effect' (2012) 107 Northwestern University Law Review, 1.
[51] Mark Scott and Laurens Cerulus, 'Europe's New Data Protection Rules Export Privacy Standards Worldwide' *Politico* (31 January 2018) <www.politico.eu/article/europe-data-protec tion-privacy-standards-gdpr-general-protection-data-regulation/> accessed 28 March 2018.
[52] Shannon Liao, 'Major Blockchain Group Says Europe Should Exempt Bitcoin from New Data Privacy Rule' (*The Verge*, 5 April 2018) <www.theverge.com/2018/4/5/17199210/block chain-coin-center-gdpr-europe-bitcoin-data-privacy> accessed 10 April 2018.

Sometimes the promotion of innovation can be the main rationale behind legislation. For example, the 2017 Luxembourg Space Law pursues the explicit objective of being the first European legal framework to provide legal certainty in relation to space exploitation and the use of space resources.[53] It secures private operators a right to exploit resources extracted in space in order to encourage a space exploitation sector with links to the Grand Duchy.

3. Ensuring the Interoperability between New Technologies and Existing Law

Regulation ensures the interoperability between new technologies and established structures. Blockchains eventually need law to have any meaningful impact. If data and transactions stored on-chain are to have any real-world consequences they cannot exist in a parallel lawless space.[54] Cryptocurrencies that cannot be exchanged for fiat have limited use, just as many actors will not wish to rely on products that are not compliant with regulatory requirements.

The maturing blockchain space will increasingly witness the emergence of applications that can bridge the brave new world of blockchains with tested legal systems. Although law and blockchain currently seem to stand in tension, they will need to become more proximate in the future in order for distributed ledgers to be deployed at broader scale. Both technology and law are capable of adapting to another, a necessary evolution to generate the user trust necessary for bridges to emerge between blockchains and the real world.

4. Generating User Trust

Regulation further plays an important role in generating user trust vis-à-vis innovative technologies. It can 'white-list' technologies and trigger new social norms regarding their acceptability. Regulating the Internet was an 'important step in its widespread adoption'.[55] In relation to digital currencies, Janet Yellen agrees that regulatory intervention may 'increase public trust in the products'.[56] Industry is plainly aware of law's trust-enhancing role. Uber, famous for pushing back against regulation, has endorsed insurance law that applies consistently across

---

[53] <www.luxembourg.public.lu/en/actualites/2017/07/21-spaceresources/index.html> accessed 3 May 2018.

[54] See further Chapter 3.

[55] Kevin Werbach, 'Trust but Verify: Why the Blockchain Needs the Law' (2017) 33 Berkeley Technology Law Review 487, 501.

[56] Letter from Janet Yellen to Congressman Mick Mulvany (4 September 2015) <https://de.scribd .com/document/283714666/Janet-Yellen-Response-to-US-Representative-Mick-Mulvaney-on-Bitcoin> accessed 3 April 2018.

the United States.[57] This is not surprising, as insurance increases trust in its business model and uniformity decreases compliance costs.

The European Union has similarly acknowledged the trust-enhancing function of regulation in other contexts of technological change.[58] The eIDAS Regulation states that building trust in online environments is an important factor of socio-economic development, as a '[l]ack of trust, in particular because of a perceived lack of legal certainty, makes consumers, businesses and public authorities hesitate to carry out transactions electronically and to adopt new services'.[59] This remains an important issue given that fewer than a quarter of Europeans trust online businesses to protect their personal information.[60]

Suggesting that law can promote innovation does not imply, of course, that this will be an easy task. Regulators must, for instance, carefully choose the timing of their intervention. The Collingridge dilemma highlights that regulators often do not know enough about an emerging technology to make informed decisions and, once they do, they are unable to change a matured technology.[61] Further, when legal change occurs too quickly, a different set of harms arises 'by disrupting settled expectations and stifling further technological innovation'.[62] Legislating will become easier as time passes and standards and terminology settle. The International Organization for Standardization (ISO) is already working on technical and interoperability standards for distributed ledger technologies that might remedy some of these technical and terminological difficulties.[63] There is a risk, however, that premature standards calcify bad technology. The challenge is thus to engage with technological change early on while safeguarding flexibility by improving identified policies as innovation matures.

Following this general overview of considerations concerning the interaction between regulation and innovation I now turn to evaluate early regulatory strategies that have been adopted in relation to blockchain technology.

II. EXAMPLES OF BLOCKCHAIN REGULATION TO DATE

Various regulatory strategies have been adopted to date. In this section, I classify them in accordance with various typologies to determine their respective advantages and shortcomings.

---

[57] TNC Insurance Compromise Model Bill (24 March 2015) <https://newsroom.uber.com/intro ducing-the-tnc-insurance-compromise-model-bill/> accessed 13 March 2018.

[58] Recital 1 of Regulation 910/2014 on electronic identification and trust services for electronic transactions in the internal market and repealing Directive 1999/93/EC (2014) OJ L 257/73.

[59] ibid.

[60] Margarete Vestager, Speech of 12 October 2017, Bpifrance Inno Génération <https://ec .europa.eu/commission/commissioners/2014-2019/vestager/announcements/setting-innovation- free_en> accessed 20 January 2018.

[61] David Collingridge, *The Social Control of Technology* (Frances Pinter 1980).

[62] Mandel, 'Legal Evolution in Response to Technological Change' (n 20) 225.

[63] See ISO/TC 207.

A. *Wait and See*

Many regulators have chosen to observe how the technology unfolds while continuing to apply existing legal frameworks. This approach enables regulators to discern developments without the need to make explicit pronouncements. In early 2017 the European Commission announced that it was 'actively monitoring' blockchain technology.[64] Its strategy includes the organization of workshops and the financing of pilot projects.[65] The wait-and-see approach definitely does not equal passivity (an approach to be avoided at all costs). While no new regulation is issued and old legal principles continue to apply, a regulator assembles information and acquires knowledge through the consultation of stakeholders and experts and by assessing developments in other jurisdictions. A formalized example of this approach is the UK Law Commission's work on smart contracts, electronic signatures and automated vehicles.[66] Similarly, the EU Blockchain Observatory and Forum was established to gather experts to monitor developments.[67] These are laudable efforts considering that genuine information gathering must precede any regulatory efforts. This process can subsequently give way to different policies, as, in light of the evidence collected, it may be appropriate to continue applying existing rules or devise new ones.

It is true that during a wait-and-see period actors can operate in a quasi-'lawless' zone. This can be a negative development, and when such freedom is abused courts should be the point of call. It can also be seen in a positive light, however, as operating in a grey zone is common for new business models. There was once uncertainty as to whether Google's referencing of full-text web pages without prior permission breached copyright law.[68] Kevin Werbach notes that, if Google had waited for permission, it might never have launched.[69] Others have stressed that the online availability of pornography, albeit unlawful under existing

---

[64] Luke Parker, 'European Commission "actively monitoring" Blockchain Developments' (*Brave New Coin*, 17 February 2017) <https://bravenewcoin.com/news/european-commission-actively-monitoring-blockchain-developments/> accessed 13 March 2018.

[65] Chuan Tian, 'European Commission Hosts Blockchain Summit with Industry Focus' (*coindesk*, 18 July 2017) <www.coindesk.com/european-commission-hosts-blockchain-workshop-industry-focus/> accessed 13 March 2018.

[66] Law Commission, '14 New Areas of Law set for Reform' (2017) <www.lawcom.gov.uk/13th-programme-of-law-reform/> accessed 28 March 2018.

[67] European Commission, 'European Commission launches the EU Blockchain Observatory and Forum' (Press Release, 1 February 2018) <https://ec.europa.eu/digital-single-market/en/news/european-commission-launches-eu-blockchain-observatory-and-forum> accessed 10 April 2018.

[68] A US court later confirmed that this was not the case; see *Field v Google, Inc.*, 412 FSupp 2d 1106 (D Nev 2006).

[69] Kevin Werbach, 'The Song Remains the Same: What Cyberlaw Might Teach the Next Internet Economy' (2017) 69 Florida Law Review 887 (hereafter Werbach, 'The Song Remains the Same').

obscenity laws, was a major factor in driving Internet adoption and subsequent technological development.[70] Blockchain developers have been congratulated for having the courage to 'build things before they have permission to do so'.[71] There is undeniably truth in this statement, yet this is also a question of degree. While small infringements can be forgiven, an openly defiant approach probably will not.

Wait and see is a common reaction to technological change. The European Commission also pursued this tactic in relation to sharing economy platforms.[72] It opted for providing general guidance and evaluating developments while leaving it up to the ECJ to determine how these new business models are to be reconciled with EU law.[73] In *Uber Spain*, the ECJ's Grand Chamber recently decided that Uber qualifies as a transportation company and that member states can regulate it as such.[74] In *Uber France* it confirmed that member states may prohibit such services and punish non-observation with criminal sanctions.[75] This highlights the pitfalls of an extended application of the wait-and-see approach, in that it leads to legal questions of general application being decided on a case-by-case basis, often merely delaying the issuing of general principles.[76] Each regulatory strategy hence has its time. While wait and see certainly constitutes a wise approach in the very early days of an innovative technology, over time it must give way to more defined strategies. In any case, this observational and educational stance must go hand in hand with the application of existing legal frameworks.

B. *The Application of Existing Legal Frameworks*

It goes without saying that existing legal frameworks apply to new technologies. This can be observed in connection with Silk Road, a now inactive online black market for illegal items and services that relied on Bitcoin for payment. The site was shut

---

[70] Johnson Peter, 'Pornography Drives Technology: Why Not to Censor the Internet' (1996) 49 *Federal Communications Law Journal* 217.

[71] [CateTV] (17 February 2018) 'Erik Voorhees thanking developers for having the "Courage to build things before they have permission to do so!" Things said at #ETHDenver' [Tweet] <https://twitter.com/CateTV/status/965020637063532544> accessed 3 April 2018.

[72] See European Commission, 'A European Agenda for the Collaborative Economy' COM (2016) 356 final (hereafter European Commission, 'A European Agenda for the Collaborative Economy').

[73] ibid. For an evaluation of the legal implications of this phenomenon, see Nestor Davidson et al., *The Cambridge Handbook of the Law and Regulation of the Sharing Economy* (Cambridge University Press 2018).

[74] Case C-434/15 *Uber Spain* [2017] EU:C:2017:981.

[75] Case C-320/16 *Uber France* [2017] EU:C:2018:221.

[76] As a result of *Uber Spain*, the EU and member states must now decide whether there is a need for new legislation.

down in 2013 and the founder was subsequently sentenced to life in prison without parole.[77] To determine whether existing legal frameworks apply, an exercise in legal classification is necessary. Legal classification has allowed the US Internal Revenue Service to conclude that Bitcoin amounts to property rather than a currency and is, as a consequence, subject to the existing property law regime.[78] In *Hedqvist* the European Court of Justice clarified that, when a Bitcoin exchange offers crypto-to-fiat services, it is exempted from value added tax on the basis of the currency exemption.[79] Legal classification is often far from straightforward, however. In *Hedqvist* the ECJ considered it to be common ground that Bitcoin 'has no other purpose than to be a means of payment', a statement that has become questionable as Bitcoin is now predominantly seen as a store of value.[80]

The legal classification of an innovative technology can have wide-ranging and long-lasting effects, as illustrated by Skype. The US Federal Communications Commission was unwilling to classify Voice Over Internet Protocol (VOIP)[81] as a telecommunications service, based on a desire to shield new market entrants from regulation and to promote innovation.[82] Similarly, PayPal could flourish because of the decision not to regulate it as a bank.[83] Commentators have observed that the key for success of both business models 'was that regulators were convinced these new entrants actually promote public policy goals, and that necessary obligations could be enforced without forcing them into legacy regulatory classifications'.[84] This underlines that classification is often not a neutral exercise but, rather, one informed by surrounding policy considerations.

When classification indicates that existing law should apply, enforcement can occur through mechanisms targeted specifically to the new context. Pump-and-dump schemes in the crypto-world are, unsurprisingly, caught by an established prohibition of such practices.[85] The US Commodities Futures Trading Commission announced a whistle-blowing scheme in 2018 that promises a monetary reward

---

[77] Andy Greenberg, 'Silk Road Creator Ross Ulbricht Loses Life Sentence Appeal' (*wired*, 31 May 2017) <www.wired.com/2017/05/silk-road-creator-ross-ulbricht-loses-life-sentence-appeal/> accessed 13 March 2018.

[78] This guidance is available at <www.irs.gov/uac/newsroom/irs-virtual-currency-guidance> accessed 13 March 2018.

[79] Case C-264/14 *Skatteverket v David Hedqvist* [2015] EU:C:2015:718.

[80] ibid. para 52.

[81] VOIP refers to methods of delivering voice communications and multimedia sessions over IP networks such as the Internet.

[82] Werbach, 'The Song Remains the Same' (n 69) 887.

[83] ibid.

[84] ibid. 925.

[85] Pump-and-dump schemes are old techniques that have, for instance, been used in boiler rooms. In the cryptoasset context, these schemes are organized at scale through social media where scammers coordinate for first buy ('pump') a certain asset and then sell ('dump') it after an increase in price.

to the whistle-blower.[86] This enforcement tactic leverages the fact that these schemes are often organized through social media between parties who may know each other. Where there is some uncertainty as to how existing legal frameworks are to be applied to changing facts, policy-makers may wish to issue guidance in relation to a given phenomenon.

C. Issuing Guidance

When there is uncertainty as to how existing legal frameworks are to be applied to a new technology, various options for clarification are available. These can be mere 'signalling' efforts, or they may take the form of more formalized guidance that can have a broadening or narrowing effect.

When a regulator adheres to a wait-and-see approach and is not yet ready to issue a clear position it can, nonetheless, provide soft informal guidance through 'signalling'. This has recently happened in relation to shadow banking, with the European Commission stating that this sector 'should not be seen solely in terms of the risks that it poses; it is also essential to acknowledge the important role that it plays within the financial sector'.[87] Similarly, a regulator may issue statements of best practices to guide an emergent industry to act in a compliant manner or issue interpretative guides that outline the regulatory agency's interpretation of existing law in relation to this technology.

Agency threats are a stronger form of signalling. They occur when an agency provides 'some warning of agency action related to either ongoing or planned behaviour'.[88] Threats go beyond policy guidelines, studies and reports as they announce concrete enforcement actions if certain circumstances are met. Agency threats are appropriate when an industry is undergoing rapid change in conditions of high uncertainty, as they offer an alternative to 'silence on the one hand and regulation and adjudication on the other'.[89] Through such communication, regulators provide guidance regarding a new technology without relying on the legislation hammer, enabling them to subsequently reconsider their stance. No-action letters are an alternative course of action, whereby a regulator guarantees to an undertaking that, should it engage in a proposed course of action that is (potentially) incompatible with law, no enforcement action will be taken.[90]

---

[86] Commodity Futures Trading Commission, 'Customer Advisory: Beware Virtual Currency Pump-and-Dump-Schemes' (2018) <www.cftc.gov/idc/groups/public/@customerprotection/documents/file/customeradvisory_pumpdump0218.pdf> accessed 14 March 2018.

[87] European Commission, 'Communication from the Commission to the Council and the European Parliament Shadow Banking – Addressing New Sources of Risk in the Financial Sector' COM (2013) 0614 final.

[88] Tim Wu, 'Agency Threats' (2011) 60 Duke Law Journal 1841, 1843.

[89] ibid. 1842.

[90] Thomas Lemke, The SEC No-Action Letter Process (1987) 42 The Business Lawyer 1019.

Regulators may also rely on more formalized mechanisms, such as the issuing of guidance. After having gathered initial insights they may decide to issue formal guidance on the application of legal frameworks. For example, the US Securities and Exchange Commission (SEC) has made it clear that coins or tokens can be considered as securities if the existing legal test is applied to ICOs.[91] Clarification would also be an appropriate course of action in relation to some of the points of tension between blockchains and the GDPR observed in Chapter 4.[92]

Guidance and signalling present the benefit that the market is slowly informed about the direction of regulators' approach, preventing stupefaction when it is formalized. While guidelines provide valuable information for industry, they also come with disadvantages. As soft law, they can subsequently be disregarded by the judiciary. Such was the case when the ECJ disregarded prior guidance by the Commission as to how the notion of an information society service should be interpreted in the context of the platform economy.[93] In the past few years a new regulatory technique has emerged, that of a regulatory sandbox, through which regulators seek to innovate law in the face of technological innovation.

D. *Regulatory Sandboxes*

A regulatory sandbox can be defined as a setting in which innovators can test their product or business model while being temporarily exempted from a number of legal requirements.[94] In exchange, these actors are often obliged to operate their business model in a restricted manner, such as through a controlled number of clients or risk exposure, and under close regulatory supervision. The process is designed to allow regulators to observe and learn while providing legal certainty to industry. Projects benefit from more lenient regulatory constraints and close dialogue with agencies.

Sandboxing is a tool designed to bring innovations to market more quickly while safeguarding public interest considerations. The approach was debuted by the United Kingdom in 2015, which approved the first sandboxed fintech services in 2016.[95] The British framework allows innovators to test new technologies in a lightly

---

[91] This guidance is available at <www.sec.gov/oiea/investor-alerts-and-bulletins/ib_coinofferings> accessed 13 March 2018.

[92] Industry can in this context sometimes force regulators' hands to issue such guidance through lobbying, media attention or strategic litigation.

[93] European Commission, 'A European Agenda for the Collaborative Economy' (n 72) 6. Opinion of AG Szpunar in Case C-434/15 *Uber Spain* [2017] EU:C:2017:364.

[94] The terminology is a play on the term 'development sandbox' that denotes a safe environment for developers to work on software.

[95] More information about this process can be found online under <www.fca.org.uk/firms/regulatory-sandbox> accessed 13 March 2018.

but clearly regulated environment under close supervision and for a defined period of time.[96] The technique has since spread to other jurisdictions.

The Swiss Financial Markets Supervisory Authority has created a new licensing category for innovative companies, which includes a licence-exempt sandbox.[97] Singapore also operates a regulatory sandbox, which aims to 'provide the appropriate regulatory support by relaxing specific legal and regulatory requirements'.[98] The Netherlands has inaugurated a similar scheme in order to 'offer more room for innovation'.[99] Its sandbox offers 'alternative interpretations within the legal framework of open standards or formal dispensation from specific legal requirements'.[100] Australia, Canada, Hong Kong and Taiwan have adopted similar schemes.[101] In the United Kingdom, the sandbox idea is now also being applied outside the fintech context, as the regulator for the electricity and downstream natural markets (Ofgem) has launched a sandbox.[102] The European Commission has expressed support for national sandboxes and is pondering its own role in potentially facilitating cross-border solutions in relation to fintech.[103] It is worth noting that the European Commission is also considering using a regulatory sandbox in the AI context.[104]

Regulatory sandboxing comes with its own set of advantages and disadvantages. Sandboxes can be black boxes that lack transparency. Equality is another concern, as in a sandbox setting some economic operators benefit from advantages not available to others. This risks being seen as incompatible with the rule of law, so it would not be surprising if judicial review actions were initiated against some of these schemes. The selectivity of admission to a sandbox also highlights the challenges for these schemes to be technology- and business-model-neutral. A further problem resides in the fact that regulators are called upon to determine what is 'innovative' in deciding which projects can be included. Indeed, usually only products deemed innovative

---

[96] ibid.

[97] 'FINMA reduces obstacles to FinTech' (*finma*, 17 March 2016) <www.finma.ch/en/news/2016/03/20160317-mm-fintech/> accessed 14 March 2018.

[98] 'FinTech Regulatory Sandbox: Introduction' (*MAS*) <www.mas.gov.sg/Singapore-Financial-Centre/Smart-Financial-Centre/FinTech-Regulatory-Sandbox.aspx> accessed 14 March 2018.

[99] <www.dnb.nl/en/binaries/More-room-for-innovation-in-the-financial%20sector_tcm47-361364.pdf?2018050113> accessed 3 May 2018.

[100] ibid. 2.

[101] <www.iam-media.com/reports/detail.aspx?g=ccb604f5-1194-4d8d-89c0-cc44306f74da> accessed 3 May 2018; <www.securities-administrators.ca/industry_resources.aspx?id=1588> accessed 3 May 2018; <http://asic.gov.au/for-business/your-business/innovation-hub/regulatory-sandbox/> accessed 3 May 2018; <www.hkma.gov.hk/eng/key-functions/international-financial-centre/fintech-supervisory-sandbox.shtml> accessed 3 May 2018.

[102] See further <www.ofgem.gov.uk/about-us/how-we-engage/innovation-link> accessed 15 January 2018.

[103] European Commission, 'FinTech: A More Competitive and Innovative European Financial Sector' (Consultation Document), 1.

[104] European Commission, 'Communication Artificial Intelligence for Europe' (2018) <https://ec.europa.eu/digital-single-market/en/news/communication-artificial-intelligence-europe> accessed 3 May 2018.

are admitted to the sandbox, obliging regulators to pass judgement on this rather fluffy criterion.

Further, the fact that actors transition from a general legal regime applicable to all to a selective and privileged regime available only to the few raises challenges in relation to on-boarding and off-boarding. For example, what about consumers who used a certain service before the firm entered into the sandbox, thinking their relations would be covered by the generally applicable regime, but they no longer are? Similarly, there is as yet insufficient data available to determine the intricacies of transitioning back from the privileged to the general regime. Further, there is always a risk that the supported product is not viable outside the sandbox context as it is simply unable to match its business model with existing law. In the European Union, member states are limited, moreover, in what they can do in a sandbox context, as the supremacy of supranational law stands in the way of sandboxes that disregard EU law.[105] This is an important limitation that is often ignored in related debates.

Regulatory sandboxes, at least in their current form, are also limited to a single jurisdiction, which can create considerable difficulty. Indeed, when a service lacks the standardization associated with regulation, the sandboxed activity becomes unfit for the cross-border provision of services.[106] Cross-jurisdictional sandboxing initiatives might be a solution, even if a distant one. The UK Financial Conduct Authority (FCA) recently expressed interest in a 'global sandbox'.[107] While global consensus on this matter is hard to imagine, the European Commission could encourage such projects among all or at least some member states. As highlighted below, there are also alternative avenues, such as the creation of a so-called 28th regime, an option examined below.

E. *Regulatory Cooperation*

While some policy challenges triggered by DLT can be jurisdiction-specific, many are not. It is thus not surprising that regulators have chosen to cooperate in this context. The Chinese and Australian securities regulators have signed an information-sharing agreement in relation to fintech, aimed at promoting innovation.[108]

---

[105] In accordance with the principle of supremacy, EU law prevails over national law in case of conflict.

[106] Dirk Zetzsche et al., 'Regulating a Revolution. From Regulatory Sandboxes to Smart Regulation' (2017) University of Luxembourg Law Working Paper Series 2017-006, 40 <https://papers.ssrn .com/sol3/papers.cfm?abstract_id=3018534> accessed 3 April 2018.

[107] Financial Conduct Authority, 'Global Sandbox' (14 February 2018) <www.fca.org.uk/firms/ regulatory-sandbox/global-sandbox> accessed 28 March 2018.

[108] Adam Reese, 'Chinese and Australian Securities Regulators Ink FinTech Cooperation Agreement' (*ethnews*, 9 November 2017) <www.ethnews.com/chinese-and-australian-securities-regula tors-ink-fintech-cooperation-agreement?utm_source=ETHNews+-+NEWS&utm_campaign= abf0540902-Martin+Swende+on+Parity%3B+China+%26+Australia+Fintech&utm_medium= email&utm_term=0_1d28ae12bd-abf0540902-84349401> accessed 14 March 2018.

Singapore and Switzerland have cooperated on fintech rules[109] while various forms of cooperation also exist between EU member states.[110] Such cooperation echoes the very nature of current forms of technological innovation, which is transnational rather than limited to a single jurisdiction. The OECD has already called for cooperation, especially regarding the question of how to tax cryptoasset exchanges.[111] In April 2018 22 EU member states signed a declaration on the establishment of a European Blockchain Partnership, in the context of which member states plan to cooperate to prevent fragmented approaches.[112]

Cooperation triggers dialogue, which improves understanding of a new technology. It is, accordingly, not surprising that the technique is not limited to the blockchain context but can also be observed in other domains of technological change. For instance, the Declaration of Amsterdam encourages member states to create possibilities for the large-scale cross-border testing of connected and automated driving technologies 'based on a learning-by-experience approach'.[113] It is also important to stress, however, that even this approach comes with limitations. It is one thing to create such initiatives yet it is quite another to successfully do so in relation to structural limitations and divergences in applicable legal frameworks. Sometimes the best option is good old-fashioned legislation.

F. New Legislation

Some jurisdictions have already enacted new legislation in relation to DLT. These moves have been primarily motivated by a desire to attract corresponding companies and capital to the jurisdiction. It is, in essence, a strategy of legislative marketing. While such legislative marketing can establish a jurisdiction as a blockchain-friendly venue, it also comes with considerable disadvantages. When technology is still little understood and swiftly developing, premature legislation risks being ill-suited and in

---

[109] Jonathan Keane, 'The State of ICO Regulation? New Report Outlines Legal Status in 6 Nations' (*coindesk*, 13 July 2017) <www.coindesk.com/state-ico-regulation-new-report-outlines-legal-status-6-nations/> accessed 13 March 2018.

[110] Memorandum of Understanding between the Ministry of Finance of the Republic of Estonia and the Ministry of Finance of the Republic of Latvia and the Ministry of Finance of the Republic of Lithuania in respect of their Co-operation for Regional Capital Market Development in the Baltics (6 November 2017).

[111] OECD, 'OECD Secretary-General Report to G20 Finance Ministers and Central Bank Governors' (2018) <www.oecd.org/tax/OECD-Secretary-General-tax-report-G20-Finance-Ministers-Argentina-March-2018.pdf> accessed 28 March 2018.

[112] European Commission, 'European Countries Join Blockchain Partnership' (2018) <https://ec.europa.eu/digital-single-market/en/news/european-countries-join-blockchain-partnership> accessed 3 May 2018.

[113] Declaration of Amsterdam, 'Cooperation in the Field of Connected and Automated Driving' (14 April 2016), point II.h.

need of subsequent revision. Even writing legislation may prove challenging, as terminology remains unsettled, which may also lead to complications in relation to the application of such legislative frameworks.[114]

A number of examples of said approach can be pinpointed. In March 2017 Arizona issued legislation that qualifies signatures secured through blockchains and smart contracts as electronic signatures.[115] Russia is creating a legal framework to legalize ICOs.[116] Vermont has considered legislation to make blockchain records admissible evidence in courts.[117] France has authorized debt-based crowdfunding recorded on the blockchain.[118] Spain is thinking about tax breaks for blockchain firms.[119] Portugal doesn't charge capital gains tax on crypto-income.[120]

States are competing not just for capital but, increasingly, also for (control over) data and data-processing systems. It is accordingly not surprising that jurisdictional competition has emerged in relation to blockchain. To illustrate, British MEPs have opined that London will need blockchains in order to 'stay relevant' after Brexit.[121] These initiatives echo the sentiment that 'regulation enables firms in countries that regulate first to take the lead in selling new technologies to countries that follow'.[122] Over the past months numerous proposals and new laws have emerged. Many of these projects underline the pitfalls of creating legislation at an early stage, when the technology itself and related terminology and understanding remain unsettled. The State of Arizona draft bill HB2417 defines blockchain technology as follows:

> 'Blockchain technology' means distributed ledger technology that uses a distributed, decentralized, shared, and replicated ledger, which may be public or private,

---

[114] Angela Walch, 'The Path of the Blockchain Lexicon' (2017) 36 Review of Banking & Financial Law 713.

[115] Stan Higgins, 'Arizona Governor Signs Blockchain Bill into Law' (*coindesk*, 31 March 2017) <www.coindesk.com/arizona-governor-signs-blockchain-bill-law/> accessed 14 March 2018 (hereafter Higgins, 'Arizona Governor Signs Blockchain Bill into Law').

[116] 'Russia is Creating a Regulatory Framework to Legalize ICOs' (*altcointoday*, 20 July 2017) <www.altcointoday.com/russia-legalize-icos/> accessed 14 March 2018.

[117] Higgins, 'Arizona Governor Signs Blockchain Bill into Law' (n 115).

[118] Diana Ngo, 'France Issues New Ruling for Mini-Bonds Trading on Blockchain Platforms' (*BTCManager*, 12 May 2016) <https://btcmanager.com/france-issues-new-ruling-for-mini-bonds-trading-on-blockchain-platforms/> accessed 14 March 2018.

[119] Esteban Duarte, 'Spanish Party Weighs Tax Incentives to Lure Blockchain Firms' (*Bloomberg*, 15 February 2018) <www.bloomberg.com/news/articles/2018-02-15/rajoy-s-party-weighs-tax-breaks-for-spanish-blockchain-companies> accessed 14 March 2018.

[120] Pedro Crisóstomo and João Pedro Pereira, 'Ganhos com bitcoins não pagam imposto em Portugal' *publico* (17 January 2018) <www.publico.pt/2018/01/17/tecnologia/noticia/ganhos-com-bitcoins-nao-pagam-imposto-em-portugal-1799707> accessed 3 May 2018. I am grateful to Cris Carrascosa for bringing this to my attention.

[121] Oscar Williams-Grut, 'London Needs to Embrace Blockchain Post-Brexit for the Next "Big Bang Moment"' (*Businessinsider*, 13 February 2018) <www.businessinsider.de/kay-swinburne-mep-uk-should-embrace-blockchain-post-brexit-for-next-big-bang-moment-2018-2?r=UK&IR=T> accessed 14 March 2018.

[122] Jonathan Wiener, 'The Regulation of Technology, and the Technology of Regulation' (2004) 26 Technology in Society 483, 484 (hereafter Wiener, 'The Regulation of Technology').

permissioned or permissionless, or driven by tokenized crypto economics or token-less. The data on the ledger is protected with cryptography, is *immutable* and auditable, and *provides an uncensored truth*.[123]

Needless to say, there are numerous problems with such a definition, which will not easily be workable for courts due to its complexity. In particular, the references to blockchain being immutable and providing an 'uncensored truth' are baffling and based on a profound misunderstanding of the technology. Such statements misrepresent what blockchains actually do. First, blockchains are not immutable, as explained in the introductory chapter. Second, distributed ledgers are not a crystal ball revealing truth; they simply record information and store it in a replicated and hard-to-amend fashion. They also replicate the 'garbage in, garbage out' problem. To illustrate, if I register a file (or hash thereof) on-chain that claims that I practise all intermediary series in Ashtanga yoga and have successfully crossed the Alps on foot then that's just wishful thinking, not an 'uncensored truth' – despite it being on the blockchain.

Sometimes such legislative efforts are not really necessary. For instance, several US states are passing legislation designed to legally recognize smart contracts, meaning that contracts cannot be invalidated just because they are executed through automated code.[124] This is already the current state of contract law in the United States, however, making such schemes unnecessary and likely to add confusion and remove legal certainty. The reason why such legislation is passed is largely to attract entrepreneurs and investment, which is why they can be thought of as efforts in legislative marketing.

Europe has not been immune to such strategies. The Swiss 'Zug Cryptovalley' ecosystem initiative has long sought to attract innovators with 'low taxes and friendly regulations' and 'friendly, accessible and supportive government'.[125] More recently Malta has announced legal reform in relation to DLT. It proposes to consider blockchains and smart contracts as 'technology arrangements' that are to have legal personality.[126] While the intentions behind this proposal remain unclear, it appears questionable whether these systems and their legal implications are sufficiently understood to proceed to such a move.[127]

---

[123] Emphasis added.
[124] Mike Orcutt, 'States that are Passing Laws to Govern "Smart Contracts" Have No Idea What They're Doing' (*MIT Technology Review*, 29 March 2018) <www.technologyreview.com/s/610718/states-that-are-passing-laws-to-govern-smart-contracts-have-no-idea-what-theyre-doing/> accessed 30 March 2018.
[125] <https://cryptovalley.swiss/>.
[126] Maltese Parliamentary Secretariat for Financial Services, Digital Economy and Innovation, 'Malta a Leader in DLT Regulation' (Consultation Paper), 17–18.
[127] There is no denying that in the short term, this strategy has achieved its objective: a few days after announcing the reform a large cryptoasset exchange announced plans to relocate to the island. The Prime Minister tweeted: Joseph Muscat [JosephMuscat_JM] (23 March 2018) 'Welcome to #Malta @binance. We aim to be the global trailblazers in the regulation of blockchain-based businesses and the jurisdiction of quality and choice for world class fintech

Although it is understandable that states resort to such legislative marketing, this can be short-sighted, as what is needed to attract a sustainable blockchain industry is good rather than fast regulation. It is worth recalling that Internet companies did not end up settling in Sealand but, rather, in jurisdictions with adequate legal and institutional frameworks.

The pitfalls of premature legislation that imposes too high a burden on industry are illustrated by New York State's BitLicence scheme. The 2015 law requires entities that engage in virtual currency operations not covered by an exemption to obtain a licence.[128] In two years only three licences were granted (to Circle, Ripple and Coinbase).[129] Application costs have been said to be prohibitive for smaller players and start-ups, which have preferred to move to other jurisdictions.[130] California had planned a similar scheme, California bill AB 1326, which was dropped, however, in the face of arguments that it would discourage innovation.[131] It is worth noting that, in light of criticisms related to the BitLicence scheme, there are currently considerations to review it altogether.[132] Rather than having provided stability to the nascent blockchain industry, the scheme thus added complication and drove some actors to other jurisdictions. This danger looms large whenever premature legislation is adopted.

This is not to say that the adoption of legislation is always misguided. Sometimes it is indeed the best option. The inclusion of cryptocurrencies in the framework of EU money-laundering legislation can be seen in this light. Here the underlying objective and means of achievement are undisputed, and this legislative updating accordingly creates valuable legal certainty.

The above overview has examined some of the regulatory strategies adopted in relation to blockchains to date. Up until now most states have opted for one-point interventions rather than a comprehensive regulatory strategy. In order to successfully make sense of the emergence of new technologies with a disruptive potential, however, comprehensive strategies are needed. Below, I debate the respective advantages of the conventional options of command-and-control legislation and self-regulation, and then suggest that an alternative regime of polycentric

---

companies – JM @SilvioSchembri' [Tweet] <https://twitter.com/JosephMuscat_JM/status/977115588614086656> accessed 3 April 2018.

[128] New York Compilation of Codes, Rules and Regulations title 23 § 200.1 et seq <www.dfs.ny.gov/legal/regulations/adoptions/dfsp200t.pdf> accessed 14 March 2018.

[129] See Michael del Castillo, 'Bitcoin Exchange Coinbase Receives New York BitLicense' (*coindesk*, 17 January 2017) <www.coindesk.com/bitcoin-exchange-coinbase-receives-bitlicense/> accessed 14 March 2018.

[130] Yessi Bello Perez, 'The Real Cost of Applying for a New York BitLicense' (*coindesk*, 13 August 2015) <www.coindesk.com/real-cost-applying-new-york-bitlicense> accessed 14 March 2018.

[131] Lyria Bennett Moses, 'Agents of Change: How the Law "Copes" with Technological Change' (2011) 20 Griffith Law Review 763.

[132] Leigh Cuen, 'This New York Lawmaker wants to end the BitLicense' (*coindesk*, 20 March 2018) <www.coindesk.com/meet-the-new-york-lawmaker-who-wants-to-replace-the-bitlicense/> accessed 28 March 2018.

co-regulation, which accounts for the regulatory advantages of code, should be preferred. I set out this model's specific characteristics and explain how it could be translated into practice in serving as the backbone of the creating of a so-called 28th regime.

III. POLYCENTRIC CO-REGULATION

When new regulation is considered, policy-makers need to answer three related questions. First, what is the regulatory objective? Second, what is the appropriate regulatory access point to realize that objective? Third, what regulatory technique is best suited to make the regulatory access point fulfil the objective in the most efficient manner? The first point is highly context-specific and the second point was discussed in Chapter 2. In the remainder of the present chapter I engage with the third aspect: regulatory techniques.

Regulation is conventionally treated as if 'it comes in one type and has only one effect on technology, like an engine transmission that can shift into only forward or reverse'.[133] This is not the case, however, as various alternatives are available. Below, I contrast command-and-control regulation, self-regulation and co-regulation to examine the respective advantages and disadvantages.[134] I will put forward an argument in favour of polycentric co-regulation, arguing that this technique is best suited to contexts of technological change. The notion refers to a situation in which public authorities voluntarily involve the private sector and other stakeholders in the drafting, implementation and enforcement of norms. It further relies on the regulatory potential of code in law-making, implementation and enforcement. Before elaborating on that point I first set out the go-to options of command-and-control legislation and self-regulation.

A. *Command-and-Control Legislation*

Command-and-control regulation, also referred to as top-down regulation, is what typically comes to mind when thinking about regulating economic behaviour: legislation. It has been defined as 'regulation by the state, which is often assumed to take a particular form, that is the use of legal rules backed by criminal sanctions'.[135] The European Union's regulatory activity is generally associated with

---

[133] Wiener, 'The Regulation of Technology' (n 122) 483.

[134] These concepts operate on a spectrum. On this, see further Tony Prosser, 'Self-Regulation, Co-Regulation and the Audio-Visual Media Services Directive' (2008) 31 Journal of Consumer Policy 99, 99.

[135] Julia Black, 'Decentring Regulation: Understanding the Role of Regulation and Self-Regulation in a "Post-Regulatory" World' (2001) 54 Current Legal Problems 103, 105.

secondary legislation crafted under the ordinary legislative procedure.[136] This echoes the fact that law is traditionally state- or EU-centred, unified, hierarchical and unpinned by the rule of law.[137] Regulation should be simple, constant and predictable, and these objectives are conventionally fulfilled through homogeneously applying legislation.

As a consequence, EU law 'has tended to stand in awe of [the] traditional conception of law'.[138] This is rooted in the fact that 'not only are those attributes of a traditional conception of law consistent with the ever closer integration motif, but they speak too of power and uncompromising authority, in real as well as symbolic terms, and never is power and authority more desired than when it is contested, as in the case of the EU'.[139] In light of the above, top-down legislation could be considered the natural and evident method of blockchain regulation. Secondary legislation creates uniformity across the European Union in preventing a fragmentation of national rules and procedures that may limit market access, elements that are particularly burdensome for smaller players.[140] There are considerable disadvantages to this approach, however.

First, a period of rapid technological transmutation is characterized by pronounced information asymmetries. It is true that information gathering always plagues any law-maker.[141] Fact selection in regulatory debates can be tricky and embed agency capture and minoritarian bias (although new data solutions can help remedy some of these problems).[142] This issue is nonetheless particularly salient in relation to DLT, as not only are information and expertise sparse but there is also staggering uncertainty in relation to future developments. The resulting lack of available information may lead to troublesome fact-selection and advice and the adoption of ill-suited legislative terminology.

Second, the rules adopted may not be enforceable or be very onerous to enforce, especially when they are based on a misunderstanding of the technology and its limitations. Courts called upon to interpret the definition of blockchain as an 'immutable ledger of truth' will not face an easy task. Such legislation reinforces an existing lack of legal certainty. Third, specific legislation could simply add more

---

[136] Article 294 TFEU.

[137] Michael Wilkinson, 'Three Conceptions of Law: Towards A Jurisprudence of Democratic Experimentalism' (2010) Wisconsin Law Review 673, 673–74.

[138] Joanne Scott and David Trubek, 'Mind the Gap: Law and New Approaches to Governance in the European Union' (2002) 8 European Law Journal 1, 9.

[139] ibid. 10.

[140] For a similar argument in relation to online platforms, see European Commission Staff Working Document, 'A Single Market Strategy for Europe: Analysis and Evidence', SWD (2015) 202 final, 6.

[141] Stephen Breyer, *Regulation and its Reforms* (Harvard University Press 1984) 109–18.

[142] See further Mark Fenwick, Wulf Kaal and Erik Vermeulen, 'Regulation Tomorrow: What Happens when Technology is Faster than the Law?' (2016) University of St Thomas (Minnesota) Legal Studies Research Paper No. 16–23 <https://papers.ssrn.com/sol3/papers.cfm?abstract_id=2834531> accessed 10 April 2018.

regulatory constraints to an already complex framework, and maybe excessive compliance burdens for the concerned actors. Fourth, command-and-control legislation is often rigid and lacks the required flexibility to enable law to adapt to change. In 1981 Richard Stewart warned that 'existing command-and-control regulatory tools must be modified or replaced in order to reduce adverse impacts on market innovation and to provide incentives for social innovation'.[143] That lesson is still valid today. Although we cannot be sure what the eventual impact of DLT will be, we do know that the blockchains of the future cannot be identical to those of the present.

With regard to a constantly evolving technology, flexible frameworks are called for. While top-down legislation may be our go-to option we must be wary of idealizing it as always constituting the most advantageous mode of economic regulation. Although it is tempting to suggest that it is the most democratic and legitimate mode of regulation, reality casts doubt on such simplistic statements, particularly in the context of a supranational law-making process shaped by opaque trilogues.[144] Top-down regulation furthermore tends to rely on a few 'well-educated, specially trained, and publically appointed professionals', leaving little room for multi-stakeholder deliberation and compromise.[145] This is even more acute given that DLT expertise remains scarce and, due to distributed ledger's cryptoeconomic set-up, many are personally invested in the success of one project or another. To counterbalance this a larger stakeholder pool is needed. Equally, while we presume that all regulation is designed to enhance the public good, we have long known that regulation can also be designed to enhance the interests of lobbyist or other entrenched stakes.[146]

The above observations accordingly question whether top-down legislation will really enable regulators to moderate between the dilemma of not stifling innovation, on the one hand, and not leaving innovative practices unregulated, on the other.[147] In light of the identified issues, I move on to consider alternative options.

B. *Self-Regulation*

Chapter 3 has highlighted that blockchains are (self-)regulating entities, as they determine the rules of engagement in relation to the network and define possible

---

[143] Richard Stewart, 'Regulation, Innovation, and Administrative Law: A Conceptual Framework' (1981) 69 California Law Review 1256, 1261.

[144] Deirdre Curtin and Päivi Leino, 'In Search of Transparency for EU Law-Making: Trilogues on the Cusp of Dawn' (2017) 54 Common Market Law Review 1673.

[145] Orly Lobel, 'The Renewal Deal: The Fall of Regulation and the Rise of Governance in Contemporary Legal Thought' (2004) 89 Minnesota Law Review 342, 371.

[146] George Stigler, 'The Theory of Economic Regulation' (1971) 2 Bell Journal of Economics and Management 1, 3; Fred McChesney, 'Rent Extraction and Rent Creation in the Economic Theory of Regulation' (1987) 16 Journal of Legal Science 1.

[147] Sofia Ranchordás, 'Does Sharing Mean Caring? Regulating Innovation in the Sharing Economy' (2015) 16 Minnesota Journal of Law, Science & Technology 413.

behaviour. These characteristics call for an examination of whether self-regulation may be an appropriate regulatory technique for distributed ledgers.

In the EU context, self-regulation has been defined as 'the possibility for economic operators, the social partners, non-governmental organisations or associations to adopt amongst themselves and for themselves common guidelines at European level (particularly codes of practice or sectoral agreements)'.[148] Julia Black describes self-regulation as 'the situation of a group of persons or bodies, acting together, performing a regulatory function in respect of themselves and others who accept their authority'.[149] This is distinguished from 'individualised regulation', which is 'regulation which is tailored to the individual firm'.[150] Self-regulation hence refers to a situation in which regulation is devised through the collaboration of private actors with no or little involvement from the state.

Self-regulation can assume various forms. It can be mandated by public authorities or adopted voluntarily. The incentives for self-regulation vary, as it can echo an attempt to operate under set internal standards, align industry behaviour or counter threats of statutory intervention by public authorities. Self-regulation has been relied on in complex sectors such as nuclear energy and finance, confirming its suitability in contexts of intricacy.[151] It has also found application in the platform economy, where platforms have become the de facto 'rule-makers'.[152] Some consider that technological change alleviates the need for top-down legislation, 'with these recent innovations likely doing a much better job of serving consumer needs'.[153] For example, digital platforms have been compared to governments, because, 'like governments, each platform is in the business of developing policies which enable social and economic activity'.[154] Due to internal data pools, actors in the data economy have a better empirical understanding of their business model and its implications than regulators, and software is an efficient means of enforcement.[155]

Code creates binding rules that may be known to all and nudge individuals into adopting a certain behaviour. Uber has been said to be engaged 'in an extraordinary behind-the-scenes experiment in behavioral science to manipulate [its drivers] in the

---

[148] European Commission, Interinstitutional Agreement on Better Law-Making [2003] OJ C 321/01, para 22.

[149] Julia Black, 'Constitutionalising Self-Regulation' (1996) 59 Modern Law Review 24, 27.

[150] ibid. 27.

[151] Neil Gunningham and Joseph Rees, 'Industry Self-Regulation: An Institutional Perspective' (1997) 19 Law & Policy 363; Elizabeth Howlett et al., 'The Role of Self-Regulation, Future Orientation and Financial Knowledge in Long-Term Financial Decisions' (2008) 42 Journal of Consumer Affairs 223.

[152] Marta Cantero Gomito, 'Regulation.com. Self-Regulation and Contract Governance in the Platform Economy: A Research Agenda' (2017) 9 European Journal of Legal Studies 53.

[153] Christopher Koopman et al., 'The Sharing Economy and Consumer Protection Regulation: The Case for Policy Change' (2014) 1 <www.mercatus.org/publication/sharing-economy-and-consumer-protection-regulation-case-policy-change> accessed 28 March 2018.

[154] ibid.

[155] See further Chapter 3.

service of its corporate growth', most notably through psychological inducements to influence when, where and how they work.[156] This highlights that, under a model of pure self-regulation, code regulates behaviour without external restrictions designed to protect public policy goals.

The European Commission has advocated self-regulation in relation to the Digital Single Market. Concerning data porting, it encourages self-regulatory measures that do not create a new right of porting but, rather, rely 'on self-regulation for transparency on the technical and operational conditions relating to portability'.[157] The option has also been suggested for other objectives. The proposed Regulation on the free flow of non-personal data foresees that the Commission shall 'encourage and facilitate the development of self-regulatory codes of conduct at Union level, in order to define guidelines on best practices'.[158] Much hope is accordingly placed in self-regulation as an efficient means of guiding technological change. Standardization in particular will likely replace law in many instances in future years.

Self-regulation has, unsurprisingly, attracted wide support from insiders of the data economy. Nick Grossman, a general manager at the venture capital firm Union Square Ventures, advocates a 'Regulation 2.0' model that juxtaposes the 'bureaucracy, friction and permission' of current regulatory paradigms with the 'transparency, accountability and innovation' of Regulation 2.0.[159] He maintains that access restrictions such as licences are expensive and burdensome and should be replaced with *ex post* evaluations through the evaluation of 'large volumes of real-time data to hold actors accountable'.[160] This suggests that the data economy calls into question existing regulatory barriers to market entry but, equally, that they open new forms of inspection and enforcement in relation to blockchains.

A number of self-regulatory projects have already been initiated in relation to DLT, including in South Korea.[161] Another initiative emanates from the United States. Here, Gemini, a licensed cryptoasset exchange and custodian based in New York, has recently proposed a self-regulatory organization for the US virtual currency

---

[156] Noam Scheiber, 'How Uber Uses Psychological Tricks to Push Its Drivers' Buttons' *New York Times* (2 April 2017) <www.nytimes.com/interactive/2017/04/02/technology/uber-drivers-psycho logical-tricks.html?_r=0> accessed 28 March 2018.

[157] European Commission, 'Proposal for a Regulation of the European Parliament and of the Council on a framework for the free flow of non-personal data in the European Union' COM (2017) 495 final, 8.

[158] Article 6 (1) European Commission, 'Proposal for a Regulation of the European Parliament and of the Council on a framework for the free flow of non-personal data in the European Union' COM (2017) 495 final.

[159] Nick Grossmann, 'White Paper: Regulation, the Internet Way' (*Data Smart*, 8 April 2015) <https://datasmart.ash.harvard.edu/news/article/white-paper-regulation-the-internet-way-660> accessed 3 April 2018.

[160] ibid.

[161] Helen Partz, 'Korean Blockchain Association Reveals Self-Regulatory Rules for 14 Member Exchanges' (*Cointelegraph*, 17 April 2018) <https://cointelegraph.com/news/korean-block chain-association-reveals-self-regulatory-rules-for-14-member-exchanges> accessed 3 May 2018.

industry.[162] The chairman of the Commodity Futures Trading Commission applauded this initiative, portraying it as 'energetic leadership and [a] thoughtful approach' that would 'add the most integrity to these markets'.[163] Indeed, at an early stage of the technology's development such processes can be helpful, as they create awareness around regulation, disincentivize 'lawless' behaviour and generate information as to where regulation is needed most.

In the long run, however, self-regulation is 'unlikely to sufficiently resolve the market failures that will ultimately allow illicit and fraudulent uses of decentralized technologies to occur'.[164] Blockchains' transformation into self-regulating oligopolies acting outside any oversight mechanisms should not be encouraged. Isolated self-regulation not only lacks transparency but also fails to account for the interests of external actors. It also risks being nothing but pleasant language, put to the side when problems actually arise.[165] Further, when self-regulation applies there is a need for counterbalances that safeguard public interests. In a climate of 'pressures for deregulation, the regulatory authorities must ensure that the pendulum does not swing too far in favour of innovation, at the expense of compliance'.[166]

I must at this stage return to the theme of information asymmetries. As blockchain expertise is scarce, individual actors simply do not have 'the knowledge required to solve complex, diverse, and dynamic problems, and no single actor has the overview necessary to employ all the instruments needed to make regulation effective'.[167] From the perspective of EU law, it must be stressed, moreover, that there is a risk that self-regulation breaches competition law.[168] The absence of uniform regulatory standards under self-regulatory models can further result in case-by-case litigation to

---

[162] Cameron Winklevoss, 'A Proposal for a Self-Regulatory Organization for the U.S. Virtual Currency Industry' (*Gemini*, 13 March 2018) <https://gemini.com/blog/a-proposal-for-a-self-regulatory-organization-for-the-u-s-virtual-currency-industry/> accessed 28 March 2018.

[163] US Commodity Futures Trading Commission, 'Statement of CFTC Commissioner Brian Quintenz on a Proposal by Cameron and Tyler Winklevoss for a Virtual Commodity SRO' (13 March 2018) <www.cftc.gov/PressRoom/SpeechesTestimony/quintenzstatement031318> accessed 3 April 2018.

[164] Carla Reyes, 'Moving Beyond Bitcoin to an Endogenous Theory of Decentralized Ledger Technology Regulation: An Initial Proposal' (2016) 61 Villanova Law Review 191, 194 (hereafter Reyes, 'Moving Beyond Bitcoin').

[165] Despite its code of conduct prohibiting any form of sexual contact between riders and drivers, Uber has been accused of not reporting sexual assault committed by one of its drivers while driving for the platform, allowing the driver to strike again thereafter. See Press Association, 'Uber Failing to Report Sex Attacks by Drivers, Says Met Police' *The Guardian* (13 August 2017) <www.theguardian.com/technology/2017/aug/13/uber-failing-to-report-sex-attacks-by-drivers-says-met-police> accessed 28 March 2018.

[166] Holly Powley and Keith Stanton, 'The Future of Banking Regulation' (*University of Bristol Law School Blog*, 24 April 2017) <https://legalresearch.blogs.bris.ac.uk/2017/04/the-future-of-banking-regulation/> accessed 13 March 2018.

[167] Julia Black, 'Decentring Regulation: Understanding the Role of Regulation and Self-Regulation in a "Post-Regulatory" World' (2001) 54 Current Legal Problems 103, 107.

[168] Imelda Maher, 'Competition Law and Transnational Private Regulatory Regimes: Marking the Cartel Boundary' (2011) 38 Journal of Law and Society 119. For this to be the case there would

determine applicable rules, which is undesirable for both industry and the regulator.[169] A further concern regarding self-regulation by industry incumbents is that they may regulate in a manner that makes market entry difficult for future competitors. There is a risk that they exercise such tasks to maximize power vis-à-vis other market participants and impose regulatory burdens on smaller competitors.[170]

Even critics of regulation argue that saying that 'a disembodied free market, one which does not rest upon government force, will function effectively is certainly a mistake of epic proportions, is not an anarchist myth'.[171] Pure forms of self-regulation without public oversight lack incentives to protect the rights and interests of others, including fundamental rights, as they are centred around self-interested cost minimization and the avoidance of potential liability.[172] While there are arguments in favour of alternative regulatory solutions adapted to the digital economy, pure forms of self-regulation are undesirable. I thus continue my quest for an appropriate regulatory paradigm by looking towards co-regulation, which unites the flexibility of self-regulatory approaches with the public policy objectives of command-and-control legislation.

C. *Polycentric Co-Regulation*

Jonathan Wiener considers that there is a need to stimulate policy entrepreneurs who are willing to 'develop and test new forms and approaches to regulation for greater effectiveness, less cost, less caustic side-effects, and other desirable attributes'.[173] The starting point of this pursuit must be the recognition that there is no single best regulatory technique but, rather, that there are 'different regulatory designs for different problems, societies, and institutional settings.[174]

New governance options recognize this. Gráinne de Búrca has shown that two different kinds of impetus mandate reliance on new governance methods: (i) strategic uncertainty, defined as complex policy problems that have not 'shown themselves to be readily amendable to resolution whether through hierarchy,

---

need to be coordination between different would-be competitor platforms that limits competition between them.

[169] Edward Glaeser and Andrei Shleifer, 'The Rise of the Regulatory State' (2003) 41 Journal of Economic Literature 401, 402–03.

[170] Luca Belli, Pedro Augusto Francisco and Nicolo Zingales, 'Law of the Land or Law of the Platform? Beware of the Privatisation of Regulation and Police' in Luca Belli and Nicolo Zingales (eds), *Platform Regulations: How Platforms Are Regulated and How They Regulate Us* (FGV Direito Rio 2017) 46 (hereafter Belli et al., 'Platform Regulations').

[171] Richard Epstein, 'Can Technological Innovation Survive Government Regulation?' (2013) 36 Harvard Journal of Law and Public Policy 87, 88.

[172] Belli et al., 'Platform Regulations' (n 170) 46, 60.

[173] Wiener, 'The Regulation of Technology' (n 122) 483, 495.

[174] ibid. 495.

market or otherwise'; and (ii) interdependence between various regulatory regimes.[175] We can readily pinpoint these elements in relation to blockchains. There is strategic uncertainty, as distributed ledgers are likely to give rise to complex policy problems. There also is interdependence between multiple regulatory regimes, considering that a blockchain is a general-purpose database that can be used for a wide variety of purposes.

It has, equally, been suggested that 'the intensity with which a given problem presents may be likely to affect the vitality and success of an experimentalist-governance solution'.[176] While chronic problems may be best addressed by command-and-control legislation, new governance methods are better suited for acute and novel issues that are subject to rapid change. Indeed, 'the fast-paced, iterative world of disruption does not mesh easily with the deliberative, slow-moving process of traditional rulemaking'.[177]

In this section I formulate a broad framework that may enable the European Union to become a policy entrepreneur in contexts of technological change burdened with uncertainty. I will take the tested concept of co-regulation and adapt it to this specific context by suggesting that processes leading up to norm definition must be polycentric in nature and that the benefits of code ought to be leveraged at the law-making, implementation and enforcement stages. I now turn to introduce the various building blocks of that concept.

1. Co-Regulation

In the EU context, co-regulation has been defined as a 'mechanism whereby an [EU] legislative act entrusts the attainment of the objectives defined by the legislative authority to parties which are recognized in the field (such as economic operators, the social partners, non-governmental organizations, or associations)'.[178] Co-regulation denotes various regulatory techniques whereby 'the regulatory regime is made up of a complex interaction of general legislation and a self-regulatory body'.[179] This interplay between the regulator and the regulated explains why it has also been referred to as 'regulated self-regulation'.[180] The collaborative process

---

[175] Gráinne de Búrca, 'New Governance and Experimentalism: An Introduction' (2010) Wisconsin Law Review 227, 232.
[176] ibid. 233.
[177] Alice Armitage, Andrew Cordova and Rebecca Siegel, 'Design-Thinking: The Answer to the Impasse Between Innovation and Regulation' (2017) UC Hastings Research Paper No. 250, 15 <https://papers.ssrn.com/sol3/papers.cfm?abstract_id=3024176> accessed 10 April 2018.
[178] European Commission, 'Interinstitutional Agreement on Better Law-Making' [2003] OJ C 321/01, para 18.
[179] Christopher Marsden, *Internet Co-Regulation* (Cambridge University Press 2011) 46.
[180] Wolfgang Schulz and Thorsten Held, *Regulated Self-Regulation as a Form of Modern Government: An Analysis of Case Studies from Media and Telecommunications Law* (John Libbey Publishing 2004) (hereafter Schulz and Held, 'Regulated Self-Regulation').

inherent to co-regulation acknowledges the complex interaction between the state, the market and technology and reflects the spirit of new governance approaches that emphasize the benefits of involving a large pool of stakeholders in the articulation, execution and oversight of regulation.[181] Under a co-regulatory model, public authorities voluntarily involve the private sector in the creation, implementation and enforcement of norms. I present a refined vision of co-regulation that involves a broad pool of stakeholders (it is polycentric) and adapted to the particularities of the technology that is regulated (it relies on code).

Under a model of co-regulation, the European Union defines legislative standards that are subsequently implemented by the private sector. It hence reflects new governance features.[182] These include (i) participation and power sharing, as power is not monopolized but shared; (ii) a preference for diversity and decentralization, as the impossibility of uniform regulation is acknowledged; and (iii) deliberation among multiple stakeholders takes place, as the European Union doesn't regulate in isolation. The resulting rules would, moreover, be characterized by (iv) flexibility and revisability, as they are constantly evaluated and can be swiftly adapted; and (v) experimentation and knowledge creation, as the various concrete applications of the general standards will reveal manifold indicators as to the suitability of a given standard.[183]

Co-regulation is no stranger to EU law. Although the Union is seldom seen to overtly embrace co-regulatory solutions, Charles Sabel and Jonathan Zeitlin have shown that it often relies on framework goals that lower units are given freedom to achieve.[184] Co-regulation has already been used regarding the Internet.[185] The E-Commerce Directive has been portrayed as a co-regulatory legal framework as it entrusts the private sector with the enforcement of norms on the Internet.[186] Co-regulation is a continuous process that embraces experimental learning and uncertainty. It is naturally designed to adapt over time, as the defined standards are constantly evaluated and reviewed.[187]

Co-regulation further involves constant dialogue, assessment and review, which create informational and adaptability advantages. It is paramount to stress that co-regulation does not amount to deregulation. Public authorities are involved at all

---

[181] Raymond Brescia, 'Regulating the Sharing Economy: New and Old Insights into an Oversight Regime for the Peer-to-Peer Economy' (2016) 95 Nebraska Law Review 87, 134.

[182] For an exposé, see Orly Lobel, 'The Renewal Deal: The Fall of Regulation and the Rise of Governance in Contemporary Legal Thought' (2004) 89 Minnesota Law Review 342.

[183] These characteristics were identified fifteen years ago by Scott and Trubek with respect to new governance. Joanne Scott and David Trubek, 'Mind the Gap: Law and New Approaches to Governance in the European Union' (2002) 8 European Law Journal 1, 4–6.

[184] Charles Sabel and Jonathan Zeitlin, 'Learning from Difference: The New Architecture of Experimentalist Governance in the EU' (2008) 14 European Law Journal 271, 273.

[185] Eighth CoP plenary meeting <https://ec.europa.eu/digital-single-market/en/news/eighth-cop-plenary-meeting> accessed 14 March 2018.

[186] <https://papers.ssrn.com/sol3/papers.cfm?abstract_id=1282826> 5.

[187] Schulz and Held, 'Regulated Self-Regulation' (n 180).

stages of the process, from the definition of the legislative framework to the complex review mechanisms. The threat of command-and-control legislation constantly looms in the background, moreover, as an incentivizing mechanism for collaboration and compliance or an alternative when co-regulation proves unsuccessful.[188] While co-regulation has elements of non-state law it is backed by robust public involvement through the definition of the corresponding legislative framework and review processes.[189] It is in this respect worth noting that the General Court held in *UEAPME* that co-regulation is legitimate only when stakeholders' 'representativeness' is given.[190]

As a middle way between self-regulation and command-and-control regulation, co-regulation presents a number of advantages. First, and unlike self-regulation, it is designed specifically to *safeguard public policy objectives*. Through the involvement of public authorities, a variety of normative considerations inform the regulatory process, making sure that public policy objectives aren't sidelined by private self-interest. Co-regulation reflects the fact that the involvement of private actors in regulatory processes must be counterbalanced by public oversight. Experience has indeed shown that, when the private sector is granted too much regulatory authority, the protection of individual rights suffers.[191]

Second, the co-regulatory solution, involving diverse stakeholders (as advocated just below), can be a means of managing *information asymmetry* in contexts of rapid technological development. As Maria Weimer has argued, the 'uncertainty and ignorance often surrounding new technologies' opens up space for 'politicization and the exercise of wide regulatory discretion'.[192] Max Weber alerted us that real market participants 'have a far greater rational knowledge of the market and interest [in the] situation than the legislators and enforcement officers whose interest is only ideal'.[193] In a context of co-regulation, information gathering is easier because some of the involved actors have first-hand information of ongoing developments.[194] Involving multiple stakeholders can ensure that regulation is 'reflexive': understood by the autonomous social systems it regulates.[195]

Third, co-regulation is inherently *flexible*. Flexibility is necessary to keep up with the pace of change. It also allows for regulatory experimentalism, which is

---

[188] ibid. 63.
[189] Hanneke van Schooten and Jonathan Verschuuren, *International Governance and Law: State Regulation and Non-State Law* (Edward Elgar 2008), 2.
[190] Case T-135/96, *UEAPME v Council* [1998] EU:T:1998:128.
[191] Belli et al., 'Platform Regulations' (n 170) 41.
[192] Maria Weimer, 'The Origins of "Risk" as an Idea and the Future of Risk Regulation' (2017) 8 European Journal of Risk Regulation 10, 16.
[193] Max Rheinstein (ed and tr), *Max Weber, On Law in Economy and Society* (Harvard University Press 1954) 39.
[194] Schulz and Held, 'Regulated Self-Regulation' (n 180) 15.
[195] Günther Teubner, 'Justification: Concepts, Aspects, Limits, Solutions', in Robert Baldwin et al., *A Reader on Regulation* (Oxford University Press 1998); Günther Teubner, *Law as an Autopoetic System* (Oxford University Press 1993).

particularly valuable in this fast-changing and diverse industry.[196] Co-regulation, with its continued assessments and reports, can identify best practices and stimulate mutual learning. The need for adaptive legal frameworks in relation to blockchain is evident. The European Union has also adopted this strategy in relation to other aspects of the data-driven economy. To further the free movement of non-personal data across member states, the Commission advocates a principle-based approach to ensure 'that the framework is flexible so that it can take into account the evolving needs of users, providers and national authorities'.[197] In relation to automated driving, the Union has emphasized the need for a legal framework that offers 'sufficient flexibility to accommodate innovation'.[198] In line with Michel Callon's thinking that regulation should not be seen as a final event but, rather, as an open-ended process, co-regulation explicitly acknowledges that no actor has all the answers and that regulatory principles need to be evaluated and revised when necessary.[199]

Fourth, co-regulation allows for *early intervention*. Technology is malleable in its early stages of development.[200] It is crucial for multi-stakeholder debates to materialize at this stage, as over time 'the product or process reaches a point of stabilization or closure'.[201] Early dialogue between regulators and the regulated has benefits for all parties. It allows regulators to better understand the technology and make sure that it develops in a manner compatible with public policy objectives. In a context of self-regulation there is little room for such deliberation, as the state is largely absent, whereas a command-and-control framework can be adopted only when the technology has matured and concepts and terminology are more settled. Co-regulation can explicitly start the regulatory process early on as an open-ended initiative.

Finally, co-regulation allows for the *reconciliation of the stark centralizing and decentralizing forces* that characterize blockchain technology. Blockchains are at once local (from the perspective of nodes) and global (if we consider the entire network). They can be extremely centralized on the infrastructure level while extremely centralized at the governance level.[202] Just as the blockchains of the future will probably combine the benefits of centralization and decentralization, regulators must do the same. Carla Reyes has underlined that '[r]egulation that

---

[196] Sofia Ranchordás, 'Innovation Experimentalism in the Age of the Sharing Economy' (2015) 19 Lewis & Clark Law Review 871.

[197] Recital 7 of European Commission, 'Proposal for a Regulation of the European Parliament and of the Council on a framework for the free flow of non-personal data in the European Union' COM (2017) 495 final (emphasis added).

[198] Declaration of Amsterdam, 'Cooperation in the Field of Connected and Automated Driving' (14 April 2016), point II.a.

[199] Michel Callon, Pierre Lasoumes and Yannick Bathe, *Acting in an Uncertain World: Essay on Technical Democracy (Inside Technology)* (MIT Press 2011).

[200] Wiebe Bijker, *Of Bicycles, Bakelites, and Bulbs: Toward a Theory of Sociotechnical Change* (MIT Press 1995).

[201] Moses, 'Regulating the Face of Sociotechnical Change' (n 21) 581.

[202] See Chapter 7.

focuses on the centralized actors in a decentralized ecosystem will simply not be able to keep pace'.[203] Co-regulation captures the fact that behaviour is governed by a web of legal, social, technical and economic standards. It unites these various forces instead of leaving them to operate in isolation.

Although co-regulation presents numerous advantages compared to self-regulation and command-and-control regulation, the technique can be improved further when it rests on a polycentric decision-making process and relies on the regulatory advantages of code.

2. Polycentricity

Through co-regulation we can move away from a homogeneous top-down model towards a decentralized, reflexive, collaborative and cooperative framework that is process-orientated and shaped by standards. In order to truly reap the benefits of such a collaborative approach, however, a larger variety of stakeholders than just the state and firms should be involved at the law-making and evaluation stages. As life moves from 'walls' to 'webs', law should follow.[204] Co-regulation generates pluralism, as binding rules emerge from the interaction of multiple actors outside the hierarchical state structure.[205] In order for this process to be genuinely inclusive, it should unite all relevant stakeholders, a decentralized setting ultimately mirroring the nature of blockchains themselves.

Polycentricity is inherent to new governance models as, unlike traditional conceptions of law that rely on a unitary source of authority, such approaches are predicated upon a dispersal and fragmentation of authority, resting on fluid systems of power sharing.[206] Polycentric decision-making allows for the concentration of knowledge, which is naturally dispersed across society.[207] It is, furthermore, in line with the European Union's 2015 Better Regulation Agenda, which promotes evidence-based regulation, including broader consultations and civic engagement.[208] Polycentricity enables a reflexive, flexible cooperative and incremental law-making

---

[203] Reyes, 'Moving Beyond Bitcoin' (n 164) 221.

[204] This metaphor originates in Thomas Friedman, *The Lexus and the Olive Tree: Understanding Globalization* (Farrar, Straus and Giroux 1999) 39–58.

[205] Poul Kjaer, 'The Metamorphosis of the Functional Synthesis: A Continental European Perspective on Governance, Law, and the Political in the Transnational Space' (2010) Wisconsin Law Review 489, 489 ('States remain a central form of ordering but only one among several.').

[206] Joanne Scott and David Trubek, 'Mind the Gap: Law and New Approaches to Governance in the European Union' (2002) 8 European Law Journal 1, 8.

[207] Cass Sunstein, *Infotopia: How Many Minds Produce Knowledge* (Oxford University Press 2006); Henrik Serup Christensen et al., 'Does Crowdsourcing Legislation Increase Political Legitimacy? The Case of Avoin Ministeriö in Finland' (2015) 7 Policy and Internet 25.

[208] Communication from the Commission to the European Parliament, the Council, the European Economic and Social Committee and the Committee of the Regions, 'Better Regulation for Better Results – An EU Agenda', COM (2015) 215.

process that unites public and private actors, improving the likelihood of the developed principles being both dynamic and adaptable.

Further, polycentric co-regulation generates feedback effects and enhances information for regulators, as it comes from a wide variety of sources. The European Commission is currently establishing draft ethics guidelines for AI and considers that these should be defined in a polycentric effort involving many stakeholders. It has argued that, given the scale of the challenges associated with AI, 'the full mobilisation of a diverse set of participants, including businesses, consumer organisations, trade unions, and other representatives of civil society bodies, is essential'.[209] The same must be true in relation to blockchains.

Regulation operates in an ecological system made up of a 'larger interconnected web of nodes and strands into which regulation seeks to introduce change'.[210] Limiting the process to regulators and the regulated provides an incomplete picture of this web. In relation to the Internet, Ian Brown and Christopher Marsden note that '[t]he public interest is not always well represented by the government or corporate interest, especially in a dynamic and generation dividing a set of technologies'.[211] While the benefits of involving many stakeholders are undisputed, the methods of doing so are not. Representatives of the private blockchain sector already often engage in formal and informal discussions with regulators. This, in fact, appears to generate greater mutual understanding. To illustrate, Vitalik Buterin has admitted that '[g]rowing up libertarian and then going out into the world and noticing that actual regulators were nicer to me than many "cypherpunks" was very disorienting'.[212]

In a co-regulatory process, the number of intervening actors can be radically expanded, as technology facilitates stakeholder involvement in ad hoc consultations.[213] As such, co-regulation can be more consistent with democratic, participatory and representative ideals, especially when it involves many stakeholders. The process recognizes pluralism and allows for decentralization and experimentation. The European Union has long been plagued by accusations of democratic deficit and lack of legitimacy.[214] Alternative methods of governance can be seen to

[209] European Commission, 'Communication Artificial Intelligence for Europe' (2018) <https://ec.europa.eu/digital-single-market/en/news/communication-artificial-intelligence-europe> accessed 3 May 2018.

[210] Wiener, 'The Regulation of Technology' (n 122) 495.

[211] Ian Brown and Christopher Marsden, *Regulating Code* (MIT Press 2013) xvi (hereafter Brown and Marsden, 'Regulating Code').

[212] Vitalik Buterin [VitalikButerin] (14 February 2018) 'Growing up libertarian and then going out into the world and noticing that actual regulators were nicer to me than many "cypherpunks" was very disorienting.' [Tweet] <https://twitter.com/vitalikbuterin/status/963939788645478400?lang=en> accessed 3 April 2018.

[213] Article 11(4) TEU.

[214] Andreas Follesdal and Simon Hix, 'Why is there a Democratic Deficit in the EU? A Reply to Moravcsik' (2006) 44 Journal of Common Market Studies 533.

stimulate democratic deliberation in the Union.[215] In order for this to be the case, transparency as to what co-regulation is and where it is to be applied are necessary.[216] Indeed, while the Union never regulates in isolation and is influenced by industry views even outside co-regulatory contexts, the latter technique can make such engagement explicit and add transparency.

When co-regulation is applied to technological innovation, the benefits of technology should be used not just to enhance deliberation but also at the enforcement stage.

3. Coupling Co-Regulation with Technology

A model of polycentric co-regulation can be devised most efficiently when the benefits of code are harnessed at the law-making, implementation and enforcement stages.

Technological innovation can stimulate polycentric participation in the law-making phase. There are often clear advantages for actors to engage in dialogue, as regulation is unavoidable and communication channels enable them to have a voice in their determination. For other stakeholders, the incentives for engaging in a polycentric co-regulatory process may be less obvious. Software allows them to be involved more easily, however, as the same technological shift that underlies the current wave of technological development can facilitate polycentric deliberation. The reliance on new digital avenues for participation and deliberation could increase networked policy-making and widen alternative spaces and forms of policy dialogues. This would fit initiatives such as 'Lighten the Load', an online feedback form that allows citizens to express views on EU regulation at any time and on any topic.[217] The European Union is already using online consultations to gather a wide sample of views in many areas. Technology can facilitate polycentricity, since it 'may provide a new option for influencing specific laws' and can help 'large, disorganised groups poorly equipped to take advantage of existing means of political influence'.[218]

It is certainly true that online participation is not free from problems, as it creates a cacophony of voices and raises difficult questions of legitimacy and

---

[215] See further William Simon and Charles Sabel, 'Epilogue: Accountability without Sovereignty' in Gráinne de Búrca and Joanne Scott (eds), *Law and New Governance in the EU and the US* (Hart Publishing 2006).

[216] Paul Verbruggen, 'Does Co-Regulation Strengthen EU Legitimacy?' (2009) 15 European Law Journal 425, 426.

[217] <https://ec.europa.eu/info/law/better-regulation/lighten-load/suggestions/add> accessed 3 April 2018. For a critical assessment, see Francesco Sarpi, 'Better for Whom?' (2015) 3 European Journal of Risk Regulation 372, 374.

[218] Tim Wu, 'When Code Isn't Law' (2003) 89 Virginia Law Review 103, 106.

self-selection.[219] More generally, there remain 'significant questions as to the effect-iveness, accountability, and legitimacy of civil society groups in representing the public interest'.[220] Yet evidence mounts that digital tools are having a positive impact overall on civic engagement.[221] Online consultation enables speedy and broad consultation and crowdsourcing in addition to e-petitions, which are considered to improve dialogue between civil society and law-makers.[222] More widely, techno-logical innovation is impacting on democratic processes through online discussion forums, online petition sites that are now also hosted by parliaments across the European Union, and social media.[223] Ultimately, more experimentation with the electronic involvement of stakeholders in rule-making is required to determine its successes and shortcomings.[224]

Furthermore, technology can facilitate the enforcement of regulatory con-straints.[225] In 1998 Joel Reidenberg foresaw that code would change not just the substance but also the form of law, as a traditional legislative approach would be less effective in achieving results than a technological approach, 'such as the promotion and development of flexible, customized systems'.[226] Lawrence Lessig agreed that, in cyberspace, regulation is different, as, when the regulator seeks to induce a certain behaviour, 'she need not threaten, or cajole, to inspire the change. She need only change the code – the software that defines the terms upon which the individual gains access to the system, or uses assets on the system.'[227]

Code is thus also an important innovation regarding the implementation of innovation. Carla Reyes has suggested that, in the United States, a concept similar to co-regulation – 'endogenous regulation' – should be applied in the blockchain

[219] Vili Lehdonvirta, 'Crowdsourcing for public policy and government' (*Oxford Internet Institute*, 27 August 2015) <www.oii.ox.ac.uk/blog/crowdsourcing-for-public-policy-and-government/> accessed 3 April 2018.

[220] Brown and Marsden, 'Regulating Code' (n 211) 3.

[221] Shelley Boulianne, 'Does Internet Use Affect Engagement? A Meta-Analysis of Research' (2009) 26(2) Political Communication 193, 205; Kevin Desouza and Aksay Bhagwatwar, 'Technology-enabled Participatory Platforms for Civic Engagement: The Case of U.S. Cities' (2014) 21(4) Journal of Urban Technology 25.

[222] Brian Loader and Dan Mercea, *Social Media and Democracy: Innovations in Participatory Politics* (Routledge 2012).

[223] Beth Simone Noveck, *Wiki Government: How Technology Can Make Government Better, Democracy Stronger and Citizens More Powerful* (Brookings Institutions 2010); Camilo Cris-tancho and Jose Sabucedo, 'Mobilization through Online Social Networks: The Political Protest of the Indignados in Spain' (2014) 17(6) Information, Communication & Society 750; Caroline Lee, *Do-It-Yourself Democracy: The Rise of Public Engagement* (Oxford University Press 2015).

[224] Stuart Minor Benjamin, 'Evaluating E-Rulemaking: Public Participation and Political Insti-tutions' (*Duke Law Journal*, 2006) <https://scholarship.law.duke.edu/dlj/vol55/iss5/1/> accessed 3 May 2018.

[225] See further Chapter 3.

[226] Joel Reidenberg, 'Lex Informatica: The Formulation of Information Policy Rules Through Technology' (1998) 76 Texas Law Review 3, 552, 556.

[227] Lawrence Lessig, 'The Zones of Cyberspace' (1996) 48 Stanford Law Review 1403, 1408.

context. Under a model of endogenous co-regulation, regulators not only enact legislation but also implement it through code, via an iterative and cooperative collaboration with 'core developers and with consensus from the network, so that regulation is endogenously incorporated into the decentralized ledger technology and the applications running on top of the technology'.[228] As a result of such a process, compliance is built into the code, and users have no choice but to be law-observing. When law is implemented through code, compliance is in most cases assured, especially when the technology used is tamper-proof and enables self-executing code. When such methods are used, the caveats identified in Chapter 3 must be observed, however.

Furthermore, software can be used at the law enforcement stage. Data harvesting and analysis provide real-time feedback concerning regulatory compliance, enabling regulators to (almost) react in real time.[229] In relation to digital platforms, some have suggested that law enforcement can verify compliance via data audits facilitated through application programming interfaces tailored to government auditing purposes.[230] Software thus undeniably offers new options also in respect of implementing and enforcing legal frameworks. The European Commission has recently stressed the importance of private parties providing data for regulatory control.[231] In order for this to be possible, however, governments need to secure more in-house technical expertise to manage, analyse and react to data.

4. The 28th Regime

As the adaptation of law to technological change seems inevitable, numerous options have been considered. To date, regulatory sandboxes are the most attractive avenue. Although such regimes offer numerous advantages, I also have identified related shortcomings above. In this context, it is worth pondering alternative options.

At present there is a risk of inaction or fragmentation between member states, accompanied by a race to the bottom (which can be stimulated by legislative marketing and sandboxes), creating conditions that disfavour sustainable innovation. Usually in such contexts the appropriate response would be the issuing of a supranational legal framework. This appears not to be an option, however, in a context in which the legal implications of blockchain innovation cannot yet be sufficiently assessed.

---

[228] Reyes, 'Moving Beyond Bitcoin' (n 164) 195.

[229] Wulf Kaal and Eric Vermeulen, 'How to Regulate Disruptive Innovation – From Facts to Data' (2017) 57 Jurimetrics 169.

[230] Arun Sundararajan, 'The Collaborative Economy: Socioeconomic, Regulatory and Policy Issues, Report carried out for the European Parliament's IMCO Committee' (2017) 24 <www.europarl .europa.eu/RegData/etudes/IDAN/2017/595360/IPOL_IDA(2017)595360_EN.pdf> accessed 3 April 2018.

[231] European Commission Staff Working Document, 'Impact Assessment', SWD(2017) 304 final Part 1/2, 2.

In order to ensure that there is no sitting idly by and missing the opportunity to devise the framework conditions facilitative of a sustainable distributed ledger ecosystem in the European Union, a so-called 28th regime, devised under conditions of polycentric co-regulation, emerges as an attractive option. In the words of Mario Monti, a 28th regime essentially denotes the creation of an 'EU framework alternative to but not replacing national rules'.[232] It creates an optional supranational regime that exists alongside national rules and gives rise to an option for parties to choose the former. Even though no specific comprehensive frameworks governing this asset class exist at member state level, they could be created at supranational level.

A 28th regime could be an attractive option when consensus emerges that legal reform may be appropriate in one domain but there is still no certainty as to what principles are suitable or there is a lack of political consensus to overhaul established principles of national or supranational law. It is thus an alternative that could be envisaged with respect to initial coin offerings of the treatment of the so-called utility tokens.[233]

For example, if there were to be agreement that a legal regime for the so-called utility tokens would be desirable, a 28th regime could be devised through a polycentric co-regulatory process. Through the involvement of code, the regime could be assessed more quickly and efficiently, potentially leading to the adoption of standard secondary legislation afterwards. A 28th regime is considered to expand options for those operating in a cross-border context in the Union. Whereas providers operating predominantly at national level can adhere to domestic law, those with an internal market focus can opt into the supranational regime.[234] In this specific context, it would also have the benefit of preventing fragmentation between member states and a race to the bottom.

Regulators are responsible for steering technological innovation to achieve desirable outcomes. A process of polycentric co-regulation that leverages the regulatory advantages of code could ensure that socio-institutional systems remain connected to techno-economic reality. Neither polycentric co-regulation nor the creation of a 28th regime would be a bulletproof solution. Such experimentation is not taking place in a laboratory, where risk and effects are limited, but in the real world. Nonetheless, it has the advantage of providing a frame for thinking how regulation can be adapted to technological change and how the latter can occur in a fashion that serves not just private but also public interests.

---

[232] Mario Monti, 'A New Strategy for the Single Market – At the Service of Europe's Economy and Society' http://ec.europa.eu/bepa/pdf/monti_report_final_10_05_2010_en.pdf (accessed 11 March 2018), 93.
[233] See further Chapter 1.
[234] ibid.

7

Blockchain Governance

> Magnificent for bitcoin, this worldwide adoption strengthens the credibility and value of the peer-to-peer network. A nonpolitical currency doesn't have a morality – it is simply a process for value transfer.[1]

This chapter challenges the view that blockchains have no morality. We have already observed that these systems are strongly regulated by code.[2] In addition to being heavily regulated they are also heavily politicized. I outline that, even though blockchains are frequently misunderstood as systems in which technology can replace humans and institutions and in which the strength of numbers and mathematics takes the place of human fragility, this is not actually the case. As everywhere, code is simply a human tool, used to express the objectives and beliefs of those who operate it. Bitcoin's unofficial motto is *vires in numeris,* Latin for 'strength in numbers'.[3] Yet those trusting the system in question don't, ultimately, trust numbers and mathematics but, rather, the humans behind them.

Dave Clark coined the phrase '[w]e reject kings, presidents and voting. We believe in rough consensus and running code' in 1992.[4] The motto expresses an intention to 'reject formal power'.[5] It referred to the ideology behind the Internet Engineering Task Force (IETF), an organization that promotes voluntary Internet

---

[1] Jon Matonis, 'Bitcoin Foundation Launches To Drive Bitcoin's Advancement' (*Forbes,* 27 September 2012) <www.forbes.com/sites/jonmatonis/2012/09/27/bitcoin-foundation-launches-to-drive-bitcoins-advancement/#51d0d6c3d868> accessed 14 May 2018.
[2] See Chapter 3.
[3] Carl Miller, 'What the Arrival of Bitcoin Means for Society, Politics and You' (*wired,* 16 December 2013) <www.wired.co.uk/article/bitcoin-demos> accessed 14 May 2018.
[4] Dave Clark, IETF Credo (1992) <https://groups.csail.mit.edu/ana/People/DDC/future_ietf_92.pdf> accessed 2 April 2018.
[5] Lawrence Lessig, 'Open Code and Open Societies: Values of Internet Governance' (1999) 74 Chicago-Kent Law Review 1405, 1417 (hereafter Lessig, 'Open Code').

6

standards such as HTTP.[6] Internet history nonetheless confirms that there are no spaces free of politics, ideology and hierarchy. Even when systems are designed to be exempt from such influence, reality catches up over time.

Blockchains have their own kings, presidents and voting processes. The technology replaces trust in the *known other* (other humans, institutions, intermediaries) with trust in the *unknown other* (entities and dynamics that are hard to see and understand from the outside). Even though this may not be obvious at first sight and is hidden by the *vires in numeris* spirit, power structures very much persist in respect of distributed ledgers.

I reach this conclusion through an evaluation of the process of blockchain governance, which refers to the maintenance of the corresponding protocol. Software maintenance in distributed ledger systems underlines that code isn't a God-given entity but something created by humans, which articulates the assumptions and goals of its creators. Seen from this perspective, it becomes evident that blockchain technology is merely a means of human expression rather than an alternative capable of replacing human decision-making. My observations unfold as follows. I introduce the processes of blockchain governance, explaining the need and contours of software updates. I also outline the necessity and main dimensions of this process and introduce core principles. The governance processes of the various layers of the ecosystem are examined in anticipation of a more detailed overview of governance debates in relation to the currently most important public and permissionless projects. After introducing how DLT governance has played out to date I make the point that, even though blockchains are presented as inaugurating a new era of decentralization, in reality these systems are frequently centralized at hardware and software level. By way of conclusion I reflect on the relation between blockchains and law and claim that, although a decentralized future may not be impossible, achieving it will be no small feat and will require breaking the curse of the perpetual repeating of history.

I. THE PRINCIPLES OF BLOCKCHAIN GOVERNANCE

In the blockchain context, 'governance' refers to the processes, rules and procedures relied on to maintain the protocol.[7] This encompasses actual protocol modification as well as the deliberation and decision-making processes that precede and inform that act. Blockchain systems are often portrayed as pure technical artefacts free from the untidiness of human existence, but the governance perspective displays the human and institutional processes behind these ledgers.

---

[6] In contrast to entities such as the International Standards Organization, anyone can register and attend meetings of the IETF.

[7] If we adopt the broader approach we also need to account for Internet governance as blockchains ultimately depend on protocols such as TCP/IP for the transfer of information between nodes.

Governance is no small factor in the overall development and ultimate success of a specific project. Vili Lehdonvirta has highlighted blockchains' governance paradox in stressing that, on the one hand, the perceived absence of a need for governance seems to be DLT's main value proposition while, on the other, a governance-free blockchain is doomed to fail as software bugs cannot be remedied and the protocol can never be upgraded.[8] Functional blockchain governance processes are in fact unavoidable, so as to allow these systems to efficiently react to unexpected real-world events and become more sophisticated over time.

The eventual success of blockchain-based systems will, correspondingly, 'depend on their internal capacity to instantiate new forms of governance'.[9] One may even go as far to argue that 'the promise of the blockchain economy is dependent on the implementation of effective governance mechanisms'.[10] Good governance will, accordingly, be an important competitive advantage for those able to embrace it. Indeed, when governance processes are absent, the technology can never improve or react to the unexpected circumstances that inevitably arise. Determining suitable governance norms therefore emerges as one of the key challenges that DLTs' future depends upon.

There is as much variance in distributed ledger governance processes as there is variance in blockchains and blockchain-based applications. Each of these projects must determine its own decision-making structures, and related principles are informed by multifarious contextual factors, such as whether the ledger is permissioned or unpermissioned, its underlying purpose and surrounding ideologies and norms. Even though governance dispositions diverge greatly, their common denominator is multidimensionality, which can be subdivided into seven distinct elements.

To start, various *endogenous and exogenous factors* determine the protocol's evolution. These include endogenous elements such as the decision to upgrade the protocol to furnish it with additional features or to change the characteristics thereof, such as the consensus protocol that is used. In addition, the governance of a particular blockchain is influenced by exogenous elements, including social norms (such as, arguably, fairness in the case of the The DAO hack, which is examined below) and, as we shall see, law.

---

[8]   Vili Lehdonvirta, 'The Blockchain Paradox: Why Distributed Ledger Technologies May Do Little to Transform the Economy' (*Oxford Internet Institute*, 21 November 2016) <www.oii.ox .ac.uk/blog/the-blockchain-paradox-why-distributed-ledger-technologies-may-do-little-to-trans form-the-economy/> accessed 3 April 2018.

[9]   Kevin Werbach, *The Blockchain and the New Architecture of Trust* (MIT Press 2018) 174 (hereafter Werbach, 'The Blockchain and the New Architecture of Trust').

[10] Roman Beck, Christoph Müller-Bloch and John Leslie King, 'Governance in the Blockchain Economy: A Framework and Research Agenda' (2018) 29 <www.researchgate.net/publica tion/323689461_Governance_in_the_Blockchain_Economy_A_Framework_and_Research_ Agenda> accessed 3 April 2018 (hereafter Beck et al., 'Governance in the Blockchain Economy').

A blockchain governance process is ordinarily comprised of *various steps,* which need to be neatly distinguished. In order to determine the governance structure of a particular blockchain, numerous elements must be considered. They include the identity of parties capable of suggesting changes; the avenues through which such changes can be suggested; the identity of the parties deciding on protocol upgrades; and the identity of those implementing these changes. There is increasing awareness that checks-and-balances between these various groups are needed, yet mechanisms able to realize this have been lacking until now.

Notwithstanding the specific context, *multiple actors* intercede in distributed ledger governance. Indeed, there is little point in adopting a DLT solution governed by a single party. The identity of the intervening parties diverges depending on the specific project at issue. Usually protocol maintenance is formed by core software developers, miners, node operators, users and token holders in public and permissionless systems. In private and permissioned systems, the vendor and consortium providing the system play a pivotal function. It is important to stress that these various actors usually do not share the same incentives for using the network and participating in governance. Accordingly, their interests are often not aligned. While this favours incremental change, it also may cause gridlock.

Blockchain governance is a *multi-layered process.* In the introductory chapter I introduced the various vertical layers that constitute blockchain ecosystems. These include the network layer itself, sometimes intermediate levels such as decentralized application platforms and the application layer.[11] Each of these layers needs its own governance processes to make decisions in relation to the maintenance of its specific software. While these processes operate at least to some extent independently, the governance decisions adopted by one layer can have repercussions for other layers, as illustrated through the example of the The DAO hack below. I highlight below that blockchains can be qualified as polycentric governance systems due to such multidimensionality as well as the fact that various actors contribute to the governance decisions in relation to each individual layer.

The principles that inform a specific governance arrangement emerge, moreover, from a multitude of *explicit and implicit processes.* These encompass rules that were explicitly agreed upon, such as when principles are devised at the outset of the project. Relevant rules and principles can also be explicitly endorsed after having been informally followed for a while. In addition, governance is informed by more subtle and implicit propositions. These can range from a community norm that discussions should at all times be well mannered to decisions that the minutes of certain stakeholder meetings be recorded and publicly released or that core developers consult the most important miners before a code change is proposed.[12]

---

[11] As well as the Internet protocols these layers ultimately depend on, which are not examined here.

[12] See, by way of example: <https://soundcloud.com/makerdao>.

Technology governance rules also comprise both *substantive and procedural principles*. Substantive questions can concern the range of possible options or the underlying principles that inform decisions. An example would be the prohibition of creating software specifically to enable unlawful activity. Procedural standards could include a minimum threshold for on-chain voting or an obligation for core software developers to consult certain constituencies before a decision on a given upgrade is made or that decisions must be reached within a predetermined time frame.

Finally, due to the cryptoeconomic structure of blockchains, governance often has an *economic flavour*. Distributed ledgers are anchored in economics and rely on fees to manage interactions. In light of this set-up, Primavera De Filippi and Aaron Wright have highlighted that 'every interaction with a blockchain is ultimately an economic transaction, and every party participating in the network serves as an economic actor'.[13] As a consequence, the cost of blockchain governance influences numerous network participants' behaviour.

The general principles identified above can be pinpointed to some degree with respect to each project. Determining the suitability of specific processes requires a thorough understanding of this technology and also of governance theories and experience in other fields. Although attention must be paid to the specificities of this technology and of each individual project, blockchain governance does not require a reinvention of the wheel. Rather, a determination of how existing and tested standards can be applied to this specific context is mandated. To this end, multi-disciplinary conversations are unavoidable.

To date and notwithstanding its importance, blockchain governance remains a largely uncharted field, however. Below, I introduce and discuss general themes to guide future research on these matters. Before moving on to this task, I should stress that I focus explicitly on protocol maintenance. There is a related governance question concerning how these protocols rule blockchain participants.[14] Readers interested in this should refer back to Chapter 3. I should also emphasize that I focus predominantly on the governance of the network infrastructure in public and permissionless blockchains (where governance has been discussed and tested most up until now), while occasionally discussing broader themes including governance mechanisms at the application layer and private and unpermissioned ledgers.

II. THE NECESSITY OF GOVERNANCE PROCESSES

Two prominent occurrences unfolding in relation to the Ethereum and Bitcoin projects over the past few years have underlined the inevitability of software

---

[13] Primavera De Filippi and Aaron Wright, *Blockchain and the Law* (Harvard University Press 2018) 185 (hereafter De Filippi and Wright, 'Blockchain and the Law').

[14] On this, see further Sinclair Davidson, Primavera De Filippi and Jason Potts, 'Economics of Blockchain' (2016) 7 <https://papers.ssrn.com/sol3/papers.cfm?abstract_id=2744751> accessed 20 March 2018 (hereafter Davidson et al., 'Economics of Blockchain').

maintenance. These stories confirm that even 'online peer-to-peer communities involve inherently political dimensions, which cannot be dealt with purely on the basis of protocols and algorithms'.[15] While technology can be designed to self-execute, it cannot account for and independently manage all changing circumstances. The decisions that must be taken range from the mundane and technical to determinations regarding wealth distribution on the network akin to monetary policy-making. It is accordingly hardly surprising that the selection of software design has proved highly controversial.

A. The 'The DAO' Hack

In 2016 about 11,000 individuals from around the globe invested Ether (Ethereum's native token) worth around $150 million into 'The DAO'.[16] This project's creators had constituted an automated decentralized investment platform devoid of central authority, legal incorporation and employees. The project was supposed to fund start-ups on the basis of the votes of those who had invested.[17] Backers got DAO tokens in exchange for their investment in Ether and could use tokens to vote on how the artefact was to spend its resources as well as on governance issues.[18] Some contended that The DAO offered 'complete transparency, total shareholder control, unprecedented flexibility and autonomous governance'.[19] There is no completely autonomous system divorced from the need for human intermediation, however, as proponents of the above theory would soon discover.

Overnight, an anonymous hacker siphoned off a third of all the funds held by The DAO by exploiting a bug in the code.[20] To enrich herself, the hacker used 'the terms of the existing smart contracts to accomplish something others later found objectionable, i.e. the diversion of their money'.[21] If we assume that 'code is law', no theft occurred, as the hacker simply exploited a weakness in the code. As a consequence, 'the hack was simultaneously valid as an enforceable smart contract

[15] Primavera De Filippi and Benjamin Loveluck, 'The Invisible Politics of Bitcoin: Governance Crisis of a Decentralized Infrastructure' (2016) 5(3) Internet Policy Review 2 (hereafter De Filippi and Loveluck, 'The Invisible Politics of Bitcoin').

[16] Nathaniel Popper, 'A Venture Fund with Plenty of Virtual Capital, but no Capitalist' *New York Times Dealbook* (21 May 2016) <www.nytimes.com/2016/05/22/business/dealbook/crypto-ether-bitcoin-currency.html> accessed 4 April 2018.

[17] Seth Bannon, 'The Tao of "The DAO" or: How the Autonomous Corporation is Already Here' (*TechCrunch*, 16 May 2016) <https://techcrunch.com/2016/05/16/the-tao-of-the-dao-or-how-the-autonomous-corporation-is-already-here/> accessed 14 May 2018.

[18] ibid.

[19] ibid.

[20] E. Spode, 'The Great Cryptocurrency Heist' (*aeon*, 14 February 2017) <https://aeon.co/essays/trust-the-inside-story-of-the-rise-and-fall-of-ethereum> accessed 21 March 2018 (hereafter Spode, 'The Great Cryptocurrency Heist').

[21] Max Raskin, 'The Law and Legality of Smart Contracts' (2017) 1 Georgetown Law and Technology Review 305, 337.

within the bounds of the software system and demonstrably invalid as theft in the minds of the contracting parties'.[22]

Considering the substantial funds that had been invested, this hack wasn't just an isolated event. Rather, it involved a larger, systemic dimension. A substantial amount of the Ether in circulation at the time had been invested in the automated venture capital fund, giving rise to concerns that the hack could unsettle the overall stability of the Ethereum ecosystem, especially in these very early days of the project.

Against this background, a fiery debate emerged in the community as to the appropriate steps to take. Some insisted that blockchain code ought to be immutable and that undoing the effects of the hack would go against the spirit of tamper evidence and trustless trust. Others stressed that reversing the effects of the hack would be the best option to guarantee the survival of the Ethereum project.[23] Importantly, law served as an exogenous factor influencing the decision, as it was suggested that refunding those who had lost ether would decrease the likelihood of judicial disputes and regulatory attention.[24]

The issue was ultimately put to a vote – a carbonvote, to be more specific.[25] A carbonvote is a mechanism whereby coin holders can pronounce their views on a proposal by sending tokens to addresses that represent their views.[26] Some 87 per cent of the vote was in favour of the hard fork that would reverse the hack's impact (though participation was very low).[27] Ultimately, the Ethereum blockchain was forked to reverse the effects of the theft, underlining that blockchains are in fact *mutable*.[28] The fork occurred when a majority of miners on the network mined new blocks using the updated software. In fact, the hard fork was subjected to a dual vote: first users could vote through the carbonvoting procedure, and subsequently miners voted with their computing power on the revision suggested by developers.[29] Some refused to do so, however, continuing to mine with the software's earlier version (which was rebaptized 'Ethereum Classic') to express their opposition to this human intervention in the protocol's operation.[30]

This episode awakened the community to the fact that there are no politics-free blockchains. Code isn't just code. Rather, it's a tool relied on by its creators to achieve specific goals that can be highly normative. Moreover, the event pinpointed

[22] Kevin Werbach and Nicolas Cornell, 'Contracts *Ex Machina*' (2017) 67 Duke Law Journal 313, 365.
[23] See <www.change.org/p/ethereum-hard-fork-ethereum-to-revert-the-hack-of-the-dao>.
[24] Michael del Castillo, 'The DAO Crisis: Or How Vigilantism and Blockchain Democracy Became the Best Hope for Burned Investors' (*coindesk*, 13 July 2016) <www.coindesk.com/author-daos-original-code-minimize-regulatory-backlash/> accessed 14 May 2018.
[25] Jeffrey Wilcke, 'To Fork or Not To Fork' (*Ethereum Blog*, 15 July 2018) <https://blog.ethereum.org/2016/07/15/to-fork-or-not-to-fork/> accessed 14 May 2018.
[26] <http://carbonvote.com/>.
[27] <http://v1.carbonvote.com/>.
[28] On forks, see further below.
[29] On the role of miners, see further below.
[30] Spode, 'The Great Cryptocurrency Heist' (n 20).

the absence of established governance processes and the lack of indications as to what rules and procedures should be adhered to when decisions of this nature are made. There were no set procedures to be pursued or explicit values to be accounted for. There were also no conflict-of- interest rules, despite the fact that at least some of those involved in the decision-making process were personally invested in the fund.[31]

Despite the ad hoc resolution of this crisis, the The DAO hack has had a formative impact on governance in the Ethereum ecosystem. In spring 2018 there was an ongoing debate as to whether this incident should count as precedent for subsequent governance decisions.[32] These discussions occur against the background of the so-called 'Parity bug'. Due to a vulnerability in this wallet library, over €150 million worth of Ether have been trapped after a user (accidentally) issued a command making her smart contract inaccessible.[33] The decision to be made is whether this should be remedied through an intervention at the network layer, similar to the The DAO adjustment, or not. Whether the earlier incident counts as precedent remains controversial.

B. *The Bitcoin Block Size Debate*

Satoshi Nakamoto determined that the size of each block on the Bitcoin block-chain ought to be one megabyte. This size constitutes a restriction on the number of transactions that can be grouped into each block, and, correspondingly, on the number of transactions that the entire Bitcoin network can handle. As adoption of the cryptocurrency grew, this was seen as preventing the network's scalability, and various remedies were explored, including moving some aspects of transactions off-chain or increasing the size of each block.[34] The risk is that a backlog of transactions awaiting inclusion clogs the system and renders it unusable for many purposes – defeating any prospect of the cryptocurrency being used as an ordinary means of payment.

Debates concerning how to scale Bitcoin have gone on for a very long time.[35] In this context, different reforms have been suggested. These included, among others,

---

31 For a disclosure, see Vlad Zamfir, 'The DAO Hard Fork, and the Negotiation that Couldn't Happen' (*Medium*, 20 July 2016) <https://medium.com/@Vlad_Zamfir/the-dao-hard-fork-and-the-negotiation-that-couldnt-happen-bdd2aedefe84> accessed 25 May 2018.

32 Phil Daian and Lorenz Breidenbach, 'Parity Proposals' Potential Problems' (*Hacking, Distributed*, 13 December 2017) <http://hackingdistributed.com/2017/12/13/ether-resurrection/> accessed 14 May 2018.

33 <http://paritytech.io/security-alert-2/>.

34 De Filippi and Loveluck, 'The Invisible Politics of Bitcoin' (n 15) 7–9.

35 For a detailed overview of how the debate developed over time, see Daniel Morgan, 'The Great Bitcoin Scaling Debate – A Timeline' (*Hackernoon*, 3 December 2017) <https://hackernoon.com/the-great-bitcoin-scaling-debate-a-timeline-6108081dbada> accessed 25 May 2018.

increasing the block size to eight megabytes[36] – a move that proved impossible, as the Chinese miners that control more than half the network's overall hashing power opposed the strategy.[37] Others suggested increasing the block size by 17.7 per cent per year or augmenting blog size to two megabytes as an emergency solution before longer-term solutions could be adopted.[38] A group of developers and industry leaders planned to roll out a 'SegWit2X' update according to which witness data would have been segregated from transaction data and the block size would have been doubled from one to two megabytes. While the segregation of signature data (which occupied the larger share of a block's overall storage capacity) from transaction data aroused little controversy, the block size increase eventually had to be suspended, as the organizers feared it would divide the community.[39] Despite the availability of various options, none could generate agreement from the various parties involved in the polycentric Bitcoin governance process.

The most important element to note about the Bitcoin block size debate for our purposes is that agreement between multiple parties proved impossible. According to Laura Shin, the debate 'has produced a contentious divide because the various ways to go about it all result in tradeoffs – and which compromises the different sides are willing to make reflect deep philosophical differences. Throw in accusations of censorship, racism, hypocrisy, corporate takeovers and deal-making behind closed doors, and the three-year-long battle has become a geek's version of a soap opera – if soap operas were mostly about and watched by men.'[40]

Her description underlines the fact that, because of the lack of human consensus on the block size issue, no genuine solution could ultimately be agreed on, which in turn prevented the system from becoming more scalable through an intervention at the infrastructure layer.[41] This emphasizes how current multi-party decision-making processes not only favour incremental change but may also result in gridlock, harming the technical adaptation of the network.

---

[36] For the related BIP, see <https://github.com/bitcoin/bips/blob/master/bip-0101.mediawiki>.

[37] Aaron van Wirdum, 'Chinese Exchanges Reject Gavin Andresen's 20 MB Block Size Increase' (*Cointelegraph*, 5 July 2015) <https://cointelegraph.com/news/chinese-exchanges-reject-gavin-andresens-20-mb-block-size-increase> accessed 14 May 2018.

[38] <https://github.com/bitcoin/bips/blob/master/bip-0103.mediawiki>; <https://github.com/bitcoin/bitcoin/pull/6451>.

[39] Kari Larsen et al., 'Bitcoin's "Block size" Debate: Big Blockers v. Decentralists' (19 January 2018) <www.reedsmith.com/en/perspectives/2018/01/bitcoins-block-size-debate-big-blockers-v-decentralists> accessed 14 May 2018.

[40] Laura Shin, 'Will this Battle for the Soul of Bitcoin Destroy It?' (*Forbes*, 23 October 2017) <www.forbes.com/sites/laurashin/2017/10/23/will-this-battle-for-the-soul-of-bitcoin-destroy-it/#13baa4dd3d3c> accessed 1 June 2018.

[41] It is worth noting that parallel proposals are explored at the application layer.

III. THE MECHANISMS OF BLOCKCHAIN GOVERNANCE

The two episodes of blockchain governance introduced above reveal that DLTs are systems in the making that must further develop. While there are ongoing debates regarding the future of governance on these networks, even the most basic assumptions remain disputed. Below, I highlight two main points of contention, concerning the modalities of principle design, on the one hand, and the locus on decision-making, on the other.

A. *Process versus Design*

Although blockchains are a recent innovation, the governance challenges they raise are not unprecedented. Vast bodies of experience and scholarly research have distilled governance principles for manifold technical, economic and political contexts. There is an ongoing discussion regarding whether related principles can be externally imposed on these technological systems or whether they need to develop incrementally from within. While speed and efficiency are clear arguments in favour of transplanting successful governance processes from other domains to DLT, this may not be workable in relation to public and permissionless ledgers.

Some have indeed rejected the option of imposing exogenous rules on distributed ledger ecosystems. According to Vlad Zamfir, 'it's almost always a mistake to imagine that you can design and institute a governance process, especially for an existing blockchain community with existing processes, and especially without adequate knowledge of the existing processes'.[42] Evidence from real-world politics confirms that the imposition of external norms on communities does not necessarily yield successful outcomes. Stephen Humphreys has illustrated how efforts to impose the rule of law on systems it was previously unknown to failed for lack of required norms and habits.[43] Denis Galligan, a leading law and society scholar, considers that governors and the governed subscribe to legal orders due to the existence of a special bond of trust between them, which is anchored in social relations.[44] It is thus questionable whether governance rules that do not develop incrementally from within a given community will find acceptance.

If we transpose these ideas to unpermissioned ledgers, a social contract would first need to develop in order for governance processes to formalize. Some consider that a related process is currently unfolding.[45] There are also arguments, however, that governance should be designed through the imposition of exogenous principles, as

---

[42] Vlad Zamfir, 'Against On-Chain Governance' (*Medium*, 1 December 2017) <https://medium .com/@Vlad_Zamfir/against-on-chain-governance-a4ceacd04oca> accessed 14 May 2018.

[43] Stephen Humphreys, *Theatre of the Rule of Law* (Cambridge University Press 2010).

[44] Denis Galligan, *Law in Modern Society* (Clarendon Press 2006).

[45] Vlad Zamfir, 'Dear Ethereum Community' (*Medium*, 7 July 2016) <https://medium.com/@Vlad_ Zamfir/dear-ethereum-community-acfa99a037c4> accessed 4 April 2018 ('The Ethereum

opposed to letting principles incrementally blossom over time.[46] The appeal of this option is efficiency. DLT governance questions are not unprecedented, and attempting to reinvent the wheel instead of relying on tested principles can lead to suboptimal outcomes. Governance debates are time-consuming and distract teams and communities from focusing on technology development and refining use cases.

It is likely that tension between governance development and design will continue in the near future. The appropriateness of the adopted solution depends on context. When it comes to enterprise blockchains, discussions regarding the philosophical nature of governance are much less appealing than in relation to permissionless ledgers. Further, when a project is being developed now or in the future, the *ex ante* imposition of exogenous governance principles is more straightforward than in relation to existing projects that already have history. Ultimately, the models of governance as a process and governance by design are not diametrically opposed. No one invents the world anew (even if they think they do), and existing principles will always affect novel ones (whether consciously or subconsciously). Similarly, even when a governance structure is designed *ex ante*, it will probably require adaptation over time. A second point concerning the very nature of distributed ledger governance remains unsettled, namely whether governance should occur on-chain or off-chain.

B. *On-Chain versus Off-Chain Governance*

Blockchain governance processes comprise two dimensions: on-chain and off-chain deliberations and decisions. In on-chain governance, stakeholders participate in discussions and decisions through the protocol itself. In contrast, off-chain governance refers to the processes around the protocol that contribute to its maintenance.

In on-chain governance, a decision is reached on the blockchain, and the protocol adapts automatically as a consequence thereof. Coin holders vote on-chain, and as a consequence of that vote nodes automatically install the endorsed update. In such circumstances miners exercise no agency, as they are not required to decide whether or not to install the update, which, rather, executes automatically.

The Tezos blockchain relies on such a process. In Tezos, anyone can submit a change to the governance structure through a code update.[47] An on-chain vote subsequently determines whether the proposal is accepted. If the proposal gets the green light, the update is integrated into a test network. After a certain period of time the proposal is again submitted to a confirmation vote, when the change is

---

community has an implicit, constantly evolving social contract that describes which changes to the Ethereum protocol and platform it would consider adopting.').

[46] Fred Ehrsam, 'Blockchain Governance: Programming Our Future' (*Medium*, 27 November 2017) <https://medium.com/@FEhrsam/blockchain-governance-programming-our-future-c3bfe3of2d74> accessed 14 May 2018 (hereafter Ehrsam, 'Blockchain Governance').

[47] See <https://tezos.com/pdf/position_paper.pdf>.

integrated into the protocol. This system creates incentives for users to actively engage in the governance process and maintain the ledger, as developers are rewarded with newly mined tokens.[48] Polkadot, a project that aims to connect permissioned blockchains with permissionless networks (a 'blockchain of block-chains'), equally plans to rely on such a procedure. It uses its own internal tokens to enable token holders to vote on software updates that automatically upgrade across the network if approved.[49] This structure includes a council that can block malicious proposals.[50] The effect of such a process is to bypass nodes and developers, to the benefit of coin holders.

Speed and efficiency are the main benefits of on-chain governance. The fact that coin holders vote in relation to their wealth creates, essentially, a plutocratic system, however. While one may argue that coin holders will act in the interest of the network because their wealth depends on the latter, this idea hasn't been tested.[51] It is also worth stressing that the voting majority necessarily wins. This can be problematic, for three reasons. First, voting participation can be really low. For instance, fewer than 10 per cent of coin holders participated in the carbonvote regarding the The DAO hack.[52] This raises legitimacy questions and increases the risk that a motivated party with only a small overall percentage of coins exercises decisive influence. Second, when a majority wins, there necessarily is a risk of majoritarian bias. Finally, considering the stark concentration of wealth in blockchain networks, a very small number of people can hold a majority of votes.

In light of the above, some consider off-chain governance to be a more suitable model, as it is not limited to on-chain voting and implementation but encompasses processes that take place in the real world. Off-chain governance groups a broader pool of actors and involves a wider net of normative principles. In contrast to a pure on-chain governance process, miners exercise agency in deciding whether to install new software. As a consequence, multiple factors influence software maintenance and there is no automatic execution of proposals.

The so-called improvement proposals are an important element of off-chain governance in public and permissionless systems. They allow anyone to suggest

---

[48] There are no (direct) financial rewards for developers in off-chain processes. This has a number of consequences, including the creation of incentives to start a new project released through an ICO.

[49] Rachel Rose O'Leary, 'Polkadot's Plan for Governing a Blockchain of Blockchains' (*coindesk*, 22 March 2018) <www.coindesk.com/polkadots-radical-plan-governing-blockchain-block chains/> accessed 28 May 2018.

[50] ibid.

[51] More clearly, their interest is to drive up (in the short term, depending on circumstances) the price of the token, which might not always overlap with what is best for the network in the long term.

[52] Vitalik Buterin, 'Notes on Blockchain Governance' (*Vitalik Buterin's Website*, 17 December 2017) <https://vitalik.ca/general/2017/12/17/voting.html> accessed 28 May 2018 (hereafter Buterin, 'Notes on Blockchain Governance').

software changes, which are subsequently evaluated and debated by the broader community and developers. If approved, they are proposed to miners. Bitcoin Improvement Proposals are intended to be 'the primary mechanisms for proposing new features' in Bitcoin.[53] Each BIP must have an author (called a 'champion'), who must write the BIP in the specified style, shepherd discussions and attempt to build consensus around the idea.[54] A draft BIP is then sent to the Bitcoin Core developer mailing list. The BIP editor checks whether the proposal meets the required formal specifications and assigns a BIP number.[55] BIPs are subsequently recorded in a versioned software repository on GitHub, and developers ultimately decide whether to accept it.[56] The resulting software change must then be activated on the network through miners with a majority of hashing power.[57]

Ethereum relies on Ethereum Improvement Proposals (EIPs), a process very similar to the one delineated above. Anyone can suggest an EIP. If the proposal requires a protocol change, it is discussed in the bi-weekly core developer call. In the event of approval, clients implement a hard fork patch. If all clients implement the patch, miners and users must update. When this is done, a successful hard fork occurs; if not, there may be a contentious hard fork.[58]

The actors involved in off-chain governance are, accordingly, more diverse, as they include not only coin holders and miners but also core developers and the wider community. DLT governance processes remain subject to evolution, and discussions are under way as to what the purpose and technicalities of these processes should be specifically.[59] Security concerns are also an important consideration. EIPs and BIPs enter into force when they are adopted by miners with more than 50 per cent of the network's mining power. Miners are rent seekers, however, that may not have the necessary technical expertise to evaluate a proposal. Indeed, it is not at all clear whether mining pools have in place procedures that vet code. This could trigger a situation in which a malicious actor attacks the network or diverts assets through a software modification that appears benign but is not.

---

[53] <https://github.com/bitcoin/bips/blob/master/bip-0001.mediawiki>.

[54] ibid.

[55] <https://github.com/bitcoin/bips/blob/master/bip-0001.mediawiki#BIP_Editor_Responsibilities__Workflow>.

[56] A software repository ('repo') is a storage location from which software can be retrieved and installed on a computer.

[57] Alyssa Hertig, 'Why are Miners Involved in Bitcoin Code Changes Anyway?' (*coindesk*, 28 July 2017) <www.coindesk.com/miners-involved-bitcoin-code-changes-anyway/> accessed 28 May 2018.

[58] I introduce hard forks in further detail below.

[59] Adam Reese, 'Ethereum Dev Yoichi Hirai Steps Away From Role As EIP Editor, Raises Questions About Process' (*ETHNews*, 16 February 2018) <www.ethnews.com/ethereum-dev-yoichi-hirai-steps-away-from-role-as-eip-editor-raises-questions-ab> accessed 28 May 2018.

IV. THE LAYERS OF BLOCKCHAIN GOVERNANCE

Thus far I have mainly engaged with governance in relation to the infrastructure layer. The blockchain ecosystem's additional layers also necessitate software maintenance, however. This section outlines the contours of these processes, and stresses that blockchain governance is ultimately a polycentric process. While the governance processes of each layer are independent, they are also interdependent. Indeed, a decision reached in relation to the infrastructure can have implications for applications, and vice versa.

When an application is deployed directly on a blockchain, the governance decisions made in relation to the underlying infrastructure affect the decentralized application. Conversely, when an intermediate layer in the form of a decentralized application framework is used, the governance decisions made in relation thereto also affect applications. As a consequence, each layer has an endogenous governance process, but is also affected by exogenous factors, including governance decisions made by other actors in the ecosystem, in addition to broader factors.[60] This interconnection reveals a need to create channels of communication between the different layers, and maybe also to define common standards over time.

A. *The Network Layer*

Governance principles in relation to permissioned and unpermissioned chains are noticeably distinct. Permissionless ledgers are open-source and interoperable protocols that are not centrally controlled by a single entity. By their nature, their governance conventions will thus be more complex than those applicable to permissioned systems, wherein the vendor or consortium facilitates coordination.

1. Permissioned Blockchains

As a general rule, governance systems can be designed more easily for permissioned blockchains. These projects' software is controlled by a determined party or a consortium that whitelists nodes and determines the system's rules of operation.[61] Such infrastructure is often designed for a specific purpose, and the related rules, including governance principles, are carefully designed to achieve this purpose. Governance by design is, accordingly, the default option in this context.

Although design parameters can be defined more easily for permissionless ledgers, there can easily be a temptation to favour centralization. For example, a consortium might rely on a blockchain located on nodes across the globe but the blockchain might be centrally managed by a single entity. When there is a single gatekeeper

---

[60] Below, I observe that this includes law.
[61] See, by way of example: <www.hyperledger.org/projects/fabric>.

authority, operational risk is concentrated in a single point of failure, which might moreover 'charge monopolist rents to network users or fail to treat them evenhandedly'.[62] This gatekeeper may further restrict entry to the blockchain-based marketplace and change the data that is stored on-chain.[63] If there are no safeguards against such governance shortcomings, the entire objective of relying on a distributed ledger may be defeated. Of course, the same challenge can arise in relation to hybrid infrastructures, which everyone can join and use but which are maintained by a number of trusted nodes.[64]

Some projects are developing sophisticated governance structures to optimize their products. To provide an example, the Linux Foundation's Hyperledger is governed by a technical steering committee. Contributors (anyone who contributes code, documentation or technical artefacts to the codebase) and maintainers (contributors with the ability to commit code) can be elected to the committee, the functions of which include making decisions on the technical direction of the Hyperledger project and approving proposals, as well as communication with external and industry organizations.[65] The R3 consortium's Corda project envisages using a similar concept of a network governing body.[66]

It is worth stressing that, when such projects are developed as blockchain-as-a-service arrangements, additional considerations apply. When a professional operator provides blockchain infrastructure, enterprises can test and use the technology without the cost and risk of deploying it in-house.[67] They also benefit from a flexibility analogous to cloud computing, of being able to access computational load when required (i.e. when transactions fluctuate). In turn, the BaaS provider leverages economies of scale to provide such infrastructure. For example, Microsoft Azure provides such services, as does IBM, which uses Linux Foundation's Hyperledger solution.[68]

In a BaaS context, governance considerations include whether the BaaS provider can unilaterally change software, whether a client can fork this software under the existing software licence and port the existing ledger and when and by whom the ledger can be overwritten (for instance, in forking the ledger).[69] A BaaS solution may be anchored in a public and permissionless ledger, moreover, such as

---

[62] David Yermack, 'Corporate Governance and Blockchains' (2017) 21 Review of Finance 7, 10.

[63] ibid. 12.

[64] <www.stellar.org/>.

[65] <www.hyperledger.org/about/charter>.

[66] <www.corda.net/wp-content/uploads/2018/05/corda-platform-whitepaper.pdf>.

[67] Lucas Mearian, 'Blockchain-as-a-service Allows Enterprises Test Distributed Ledger Technology' (*Computerworld*, 15 November 2017) <www.computerworld.com/article/3237465/enterprise-appli cations/blockchain-as-a-service-allows-enterprises-test-distributed-ledger-technology.html> accessed 28 May 2018.

[68] <https://azure.microsoft.com/en-us/solutions/blockchain/>; <www.ibm.com/blockchain/>.

[69] Jatinder Singh and Johan Michels, 'Blockchain as a Service: Providers and Trust' (2017) Queen Mary School of Law Legal Studies Research Paper No. 269/2017, 10 <https://papers.ssrn.com/sol3/papers.cfm?abstract_id=3091223> accessed 4 April 2018.

Ethereum-as-a-Service offerings, which can be affected by Ethereum's governance process.[70] This underlines the interconnection between the governance processes of various components, which also finds expression in the interaction between the network and application layers.

2. Unpermissioned Blockchains

Above, I have already outlined some of the elements and controversies related to the governance of permissionless ledgers. In general, governance parameters in these systems are less defined, due in part to the fact that, in contrast to permissioned systems, their principles are not determined at the outset. Further complication emerges from the decentralized control exercised over such blockchains, as well as the fact that, as they are a general-purpose technology, the specific objectives and value propositions are less defined than in relation to their private counterparts. For example, the BIP process mandates that, in order for a BIP to be considered, it must keep with 'Bitcoin philosophy'.[71] The EIP process similarly refers to 'Ethereum philosophy', yet the meaning of these expressions is far from obvious.[72] It follows that, in these contexts, both the procedures of governance and the underlying values and objectives remain undefined. Below, I evaluate these systems in further detail.

B. *Governance of the Application Layer*

Governance structures are no less imperative concerning the application layer. To illustrate, think about an Uber-like platform that is organized through a D(A)O. This idea has much appeal from a socio-economic perspective. It would create a digital co-operative through which drivers could independently organize their work and reap a larger share of the generated profits than Uber's 25 per cent.[73] There is an open question, however, as to whether such projects can be realized from a governance perspective. Indeed, in such a set-up, the drivers who collaboratively manage the platform would need to reach agreement through voting, which, depending on the voting threshold that is applied, may make it impossible to reach consensus on a given matter. It is precisely because of the inefficiencies of decentralized management that centralized institutions have emerged and currently represent the central share of organizations.

It is important to note that the infrastructure and application layers cannot be neatly separated. For instance, those deploying a smart contract on a specific

---

[70] ibid.
[71] <https://github.com/bitcoin/bips/blob/master/bip-0001.mediawiki#BIP_Editor_Responsibilities__Workflow>.
[72] It is likely that these expressions are probably just the result of copy/pasting from the Python improvement process documents. See further <www.python.org/dev/peps/pep-0001/>.
[73] <www.uber.com/de/drive/resources/payments/>.

distributed ledger have to trust not only the processes around the construction and administration of this piece of code but, further, of the underlying infrastructure, such as that execution will happen and code will not be altered.

While decentralized governance offers manifold advantages, centralized structures will always fare better from a pure efficiency perspective. The resulting question is thus how blockchain governance mechanisms can be best designed to prevent a stalemate of the entire project.

C. *Blockchain Intermediaries*

Intermediaries are similarly faced with governance challenges. To take the example of oracles, the agents that feed information to smart contract code, clear principles ought to be devised as to who operates these agents and what thresholds for decision-making are employed. Oracles can be operated by a private party, public–private cooperation or even the state. Furthermore, there must be defined processes as to what thresholds are relied on to establish whether a given fact occurred. For example, is it deemed satisfactory for one individual to state that an earthquake has occurred, or must hundreds of users in the concerned area confirm this? Will these individuals be laymen or do they need to be seismologists?

Similar governance questions will surface in relation to many other intermediaries, including smart contract arbitration systems that can be staffed by peers, experts or ordinary judges.[74] Because governance discussions have been most pronounced in relation to permissionless blockchains to date, I now turn to, and provide, a more detailed overview of the governance intricacies in these systems.

V. THE GOVERNANCE PROCESSES OF
PERMISSIONLESS BLOCKCHAINS

In permissionless systems various stakeholder groups matter for governance purposes: core software developers, miners, nodes, coin holders and other stakeholders. I review the role of the various groups, which diverges depending on whether an on-chain or off-chain governance process is used. It must be plain from the outset that the roles and incentives of the various stakeholders in governance processes are not aligned. Each group has different means of participation and acts on the basis of different self-interests.

Although blockchain governance raises many important questions, these are by and large not unprecedented. Indeed, existing concepts and theories are helpful in making sense of them. One of the most popular lenses to assess governance arrangements is Albert Hirschman's conception of 'exit, voice and loyalty', which lays out that members of an organization, whether a firm, state or other form of

---

74 See further Chapter 1.

human grouping, have two possible responses when they are less satisfied with their membership: exit (leave the organization) or voice (actively try to repair shortcomings).[75] Loyalty to the organization reduces the risk of exit. I rely on this paradigm below to evaluate the role and status of the various constituencies in distributed ledger governance.

The theory of polycentricity also provides a useful lens, as, whatever their configuration and degree of centralization (or not), blockchains are not maintained and operated by a single party. Vincent Ostrom, Charles Tiebout and Robert Warren introduced polycentricity in 1962.[76] Elinor Ostrom subsequently refined it. She argues:

> Polycentric systems are characterized by multiple governing authorities at differing scales rather than a monocentric unit. Each unit within a polycentric system exercises considerable independence to make norms and rules within a specific domain (such as a family, a firm, a local government, a network of local governments, a state or province, a region, a national government, or an international regime)[77]

Although the institutions Ostrom focused on differ from DLT and the theory is, accordingly, not a perfect match to capture my object of study, polycentricity nonetheless provides a useful frame of thinking, as it highlights that systems can be shaped through the influence of multiple governing authorities (as is the case in respect of blockchains) and, further, that these can be shaped by the interplay of public and private norms (a point I further elaborate on below when considering the status of law as an exogenous governance factor). Polycentricity is also a framework that helps make sense of the mutual influence of governance decisions at various layers. An in-depth analysis of these concepts in relation to distributed ledgers will have to be left to further research, but they help provide general frames to capture some of the dynamics evaluated below, where I examine the various stakeholder groups implicated in the governance of public and permissionless ledgers.

A. *Core Software Developers*

Anthropologist Margie Cheesman considers that 'there is a presumed trust in the code, yet a lack of attention to who writes, maintains or changes the code'.[78]

---

75 Albert Hirschman, *Exit, Voice and Loyalty: Responses to Decline in Firms, Organizations and States* (Harvard University Press 1970).

76 Charles Tiebout, Vincent Ostrom and Robert Warren, 'The Organization of Government in Metropolitan Areas: A Theoretical Inquiry' (1961) 55 The American Political Science Review. The notion also appeared in Lon Fuller, 'The Forms and Limits of Adjudication' (1978) 92 Harvard Law Review and Michael Polanyi, *The Logic of Liberty* (University of Chicago Press 1951).

77 Elinor Ostrom, 'Polycentric Systems for Coping with Collective Action and Global Environmental Change' (2010) 20 Global Environmental Change 550.

78 Margie Cheesman, 'Anticipating Blockchain for Development: Data, Power and the Future' (*Oxford Internet Institute*, 20 November 2017) <www.oii.ox.ac.uk/blog/anticipating-blockchain-for-development-data-power-and-the-future/> accessed 21 March 2018.

Core software developers (the 'core devs', in blockchain parlance) are important actors in this regard. Whereas anyone can suggest changes to the protocol of a public and permissionless ledger (such as through the BIP and EIP processes), only core developers have the commit key through which these changes can be implemented.[79] Often the avenues for reaching human consensus around these decisions are far from obvious.

In permissionless systems, 'there is no central entity that is officially charged with maintaining or fixing the software'.[80] Core development teams are loosely associated, largely coordinate through informal means and are geographically fragmented.[81] Yochai Benkler has shown that governance structures in peer-to-peer communities are typically volunteer-driven and self-organize.[82] This has shortcomings, as Angela Walch has highlighted, as 'there is no one who is responsible for keeping the Bitcoin software operational'.[83] In Bitcoin, a mailing list and the BIP process are the main communication tools between the most important developers.[84] In Hirschmanian terms, core developers exercise voice in proposing changes to a project's architecture. They have a monopoly in suggesting such changes to miners. Core developers can also exit a system when they stop developing for that project and join another project.

The informality of the processes is further revealed by the fact that the rules regarding core developer appointment and removal remain undefined. There are currently no transparent and formalized processes to become a core developer, and acting as a core developer is not subject to compliance with predetermined principles (such as conflict-of-interest rules). Similarly, no removal processes have been implemented. Although the informality of the processes may be unavoidable, and even desirable at this stage, it will inevitably give rise to complications over time.

Considering the substantial leverage core developers exercise over the overall system, it becomes obvious that trusting a blockchain presupposes trust in the individuals who write and debug code and the processes guiding them in this task. Indeed, although the role of developers is limited when an on-chain governance process is adopted, they are central actors in off-chain solutions. If we examine blockchain governance through the lens of conventional separation of powers paradigms, we can think of core developers as the entity that proposes new

---

[79] They can of course themselves submit improvement proposals also.

[80] Angela Walch, 'The Bitcoin Blockchain as Financial Market Infrastructure: A Consideration of Operational Risk' (2015) 18 NYU Journal of Legislation and Public Policy 837, 844 (hereafter Walch, 'The Bitcoin Blockchain').

[81] The first point is however often overstated. See Vitalik Buterin, 'Ethereum Foundation Internal Update' (*Ethereum Blog*, 7 January 2016) <https://blog.ethereum.org/2016/01/07/2394/> accessed 14 May 2018.

[82] Yochai Benkler, *The Wealth of Networks. How Social Production Transforms Markets and Freedom* (Yale University Press 2006).

[83] Walch, 'The Bitcoin Blockchain' (n 80) 870.

[84] Ehrsam, 'Blockchain Governance' (n 46).

legislation (which can be the legislative or executive depending on the respective constitutional context). Miners are the main judges of whether such changes are adopted.

B. *Miners*

Whereas the core developer community can only propose, miners implement protocol changes. In order for a protocol update to be successful, a majority of miners (measured in computing power) need to install the modifications put forward by the core developers. They vote on proposals in deciding which version of the software to rely on to add new blocks.

In on-chain governance, adoption automatically follows coin holder votes.[85] In off-chain governance settings, however, miners are required to independently determine their position. As a consequence, miners collectively hold a veto over the amendments suggested by core developers and are free to refuse to run the new code. It is for this reason that core developers sometimes coordinate their decisions with large mining pools.[86] When an unintended hard fork occurred on Bitcoin in 2013 core developers persuaded the largest mining pool to follow the shortest chain (in contravention of the customary longest-chain rule),[87] because it supported the old and new versions of the software.[88]

Miners are, accordingly, important actors in blockchain governance. Some have argued that '[c]ore developers and important miners wield powers that are comparable with those of the management of publicly traded companies'.[89] Yet they evade the rules regarding scrutiny, transparency and accountability that the latter face.[90] There are no directives concerning appointment and removal; miners are simply rent-seeking agents that join the network out of their own motion to benefit from the coinbase transaction and transaction fees. Importantly, there are also no rules that prevent a core developer from being a miner, or, worse, running a mining pool. Even if there were norms and rules that would prohibit such conflicts, at present no institutions have been defined that could enforce them.

---

[85] On this, see further below.

[86] Walch, 'The Bitcoin Blockchain' (n 80) 873.

[87] According to such convention, miners mine on the longest chain where an accidental hard fork emerges.

[88] Arvind Narayanan, 'Analyzing the 2013 Bitcoin fork: Centralized Decision-making Saved the Day' (*Freedom To Tinker*, 28 July 2015) <https://freedom-to-tinker.com/2015/07/28/analyzing-the-2013-bitcoin-fork-centralized-decision-making-saved-the-day/> accessed 14 May 2018.

[89] Philipp Hacker, 'Corporate Governance for Complex Cryptocurrencies? A Framework for Stability and Decision Making in Blockchain-Based Monetary Systems' (2017) 17 <https://papers.ssrn.com/sol3/papers.cfm?abstract_id=2998830> accessed 21 March 2018.

[90] ibid.

The consolidation of mining operations in the form of mining pools is a key governance concern.[91] In January 2018 the top four miners in Bitcoin and the top three miners in Ethereum controlled more than 50 per cent of the hash rate.[92] There are, moreover, suspicions that the various Chinese mining pools are actually just one entity.[93] Such centralization was not anticipated but, rather, emerged because, with the rise in valuation of these cryptoassets (and thus also mining rewards), competition increased and specialized mining hardware was developed.[94] To increase economies of scale, mining pools formed that increase the chances of mining a block and splitting the block reward. This confirms that in the blockchain world too circumstances change, and governance processes need to provide flexibility for adaptation.

It is important to note that, in addition to deciding on others' proposals, miners can also take governance into their own hands through miner-led soft forks. Hard and soft forks are a highly important element of blockchain governance that must be explained. While both cause a cleavage of the ledger, their characteristics are distinct.

Soft forks are backward-compatible (they can be reversed) protocol changes are that implemented by voluntary software updates. They are suggested and adopted by a minority of miners. Yet 'there is nothing remotely "soft" about a soft fork. Soft forks are violent affairs where a majority of miners attempt to impose their own will on a minority, who have no means of voting against the new changes.'[95] *Hard forks* are not backward-compatible (they cannot be reversed) and require all miners to update their clients, making them more democratic. Yet a hard fork also has a stronger overall effect. Under a soft fork, the old and new versions of the software can coexist. A hard fork changes the protocol so profoundly that users who have not implemented the alteration can't use the network anymore.[96] Unlike soft forks, hard forks are thus mandatory updates for anyone wishing to continue using the networks.[97]

---

[91] Adem Efe Gencer et al., 'Decentralization in Bitcoin and Ethereum' (*Hacking, Distributed*, 15 January 2018) <http://hackingdistributed.com/2018/01/15/decentralization-bitcoin-ethereum/> accessed 28 May 2018 (hereafter Gencer et al., 'Decentralization in Bitcoin and Ethereum').

[92] ibid.

[93] Emin Gün Sirer, 'Time for Bitcoin Users to Reclaim Their Voice' (*Hacking, Distributed*, 1 January 2016) <http://hackingdistributed.com/2016/01/03/time-for-bitcoin-user-voice/> accessed 4 April 2018.

[94] Today, specialized chips (Application-Specific Integrated Circuits 'ASIC') are used, often produced by companies connected to miners.

[95] Tjaden Hess et al., 'Ethereum is Inherently Secure Against Censorship' (*Hacking, Distributed*, 5 July 2016) <http://hackingdistributed.com/2016/07/05/eth-is-more-resilient-to-censorship/> accessed 28 May 2018.

[96] This can be temporary where a number of miners accept a new block that other nodes have not yet confirmed (or where the network is under attack).

[97] Hard forks don't happen in other peer-to-peer systems – here they do as the entire purpose is reaching consensus and (what renders the system possible) this cannot be done if the same protocol is not followed.

When there is no unanimous agreement on the update, the protocol splits into various copies. This occurred in the aftermath of the The DAO hard fork, when Ethereum became two different projects: Ethereum and Ethereum Classic. Similarly, when agreements concerning the Bitcoin block size debate proved difficult, some developers forked the protocol to create a new version of Bitcoin, Bitcoin Cash, in 2017.[98] The ability to fork underlines that nodes have two options in participating in blockchain governance: exercising voice (participating in governance deliberations) or exiting the system by creating an alternative system through a hard fork.[99] Miners can also exit the system by dedicating their hash power to another project.

The economic and political importance of forks must not be underestimated. When a ledger relies on open-source software, you can simply fork the protocol to design it in a way not incorporating specific elements. This constitutes a big difference with the Internet, of which there is only one.[100] Forking has significant economic implications, moreover, as, '[i]n the Web 2.0 world, forking is the equivalent of Facebook allowing any competitor to take their entire database and codebase to a competitor'.[101] When miners decide to fork they need to weigh costs and benefits, as network effects weaken with every fork. It may also undermine trust in the specific project, and maybe the technology more generally. It is for these reasons that some are currently experimenting with blockchain solutions that are unable to fork.[102] It is important to note that forking can also happen at the application layer. This drastic solution was adopted as a consequence of a dispute between the initial managers of the Arcade City application (a blockchain-based ride-sharing platform).[103]

C. *Coin Holders*

In an on-chain governance context, token holders exercise decisive influence over the protocol's development. Here, coin holders are essentially the lone

---

[98] David Glance, 'Bitcoin Splits and Bitcoin Cash Is Created. Explaining Why and What Happens Now' (*The Conversation*, 2 August 2017) <https://theconversation.com/bitcoin-splits-and-bitcoin-cash-is-created-explaining-why-and-what-happens-now-81943> accessed 28 May 2018.

[99] Albert Hirschman, *Exit, Voice and Loyalty: Responses to Decline in Firms, Organizations and States* (Harvard University Press 1970). On Hirschman's work on exit, voice and loyalty, see further Chapter 2.

[100] Carla Reyes, 'Moving Beyond Bitcoin to an Endogenous Theory of Decentralized Ledger Technology Regulation: An Initial Proposal' (2016) 61 Villanova Law Review 191, 231.

[101] Ehrsam, 'Blockchain Governance' (n 46).

[102] Marc Hochstein, 'No-Fork Guarantee? New Cryptocurrency Touts Resistance to Code Splits' (*coindesk*, March 2018) <www.coindesk.com/hedera-hashgraph-swirlds-no-fork-guarantee-cryptocurrency-touts-resistance-code-splits/amp/?__twitter_impression=true> accessed 28 March 2018.

[103] Beck et al., 'Governance in the Blockchain Economy' (n 10) 18.

decision-makers, as the protocol updates automatically as a consequence of their decision.[104] Examples include projects such as EOS and NEO, in which coin holder votes appoint the super-nodes that run the network.[105] While token holders bear enormous power in on-chain governance, they can play a more subtle complementary governance role in off-chain governance, illustrated by the carbonvote on the hard fork in the aftermath of the The DAO hack.

On-chain voting processes seduce with efficiency and speed. Yet, when ownership and voting are tightly coupled, a feudalist structure emerges wherein influence is measured in wealth. This is even more problematic when wealth is strongly concentrated. According to estimates, 1,000 accounts held 40 per cent of Bitcoins while only 100 accounts controlled 17 per cent of all coins in late 2017.[106]

Although sometimes the term 'user' is deployed to refer to a coin holder, this can be misleading, as coin holders and user interests are not naturally aligned. Users buy coins from coin holders to use the infrastructure, as a consequence of which both sets of actors have diverging preferences concerning pricing. It is true that at this moment in time there is overlap, as most users are also coin holders, but it is important to recognize that, if these projects flourish as predicted, this will change.[107] On the other hand, it is also important to bear in mind that is likely that in the future the groups of miners or validators and coin holders may increasingly overlap (such as when proof-of-stake is used as a consensus mechanism), approximating the respective interests of these groups.

Coin holders can exit the system in selling their cryptoassets. While miners that have made this decision can return to the initial project relatively easily, coin holders might have to accept significant losses depending on the market rate when they leave and join.

D. *Other Governance Participants*

We've seen that blockchain governance is essentially a polycentric process to which a multitude of actors contribute. Beyond the main stakeholder groups introduced above, more marginal groups contribute to this complex process. First, the press and prominent voices in this space can exercise influence on those actively participating. Second, users indirectly contribute to governance. For example, when a hard fork occurs and a project splits into two, users must determine which network to use. Third, exchanges play an important role in a hard fork scenario in deciding which coins or tokens to list. This matters not just for users but also for miners that need to

---

[104] Buterin, 'Notes on Blockchain Governance' (n 52).
[105] ibid.
[106] Olga Kharif, 'The Bitcoin Whales: 1,000 People Who Own 40 Percent of the Market' *Bloomberg* (8 December 2017) <www.bloomberg.com/news/articles/2017-12-08/the-bitcoin-whales-1-000-people-who-own-40-percent-of-the-market> accessed 4 April 2018.
[107] Indeed, current coin holders hold coins hoping that user numbers increase in the future.

convert their cryptoassets into fiat currency (such as to pay their electricity bills when proof-of-work is used). Since exchanges make a profit through fees, they are likely to list cryptoassets with much user demand, again underlining that users have an indirect influence on governance decisions.

The exit/voice lens is also helpful to understand users' role in the ecosystem. They can exit a given project by using another one and selling their cryptoassets. Users exercise voice in contributing to governance debates on social media or in submitting BIP or EIP proposals. It is worth noting that users may also have the option of initiating hard forks – a so-called user-activated soft fork, or UASF. Here, nodes commit to represent the views of the user community when pushing for a soft fork.

These are but some examples of how additional groups contribute to the complex polycentric distributed ledger governance processes. This overview of blockchain governance processes has revealed that, although no single party has control over related decisions, the decision-making process nonetheless remains rather centralized and controlled by a few parties.

VI. WHAT DECENTRALIZATION?

The above overview has underlined that multiple actors influence decisions regarding the maintenance of blockchain protocols in permissionless systems. Indeed, while no single party exercises control over the future configurations of a given project, protocol maintenance remains in the hand of select parties.

Distributed ledgers have been labelled a 'technology for decentralization'.[108] It is conventionally assumed that blockchains are decentralized both at software and hardware level. In blockchain networks, however, there can be centralization from both the hardware and software perspectives. Indeed, the hardware layer may be centralized when there are few nodes or when nodes are owned by a small group of individuals and stored in close geographic proximity. While it is often assumed that nodes are run by individuals in an isolated fashion, in reality they are often clustered in data centres.[109] Similarly, mining operations are also often centralized.[110]

While centralization can thus be pinpointed from a hardware perspective, at software level too 'the blockchain economy at present continues to be characterized by a high degree of centralized decision-making'.[111] Those thinking that Satoshi Nakamoto's retirement removed the risk of centralizing the governance process of a formally decentralized ledger are mistaken. There is important concentration in software development, mining and wealth distribution in relation to DLT. Going forward, such concentration may further increase, as blockchains

[108] Davidson et al., 'Economics of Blockchain' (n 14) 6.
[109] Gencer et al., 'Decentralization in Bitcoin and Ethereum' (n 91).
[110] ibid.
[111] Beck et al., 'Governance in the Blockchain Economy' (n 10) 28.

'may avoid costly consensus protocols by re-introducing trusted intermediaries that control the blockchain'.[112]

Indeed, incidents such as the 2013 accidental Bitcoin hard fork have shown that centralization and coordination between mining pools and core developers allow agreement to be reached rapidly, which can appear impossible to achieve when coordination between thousands of small independent miners is required. Historically, decentralization has been hard to achieve, precisely because of the efficiency advantages of centralized decision-making processes. The challenge for public and permissionless projects aimed at decentralization is to show that history doesn't always repeat itself. When considering the intricacies of blockchain governance, regard must also be given to the external factors influencing the process.

VII. LAW AS AN EXOGENOUS FACTOR OF BLOCKCHAIN GOVERNANCE

Governance processes are influenced by a range of contextual factors, including law. As these systems further mature and seek regulatory compliance to be attractive for a large user base, law can be expected to be an increasingly important factor. In Chapter 3 I made the argument that distributed ledgers need to be compliant with law in order to achieve large-scale adoption. Here, I underline that governance decisions already have legal implications, and claim that law is a factor influencing governance processes in both substance and form. I conclude by offering some thoughts on the intertwining between polycentric co-regulation and internal blockchain governance.

The structuring of governance processes inevitably has legal implications. With scale, litigation becomes unavoidable and institutional structures are a factor that can establish liability. Although there is often an assumption that DLT operates in a lawless space, because law is unable to keep up with this innovation, this is simply not the case. Indeed, informal cooperation in this space may qualify as accidental corporate structures, triggering related legal consequences. It has been stressed that some DLT projects can be considered as joint ventures.[113] Similarly, mining pools could be seen as partnerships, a corporate form that would make it even easier to make them addressees of legal obligations.[114]

---

[112] Jean Bacon et al., 'Blockchain Demystified' (2017) Queen Mary University of London, School of Law Legal Studies Research Paper No. 268/2017, 19 <https://papers.ssrn.com/sol3/papers.cfm?abstract_id=3091218> accessed 3 April 2018.

[113] Dirk Zetzsche et al., 'The Distributed Liability of Distributed Ledgers: Legal Risks of Blockchain' (2018) University of Illinois Law Review 1361.

[114] 'Vermont Lawyer Warns of Legal Complications Ahead for Cryptocurrency Miners' (*Crypto Investor*, 12 February 2018) <http://cryptocurrencyinvestor.net/vermont-lawyer-warns-of-legal-complications-ahead-for-cryptocurrency-miners/> accessed 28 February 2018.

Angela Walch has written about the role of core developers in blockchain governance and calls for them to be subjected to fiduciary duties.[115] This links to more general discussions as to whether software developers should be liable for the effects of their code.[116] Others have proposed that the creators of a DAO be subject to fiduciary duties to ensure compliance with disclosure requirements.[117] This underlines that the structures and procedures behind governance generate legal implications. It has also been envisaged that regulators could hold developers strictly liable for 'creating and deploying autonomous blockchain-based systems, creating incentives for developers to create more careful innovation to decrease the risk of damages'.[118]

Law is also a factor informing blockchain governance from a substantive standpoint. Law and code cannot easily be separated, as, even when parties are aggrieved through a smart contract, they will probably revert to the legal system whether this is foreseen by the smart contract or not. In order to deal with related consequences, architects of blockchain governance at network, application and intermediary level will seek to design processes that enable legal compliance. One of the factors grounding the The DAO hard fork was indeed fear of judicial disputes and regulatory attention.[119]

Blockchain architects will continue to face difficult questions, such as with regard to the treatment of illegal content such as illegal pornography or copyrighted materials. While these are questions regarding the administration of the network, they also have legal implications. Most projects will seek to be compliant in order to avoid legal hassles and achieve large-scale adoption. It is conceivable that in the years to come protocols will (at least in part) abandon the 'immutability' proposition to embrace legally mandated mutability, such as when a ledger hosts illicit content or when data must be modified in light of court decisions or legislation.

Legislation imposing specific legal requirements in relation to governance has started to emerge. The Gibraltar Financial Services Commission's Distributed Ledger Technology Regulatory Framework requires that providers respect a number

---

[115] Walch, 'The Bitcoin Blockchain' (n 80). For a similar argument in relation to data processors, see Jack Balkin, 'Information Fiduciaries and the First Amendment' (2016) 49 UC Davis Law Review 1183.

[116] Bruce Ducker, 'Liability for Computer Software' (1971) 26 Business Lawyer (ABA) 1081; T. Randolph Beard, George S. Ford, Thomas Koutsky and Lawrence Spiwak, 'Tort Liability for Software Developers: A Law & Economics Perspective' (2009) 27 Journal of Computer & Information Law 199; Karen Mercedes Goertzel, 'Legal Liability for Bad Software' (2016) 29 CrossTalk 23.

[117] Tiffany Minks, 'Ethereum and the SEC: Why Most Distributed Autonomous Organizations are Subject to the Registration Requirements of the Securities Act of 1933 and a Proposal for New Regulation' (2018) Texas A&M Law Review 405.

[118] De Filippi and Wright, 'Blockchain and the Law' (n 13) 181.

[119] Michael del Castillo, 'The DAO Crisis: Or How Vigilantism and Blockchain Democracy Became the Best Hope for Burned Investors' (*coindesk*, 13 July 2016) <www.coindesk.com/author-daos-original-code-minimize-regulatory-backlash/> accessed 14 May 2018.

of requirements, including that they have 'rules by which authority is exercised and decisions taken and implemented to manage all risk types and exposures'.[120] Providers must further ensure 'that all systems and security access protocols are maintained to appropriate high standards'[121] and that systems are in place to prevent, detect and disclose financial crime.[122]

A possible future evolution at the nexus of law and governance could be court-ordered hard forks, whereby courts would essentially be ordering developers to write new software.[123] While this strategy could ensure compliance, it will trigger controversy, as it is very interventional. There are other open questions, such as who is liable when this software update generates damage or financial loss. Moreover, implementation challenges will arise when the miners required to implement the update are situated in multiple jurisdictions.

When a model of polycentric cooperation is adopted in line with what was suggested in the preceding chapter, a blockchain or blockchain-based application's governance structures would not only serve the endogenous administration of the project but also constitute the link between the project and exogenous rules and actors. Indeed, the distinction between private rule-making and public rule-making can be difficult to draw, as legitimacy arises from the interplay of internal and external rules.[124]

VIII. THE IMPORTANCE OF GOVERNANCE FOR BLOCKCHAINS' FUTURE

Blockchain governance is a complex, multi-stage process informed by a range of considerations, including law. Evaluating DLT from the governance perspective calls for the separation of fact from fiction in relation to decentralization narratives. While there is indeed no single actor that has control over these systems, they are often portrayed to be more decentralized than they really are.

The above overview has confirmed that distributed ledgers are not only heavily regulated by code but also heavily politicized. The original Bitcoin blockchain was ideologically motivated and originated in a general climate of fatigue with traditional institutions. The governance perspective reveals that narratives of trustless trust are inherently limited, as there are always humans behind trusted code. Human coordination and communication remain messy, even when they relate to code.

---

[120] Gibraltar Financial Services Commission, 'Distributed Ledger Technology Regulatory Framework (DLT framework)' (GFSC) <www.gfsc.gi/dlt> accessed 21 March 2018.
[121] ibid.
[122] ibid.
[123] This could be an issue in jurisdictions where code is protected as speech.
[124] Werbach, 'The Blockchain and the New Architecture of Trust' (n 9) 175.

Siva Vaidhyanathan has warned of 'techno-fundamentalism', blind faith in technology to solve all problems. This warning must also be heard in relation to blockchains.[125] Indeed, as these systems mature, solid governance structures to account for the messiness of human relations must be devised. Right now the lack of centralized supervision or oversights makes decentralized architectures more likely to be co-opted or manipulated by external powers.[126] What is more, the lack of a formalized power structure makes it harder for users and observers to realize who is actually in control of the network.[127] When there are no solid human decision-making processes behind technology, it simply cannot keep up. Lacking or inadequate governance principles limit the technology's usefulness.

In spite of current weaknesses, intact governance processes are so important they can be a project's competitive advantage, as the speed of adaptation is a crucial factor in ensuring the long-term viability of a project. Achieving this is far from easy. Vitalik Buterin recently worried that 'there is a large chance that we never will come up with a blockchain governance process that is sufficiently robust that it will be capable of regularly doing things like adjusting fundamental economic parameters'.[128] Yet devising such a process is an unavoidable component of the viability of a given project. The coordination of multiple actors in polycentric processes may be far from easy, but, after all, Elinor Ostrom has shown that it is possible in at least some contexts.

Governance determines how code can be updated and how technical bugs can be solved. It also determines the interoperability between the on-chain and off-chain worlds, as governance processes are needed for blockchains to comply with law. Although the precise principles to be followed are context-specific, technology itself cannot provide adequate responses. Rather, as Lawrence Lessig has already noted, governance must be 'a mix of the regulations of code and the regulations of bodies that regulate this code. It is both machine and man.'[129]

---

[125] Siva Vaidhyanathan, *The Googlization of Everything* (University of California Press 2011).

[126] Primavera De Filippi, 'The Interplay between Decentralization and Privacy: The Case of Blockchain Technologies' (2016) Journal of Peer Production <http://peerproduction.net/issues/issue-9-alternative-internets/peer-reviewed-papers/the-interplay-between-decentralization-and-privacy-the-case-of-blockchain-technologies/> accessed 21 March 2018.

[127] ibid.

[128] Vitalik Buterin (*Medium*, 16 April 2018) <https://medium.com/@VitalikButerin/to-be-clear-im-not-necessarily-wedded-to-a-finite-supply-cap-a7aa48ab880c> accessed 28 May 2018.

[129] Lessig, 'Open Code' (n 5) 1408.

8

Conclusion

This monograph set out to examine blockchain technology from a legal and governance perspective. The resulting analysis has highlighted a number of tensions. In examining blockchain technology through an overview of its central technical components, characteristics and expected future implications, I have shown that, while the technology is said to bear enormous innovative potential, because of numerous limitations and uncertainties it is impossible to say for sure, at this moment in time, whether this promise can be realized.[1] This, of course, is a general problem, as the course of innovation can never be predicted with certainty.

Thereafter, I have presented distributed ledgers as a network that can be regulated, but that may also come to regulate us. I started by addressing claims that, due to their decentralized and transnational peer-to-peer structure and the use of encryption, blockchains cannot be regulated. In drawing parallels to early debates of Internet regulation I have rebutted that narrative, highlighting various centralized regulatory access points to the decentralized network that enable regulatory intervention.[2] At the same time, however, I have also underlined that blockchains are regulatory agents, capable of regulating both humans and machines. In pinpointing that the technology is an aspect of the increasing automation of law, the associated promises and drawbacks have been drawn out.[3]

My analysis then turned to the third tension. In evaluating the relationship between blockchains and 'data law' in the European Union, it became evident that the technology stands in tension with established legal frameworks, while having the simultaneous potential of remedying acknowledged market failures that law has to date been unable to solve on its own. This examination has unveiled that DLT can stand in considerable tension with established legal frameworks and their underlying

---

[1] See Chapter 1.
[2] See Chapter 2.
[3] See Chapter 3.

technical and economic assumptions (in the case of the GDPR and personal data).[4] At the same time, distributed ledgers could provide a technical solution in areas in which law is currently falling short of achieving desired normative objectives (in this case, promoting the sharing of non-personal data in the internal market).[5]

The final tension that has been investigated is that blockchains' success is ultimately dependent on successful endogenous rules and principles *and* exogenous regulation. In pondering the complex interaction between law, technology and innovation, I stressed the need for adequate regulation and made the case that, as technology changes, law must too. This led me to suggest that a concept of polycentric co-regulation, reconciling the established benefits of public policy protection with the newer regulatory opportunities of technology, be adopted.[6] Finally, I turned to the theme of blockchain governance to underline ongoing debates regarding the uncertainties as to how these technological artefacts, designed to replace trust in human beings, should be governed amidst realizations that technology does not eliminate the need for human consensus. I highlighted the importance of blockchain governance and the links between internal and external regulatory processes.

It may be that the most significant tension of all is that blockchains constitute a technology that can be used either for beneficial or for malicious ends. Just like any other technology, blockchains awaken both utopian and dystopian visions. The emergence of blockchain has opened up a new way of thinking about technology and its impact on our lives. Beyond the actual technology itself, the term 'blockchain' has become shorthand for broader technological change and innovation. It has become a narrative that arouses the power of collective imagination concerning broader technological change and its impact on human civilization. Technological immaturity coupled with a seemingly infinite array of possible use cases open many potential future scenarios for blockchains' use.

Distributed ledgers can bring us closer to what Gilles Deleuze has called the 'society of control', a world in which humans are increasingly managed and controlled by machines.[7] It can be co-opted by authoritarian governments as a means of suppression or leveraged to increase corporate control, to the detriment of individual freedom, and the power of the state as an embodiment of the social contract. Blockchains may also come to be relied on, however, as a tool that solves a range of socio-economic and technical problems, ultimately improving social relations and the human condition.

Blockchains' future will probably lie somewhere between the utopian and dystopian extremes of hope and fear that are currently formulated. Where exactly is up to

---

[4] See Chapter 4.
[5] See Chapter 5.
[6] See Chapter 6.
[7] Gilles Deleuze, 'Postscript on the Societies of Control' (1992) 59 The MIT Press 3. See also Lawrence Solum, 'Artificial Meaning' (2014) 89 Washington Law Review 69.

us to delineate. Technology is in itself 'neither good nor bad; nor is it neutral'.[8] Rather, it is what those who control it manipulate it to be. It is now, in the early stages of technological development when DLT remains immature and malleable in its configurations, that future usages are defined. Interdisciplinary research and multi-stakeholder dialogues are needed to make sure that future configurations advance rather than undermine law and public policy objectives.

In this monograph I have attempted to chart some of the main regulatory and governance questions that emerge in this context. My objective has been to lay the groundwork for subsequent research and discussions – a necessary step if we are to make sense of this ongoing technological transformation. My analysis has focused on the European Union and its legal order. This choice was, doubtless, driven by personal motivation. The choice is also warranted objectively, however. The European Union has set out to become a leader in new technologies. This is a challenge not just technologically and economically but also from a normative perspective. The task that has to be achieved is not limited to developing adequate technology, business models and other use cases, but to do so in a manner respectful of the public policy objectives dearly held in this part of the world. This defiance is clearly not limited to blockchains, but also extends to other fields, including biotechnology and artificial intelligence. If blockchains turn out to be what many speculate, Europe has been gifted with a unique opportunity to reap the related benefits. A robust blockchain ecosystem has started to develop in the European Union, particularly in some cities such as Berlin, as a result of a mixture of cultural and socio-economic reasons. This has, at least initially, been the result of lucky circumstances rather than any strategy intervention by the European Union or its member states. The challenge consists in maintaining and strengthening that ecosystem while encouraging it to develop in line with the widely accepted public policy aims.

---

[8] Melvin Kranzberg, 'Technology and History: Kranzberg's Laws' (1986) 27 Technology and Culture 544, 545.

Index